EARNEST EXUBERANCE IN CHAUCER'S POETICS

Textual Games in the *Canterbury Tales*

Wolfgang E. H. Rudat

The Edwin Mellen Press
Lewiston/Queenston/Lampeter

Library of Congress Cataloging-in-Publication Data

Rudat, Wolfgang E. H.
    Earnest exuberance in Chaucer's poetics : textual games in the
Canterbury tales / Wolfgang E.H. Rudat.
    p.   cm.
    Includes bibliographical references (p.) and index.
    ISBN 0-7734-9381-6
    1. Chaucer, Geoffrey, d. 1400. Canterbury tales. 2. Puns and
punning in literature. 3. Rhetoric, Medieval. 4. Sex in
literature. 5. Poetics. I. Title.
PR1875.P85R83 1993
821'.1--dc20   93-34113
                                                                    CIP

A CIP catalog record for this book
is available from the British Library.

The Edwin Mellen Press   The Edwin Mellen Press
        Box 450   Box 67
    Lewiston, New York   Queenston, Ontario
      USA 14092   CANADA L0S 1L0

The Edwin Mellen Press, Ltd.
Lampeter, Dyfed, Wales
UNITED KINGDOM SA48 7DY

Printed in the United States of America

for Hildegard Engler

CONTENTS

PREFACE
and Acknowledgments

As is suggested by the title and the content of my Introduction, "Cosmic Union, Literary Game, and Acknowledgments of *Corage*," the *real* "acknowledgments" are to be found in the Introduction, which perhaps could be considered an introductory chapter—but which also singles out some of the scholars whom I am indebted to, because I either heartily agree or just as heartily disagree with them. Thus the Introduction is rather informal in its acknowledgments, and I wish to use the Preface to make acknowledgments of a more formal kind. Ironically, the scholar with whom I express disagreement the most frequently is also the person with whom I agree the most heartily because his work has both challenged and inspired me: Thomas W. Ross, who has performed controversial but groundbreaking work on imaginatively close-reading Chaucer, both in his 1972 book on *Chaucer's Bawdy* and in his 1983 *Variorum* edition of the *Miller's Tale*. My own controversial close-reading approach puts me in a unique position to carry on Professor Ross' courageously incendiary torch.

I would also like to take this opportunity to express my gratitude to those journals which provided initial encouragement by publishing articles of mine which employed an at times unorthodox approach to Chaucer and then granted me permission to use material from those publications (listed in alphabetical order): *American Imago: A Psychoanalytic Journal for Culture, Science and the Arts* (copyright 1978 by Wayne State University Press), *Annuale Mediaevale* (1982), *Chaucer Yearbook* (October 1993), *English Language Notes* (copyright 1991 by The Regents of the University of Colorado), *Explicator* (copyright 1977 and 1983, respectively, by Meldref Publications), *Journal of Evolutionary Psychology* (April 1982, October 1982), *Neophilologus* (1980), and *Revue belge de philologie et d'histoire* (1976).

The article publications referred to above, which of course were only early stages of interpretations that I offer in the present study and, overall, represent only a small portion of this book, are listed in full bibliographical detail in the endnotes to the chapters in which I use material from them. I would like to express my indebtedness to the late Robert C. Elliott, who provided me with an understanding of the Power of Satire, not only in his book thus titled but also, "ful yoore ago," as a teacher. In turn, I am grateful to my students, who taught me while I thought I was teaching them. I am grateful to the University of Houston for making this research project possible by granting me teaching-load reductions. Last but not least, I am grateful to my wife, Karen Sjoquist Rudat, who not only put up with a scholar given to a manic-chaotic schedule but, in reading the ever-expanding manuscript versions of this book countless times, provided fresh insights of her own and common-sense suggestions for improvement.

INTRODUCTION

Cosmic Union, Literary Game, and
Acknowledgments of *Corage*

It may seem quaint that anyone would want to title with frivolous puns involving the words "acknowledgment" and *corage* the Introduction of a scholarly study intended to offer new interpretations of a few individual stories and other selected passages from the *Canterbury Tales*. But then this study, whose unifying methods and themes are the combination of sexual and theological interpretations, might never have been written in the first place if it had not been for Laura Kendrick's 1988 book, *Chaucerian Play: Comedy and Control in the Canterbury Tales*.[1] That stimulating (or should I say "teasing"?) book inspired-and-*encouraged* me[2] in my enterprise of discussing the playful spirit of the *Tales*. The nature of Kendrick's book is perhaps best described by Martin Stevens in a 1989 review-article on several recent books on Chaucer:

> Here is a book about play that is also self-consciously playful, full of audacious interpretive moves and, consequently, the liveliest, most keenly provocative book published in recent years on the *Canterbury Tales*. The book . . . takes Chaucerian play as its subject to discover what . . . making earnest out of game (and vice versa) really means . . . The reader is treated to a book that in its general appeal has a Chaucerian spirit about it.[3]

Kendrick has now opened the interpretive flood gates in a manner in which this had never been dared before, or at least not in a book-length study:[4] I myself had tried to create some such openings in the form of articles,[5] but I never had the *corage* to do it in book-form—so that in a sense Kendrick left me at the gate. I must admit to a prick of competitive stimulation, but more important than the challenge to "quyte" her is the inspiration I drew from her study, both in subject matter and in terms of approach.

Stevens makes the following comments concerning Kendrick's approach:

> [Kendrick cites] Larry Benson's 1984 Chaucer Congress paper which warned critics not to overextend their own erotic fantasies in finding vulgar puns that Chaucer never intended. The effect, according to Kendrick, was that "Benson's denials enabled him, to everyone's amusement, to dwell at length on bawdy words" . . . She adds a waggish Chaucerism of her own, "Even in this book, I might be said to be doing the same thing [as Benson], under cover of scholarship—which does not make it any less scholarly, only more duplicitous."[6]

I go beyond Kendrick's methodology mainly by giving Chaucer's text a close reading more consistently and more persistently than Kendrick does, for I am more interested than Kendrick was with holistic interpretation, holistic interpretation of specific tales as well as certain recurring motifs. Also, without extending my own erotic fantasies, I feel no need for something like what Kendrick first calls "Benson's denials" but what she herself at times seems to engage in to be on the safe side. My discovery of bawdy puns and innuendoes is based on interpretive moves which attempt to examine Chaucer's text *palimpsestically*, i.e., attempt to read it as a text where not only do earlier parts determine the meanings of later parts as is customary, but where the meanings of earlier words or phrases are retroactively informed by a live-and-lively interaction with later words or phrases.

In fact, in a book which extends the close-reading of Chaucer farther than has any previous study, my emphasis on the palimpsestic nature of

Chaucer's work will provide something that Stevens deplores as largely missing in Kendrick's "often scintillating study,"[7] namely a concern with the intertextuality between different parts of the *Canterbury Tales*—and with the voicing of the text at large. This in turn means that I will have to argue against Robert M. Jordan's denial of organic unity in Chaucer's work, a denial which Jordan made in his 1965 study, *Chaucer and the Shape of Creation: The Aesthetic Possibilities of Inorganic Structure*.[8] The particular narratives I have chosen, primarily the General Prologue, the *Miller's*, the *Prioress'*, the *Pardoner's*, the *Clerk's*, and the *Merchant's Tales*, are intended to serve as models for close-reading the rest of the *Canterbury Tales*, but they are also intended to serve as a selective rebuttal to Jordan's claim, which he repeated in 1987 in *Chaucer's Poetics and the Modern Reader*, where he observed: "It is becoming increasingly difficult to deny the ennui that threatens to envelop Chaucer studies at the appearance of every new reading of *Troilus* or every new version of the Pardoner's condition."[9] I do possess the audacity to defy Jordan's caution concerning ennui in Chaucer studies and offer a new version of the Pardoner's condition, a new version which, examining Chaucer's own text for possible both-and irony, may just turn out to be the definitive version—that is, to the extent that Chaucer wanted his readers to be able to figure out such a thing.

In my discussion of Chaucer's portrayal of the Pardoner I have drawn much encouragement from Carolyn Dinshaw's "Eunuch Hermeneutics" chapter in her 1989 study on *Chaucer's Sexual Poetics*,[10] but, more importantly, through my palimpsestic mode of reading I perceived as constituting an organic structure Chaucerian contexts which Jordan probably never would have thought could be part of an organic unity. And since my entire study is based on an 'organic reading' of the *Canterbury Tales*, I will have to disagree with Carl Lindahl's approach in his 1987 book, *Earnest Games: Folkloric Patterns in the Canterbury Tales*, in which he made the following observation:

> If folklore were to be assigned to one or the other of Chaucer's favorite pair of categories—*ernest* and *game*—nearly every twentieth-century reader would classify it exclusively as *game*. Yet, as the *Canterbury Tales* reveals, it is remarkable how often games are found to contain earnest matter. *The Host warns that one should never make earnest of game*, but he knows, and we observe, that one can always *conceal* earnest within a game. The folkloric patterns I shall discuss are the most earnest conceivable games, for the pilgrims use these traditional strategies to express their most negative and heretical thoughts—thoughts which, if given any other form, would invite frightening consequences."[11] (The italics from "*The Host*" to "*game*" are mine.)

I agree of course with what Lindahl says about the *Canterbury Tales* concealing earnest within game; in fact, I would extend the *earnest game* strategy, which allows the individual pilgrims telling a story to express their thoughts, to include the poet himself who, as I will show, expresses thoughts that are much more negative and certainly much more heretical than has been realized. I must, however, agree with the following comment which Stevens makes about Lindahl's study in his review-article: "[Lindahl's] method unfortunately oversimplifies Chaucer's churls' fiction and reconstitutes it, with a folklore bias, as a new kind of 'roadside drama,' resurrecting the specter that we have worked so hard to dispel."[12]

I have good reason to begin my study by quoting reviews of two recent books on Chaucer, even though I promise that I will engage in metacriticism only where metacriticism might actually help us with our understanding of Chaucer's text. What Stevens does not mention in his review of *Earnest Games* is that Lindahl misattributes *to the Host* the statement that "men shal nat maken ernest of game," an announcement which the poet-narrator himself makes in the Miller's Prologue (I 3186). Lindahl's attribution to the Host of spoken words which are actually part of Chaucer's written narration of the poem is indicative of a tendentiousness which neglects Chaucer's text in favor of a folk-mode reading.[13]

Lindahl is exploring the various framed stories of the *Canterbury Tales* as standing in the tradition of "Oral and *aural* transmission,"[14] as "*earnest games*, acts of play in which serious social messages were embedded."[15] It would therefore be very convenient to Lindahl's argument to have the Host who, to use Lindahl's term, stages the "games" by calling in the General Prologue upon the pilgrims to tell "Tales of . . . sentence and . . . solaas" (I 798),[16] i.e., instructing and amusing tales, be the one to make the *earnest game* warning. Thus Lindahl's misattribution of what are probably the thematically most important lines in the entire *Canterbury Tales* calls into question the validity of his interpretation of the *earnest games* as "acts of [oral] play." In fact, I wish to argue that in Chaucer's immediately preceding editorializing excuse that the Miller is a "cherl" (I 3182) and in his advice, "whoso list it nat *yheere,/Turne over the leef* and chese another tale" (I 3176-77, italics mine), the poet is actually in a ludic spirit of irony pitting his own sophisticated, written/literary "game," in the sense of fun-game rather than acted play, against the oral-folkloric tradition he is drawing upon.

If Chaucer has the plot within the story of the pilgrimage itself interact with the plots of the various tales, then such intertextuality, such an organic interrelation, may very well inform Chaucer's character portrayal both of his pilgrims and of the characters within the tales told by the pilgrims. On the other hand, if we read, for example, the fabliau of the *Merchant's Tale* as a "game" in the sense in which Lindahl interprets and uses that term, as an "act of [oral] play," we miss out on the splendidly comical interaction between that individual tale and the opening lines of the General Prologue: "Whan that Aprill with his shoures soote/The droghte of March hath perced to the roote . . . " For this interaction between the cosmic-union picture, in which the sky alias April impregnates the earth alias March, and the *Merchant's Tale* begins *after* Chaucer has had the Merchant deliver his oral presentation about an old man named January who marries a young girl named

May, and marries her expressly in order to increase the flock of God's children (IV 1448-49). It is only because of the impregnation picture with which the literary artist opens the *Canterbury Tales* that we ask the following question: does January succeed in doing to May what in the opening lines of the General Prologue April had done to March?

The cosmic-union motif will serve as one of the main unifying themes for my study, and I will use this motif in a later chapter to answer the question I just posed with regard to January and May. Meanwhile, let me point out some information about January. During the wedding festivities, long before he and his bride go to bed, January thinks to himself:

> Allas! O tendre creature,
> Now wolde God ye myghte wel endure
> *Al my corage*, it is so sharp and keene! (IV 1757-59, italics added)

January is worried that his tender wife might not be able to endure all his *corage*, which, as Thomas W. Ross notes in his 1972 study on *Chaucer's Bawdy*, means here the "capability to achieve and maintain erection—the act of valor peculiar to the bedroom."[17] But then, January knows at this point that prior to taking his bride to bed he will do something with regard to this special type of "courage":

> He drynketh ypocras, clarree, and vernage
> Of spices hoote *t'encreessen his corage*;
> And many a letuarie hath he ful fyn,
> Swiche as the cursed monk, daun Constantyn,
> Hath writen in his book *De Coitu*;
> To eten hem alle he has no thyng eschu. (IV 1807-1812, italics added)

After having taken Dutch courage of sorts, January takes his bride to bed and he again cautions her:

> "Allas! I moot trespace
> To yow, my spouse, and you greetly offende
> *Er tyme come that I wil doun descende*.
> But nathelees, considereth this," quod he,
> "Ther nys no *werkman*, whatsoevere he be,
> That may bothe *werke* wel and hastily;

This wol be doon at leyser parfitly.
It is no fors how longe that we pleye . . . "
Thus laboureth he til that the day gan dawe . . .
(IV 1828-42, italics added)

What does January mean when he apologizes to his bride that he will have to cause her discomfort before he "wil doun descende"? Or more precisely, what does *Chaucer the poet* have in mind when he has the Merchant put that statement in January's mouth?

This is one crucial passage just in the *Merchant's Tale* where any folk-loric-pattern thesis becomes reductive because it fails to do justice to Chaucer's literary artistry. The meaning intended by January is that it will take him quite a while before he is through with his bride and dismounts her body. January does not say why, but his mention of both *werkman* and *werke* suggests that he knows that what he calls "playing" between husband and wife may require some work—a suggestion which the Merchant-as-teller elaborates by concluding, "Thus laboureth he til that the day gan dawe." Chaucer, but presumably not the Merchant himself as the Merchant is not very likely to possess the theological knowledge that Chaucer does, is here alluding to a portion of St. Augustine's *The City of God* whose possible significance for Chaucer's own work has received very little critical attention. Chaucer is alluding to St. Augustine's theory, a theory whose allusive utilization in Milton's *Paradise Lost* has received a good deal of attention,[18] namely the thesis that Original Sin caused a drastic change in human sexuality. I will discuss Chaucer's allusive use of Augustinian sexual theology later in this study; suffice it for now to say that according to St. Augustine's rather graphi-cally presented theory the prelapsarian sex act was *sine labore*, without effort (*The City of God*, XIV, 26),[19] whereas the postlapsarian sex act is, like other postlapsarian activities, carried out in the sweat of man's brow.

Thus, whether or not the Merchant himself is suggesting that the old bridegroom has trouble achieving ejaculation, Chaucer certainly is suggesting it. Chaucer conveys this idea by having the Merchant's description of January's marriage consummation interact not only with St. Augustine's pronouncement of postlapsarian sex as *labor*, but also with the the opening lines of the General Prologue, where the poet presents a scene in which the life-begetting sky quite literally *descends down* into the womb of Mother Earth with a piercing ejaculation:

> Whan that Aprill with his shoures soote
> The droghte of March hath perced to the roote . . .

Significantly for our understanding of Chaucer having January make his announcement as to when the old man "wil doun descende," our poet is in the opening lines alluding to Virgil's representation of spring rainfall as the impregnation of Earth by Jupiter alias sky that is described in the Second *Georgic*:

> vere tument terrae et genitalia semina poscunt.
> tum pater omnipotens *fecundis imbribus Aether*
> *coniugis in gremium laetae descendit*, et omnis
> magnus alit magno commixtus corpore fetus.
> avia tum resonant avibus virgulta canoris,
> et Venerem certis repetunt armamenta diebus.

> In spring the soil swells and calls for life-giving seed. Then *Heaven, Almighty Father Jupiter, comes down in fruitful showers into the womb of his joyous partner*, and joining his might with her mighty body, nurtures all growths. Then pathless bushes ring with the singing of birds, and in their determined time the cattle renew their loves. (*Georgica*, II, 324-29, italics added)[20]

Why would I wish to argue that in the General Prologue Chaucer is alluding specifically to Virgil's *Iuppiter descendens* passage[21] when there are sources which may seem to offer themselves as more likely or more natural, such as the rainfall scene in the much-celebrated *Roman de la Rose*, parts of which Chaucer himself had translated if we can assume that he is the author of *The Romaunt of the Rose*?[22] Let me present my case for a Virgilian allusion first and then go into a comparison between the opening lines of the *Canter-*

bury Tales and *The Romaunt of the Rose.* While there exists an enormous amount of Chaucer scholarship which can be categorized as source-study, comparably little work has been devoted to allusion-study. The important distinction between these two critical genres, a distinction which is easily blurred or ignored, is that, whereas knowledge of the source which the literary artist is drawing upon may or may not help us better understand his or her work, a deliberate "al-lusion" to another work—i.e., a deliberate act of "playing to or toward" that other work—is an act of communication with the reader. The purpose of such a communication is to invite the reader, whom the artist is counting on to be familiar with the other work, to perform a creative act of his own by exercising his own invention and contemplating the possible relevances of the entire allusive context, i.e., to examine the alluded-to context for meanings which may not be explicit in the text but which the artist may have imported into his own work by alluding to the other work.[23] New possibilities offer themselves for interpreting Chaucer's text if we—to express it in the words which Carmela Perri used in her article "On Alluding"—"complete the allusion's unstated significance."[24]

Why, then, would I wish to argue that Chaucer is specifically alluding to Virgil's *Iuppiter descendens* passage? The answer lies essentially in the respective cause-effect sequences in the two passages, with the allusion in Chaucer operating for purposes of both comparison and contrast. In the *Georgics* passage, the cosmic union results in the procreation of physical life; in Chaucer's Prologue, the union between sky and earth compels the plant world and the animal world, represented by the birds, to reproduce and people to search for spiritual renewal: "Thanne longen folk to goon on pilgrimages" (I 12). For Virgil the spectacle of the *Iuppiter descendens*, the spectacle of cosmic union, prods the birds to sing and the cattle to mate. Yet when Chaucer writes that the birds "maken melodye,/That slepen al the nyght with open ye/(So priketh hem nature in hir corages)" (I 10-11), he is alluding to Virgil in order to extend the latter's cause-effect sequence between spring rain and sex urge in the following fashion.

The sexual connotation of the word *corage* noted earlier—here Chaucer's use of the word *corage* in the *Merchant's Tale* retroactively-organically informs the *Canterbury Tales'* opening lines—not only serves to make Chaucer's statement about the birds more sexually explicit, but it also tells us something about the pilgrims. Especially in light of the "corages"/"pilgrimages" rhyme through which Chaucer poetically connects the amorous birds with the pilgrims—"(So priketh hem nature in hir corages);/Thanne longen folk to goon on pilgrimages"—the pilgrimage to Canterbury, touched off by the witnessing of the procreative union between April and the land, is in part as sexually motivated as the singing of the birds. This sexual motivation, whose presence Chaucer highlights by importing via his allusion the Virgilian cause-effect sequence into his own poem, governs the behavior of some of the participants in the pilgrimage. The pilgrim Chaucer is also including himself in this motivation when he repeats the rhyme a few lines later and refers to himself as "Redy to wenden on my pilgrymage/To Caunterbury with ful devout corage" (I 21-22).[25] In other words, the sexual impulse is presented as extending from Chaucer the pilgrim to Chaucer-the-literary-artist writing about the pilgrimage.[26]

Such an impulse on the part of both the poet and several of the pilgrims accounts for the exuberance of bawdy stories and obscene dialogues. And I mean "exuberance" in its literal sense: the "out-pouring" of the cosmic union causes an unrestrained "out-pouring" of speech on the part of the pilgrims and an unrestrained playfulness, a joyous letting-go, on the part of the literary artist. To a modern Christian some of the bawdy material may seem too exuberant, too unrestrained, to be acceptable topics of conversation on a Christian pilgrimage, especially where Chaucer's *games* are heretically obscene in the manner in which they play on Christian doctrine and Christian notions. I will of course provide examples of such theological jokes, but at the moment I wish to use the General Prologue, whose opening lines I have attempted to explicate with the help of their interaction with the later description of the wedding night in the *Merchant's Tale*, in turn to explicate a passage in the *Merchant's Tale*.

What does it mean for our understanding of the tale that in the consummation scene Chaucer, rather than the Merchant who, as a character within the description of the pilgrimage and as the teller of January's story, is not privy to the literary artist's manipulations in the General Prologue, has January warn his bride that it will take some time before he "wil doun *descende*" (italics added)? It means that the poet is referring to his opening lines and thereby also alluding to Virgil's *descensus* passage to suggest that, unlike Jupiter, January has a problem with achieving ejaculation. This is a problem which January may or may not have been afraid would happen, but through his allusive transactions with Virgil's Second *Georgic* Chaucer is insinuating the following idea. January's ejaculation may not be as fruitful as Jupiter's, who descends "coniugis in gremium laetae," and when January's "descensus" finally occurs it certainly does not do anything to make his own spouse *joyous/laeta*, regardless of whether such a joy would eventually depend on how January's presumably less than sweet-and-piercing-to-the-root *descensus* affects May's *gremium/womb*.[27]

After presenting my case that in the opening lines, in which Chaucer sets the stage for his poem's exuberant playfulness, Chaucer alludes to Virgil, I will now look at *The Romaunt of the Rose*. Larry D. Benson has observed about the opening lines of the General Prologue:

> The celebration of the return of spring recalls the opening of *The Romaunt of the Rose*. There the description of spring, with its suggestion of fertility and rebirth, leads to "Than yonge folk entenden ay/Forto ben gay and amorous" (Rom 82-83). Here it leads to another kind of love: "Thanne longen folk to go on pilgrimages."[28]

I have just argued that in the *Canterbury Tales* the rain leads to a "love" which is not entirely of "another kind" than that of the *Romaunt*. On the other hand, it could be argued that through an allusion to *Romaunt*, 82-83 Chaucer is introducing a sexual impulse into the *Tales* and that, therefore, no allusion to the cause-effect sequence in Virgil would be needed. The problem with such an argument is that the rainfall which Chaucer mentions in the *Romaunt* passage is not exactly a powerful ejaculation picture (or, if you will, the picture of a powerful ejaculation): "the erthe wexith proud withalle,/For swote dewes that on it falle" (59-60).

The picture of sweet dews falling onto the earth is rather the picture of a Jupiter who used to be a *pater omnipotens* but has now become a January who has to take aphrodisiacs "t'encreessen his corage." Regardless of whether, when Chaucer echoes lines 59-60 in "Whan that Aprill with his shoures soote/The droghte of March hath perced to the roote," he is actually parodying the earlier rainfall picture, it is important to note here is that in the *Romaunt* passage we strictly speaking do not have a cosmic-union picture: while "the erthe wexith proud," no celestial/ethereal impregnator is explicitly mentioned. But then, since the "yonge folk" are lovers, they never had any need for a spectacular cosmic union to begin with: quite in contrast to Chaucer-the-pilgrim-narrator who at this moment is lying at the Tabard Inn "Redy to wenden on [his] pilgrymage/To Caunterbury with ful devout corage," because he has been inspired by the union between sky and earth. That is to say, unlike January, Chaucer-the-pilgrim is "Redy" even without the hot spices which "that cursed monk, daun Constantyn" had recommended in his *De Coitu*. And Chaucer-the-poet likewise is "Redy" to go.

I too am "Redy" to go, but before I shower my modern-day fellow pilgrims with some of Chaucer's risqué innuendoes I wish to reemphasize the holistic thrust of my enterprise, the combination of sexual and theological interpretations of Chaucer's text. While I am concerned with Chaucer's irony and naughty wit, I will show that he wrote the *Canterbury Tales* in a spirit of *earnest* exuberance. I will show that D. W. Robertson, Jr. was closing in on the target when he observed, in *A Preface to Chaucer* some three decades ago, that "Medieval writers were just as capable of a kind of philosophical obscenity as were later writers like Erasmus, Rabelais, Swift and Sterne," and that those medieval writers' obscenities "suggest certain very Christian conclusions."[29] And I will show that Donald R. Howard was right when he stated in 1976 that "Chaucer believed . . . that the end of literature was to teach and delight."[30]

But within the same breath Howard remarked that "The problem is the proportions of the mixture [of *teach* and *delight*]."[31] Instead of treating the proportions of the mixture as a problem, I consider the elusive mixture-proportions question a delight. It is a potential *dulce* for those readers who are willing to use a playful spirit and possess enough flexibility to be able to go with the flow in whatever direction Chaucer's spirit moves them concerning the *dulce*-versus-*utile* question. The point is that the mixture-proportions question is a challenge, a challenge actually intended by Chaucer, to the individual reader and therefore cannot and should not be given a sweeping answer. As I will demonstrate in the chapters, there is more *solaas* than readers have previously been aware of, but any discovery of new *solaas* could unearth *sentence* to match.

The *dulce*-versus-*utile* question brings us to the following questions which readers of my study are bound to ask. Could Chaucer's audience have responded to the kind of complex, interwoven allusiveness which I cite to make my arguments? Wasn't part of Chaucer's work "published" by being read aloud whereas we possess sophisticated tools—such as notes, cross-references, concordances, and now even computers—which permit us to glide back and forth through the long and complex text? Could these problems be simply solved by arguing that the possible responses of Chaucer's audience are irrelevant to the modern reader? Let me answer those questions in reverse order. No, the modern reader cannot and must not ignore the possible responses of Chaucer's contemporary reader—but my emphasis is on *reader* rather than listener. Chaucer clearly was redirecting his presumed 'audience' from simply listening to sophisticatedly reading when he punningly advised in the prologue to the *Miller's Tale*, "whoso list it nat yheere,/Turne over the leef and chese another tale." That is to say, Chaucer did not expect his interwoven allusiveness to be caught by the listener—or, for that matter, by the merely casual reader. When Chaucer wrote, "Turne over the leef," he was actually admonishing the reader to do his homework, to do what he needed to do in order to be able to appreciate the poet's art: the poet was asking for the reader's physical effort of turning over the leaf.

But then we modern readers have to bear in mind what kind of reader Chaucer was calling upon for cooperation. First of all, while Chaucer's contemporaries did not possess the tools we have today, they also did not have television and the mass of other media to preoccupy their time—so that at least the leisure class had more time for reading less material. Second, since Chaucer wrote before the invention of printing, obtaining a copy of his work was so time-consuming and expensive that, in order to get their money's worth, those who were fortunate enough to obtain it, and perhaps obtain it only for a limited amount of time, had no choice but to subject it to careful reading and re-reading, to subject it to a scrupulously scrutinizing examination, a courtesy which today we don't extend to visual programs we can videotape—or, for that matter, to the paperbacks we mothball on our bookshelves after speed-reading them.

Such a careful study and resulting appreciation of Chaucer's art was limited not only to the literate-and-educated few, but actually to those educated few who were interested in further intellectual stimulation. In fact, it could even be argued that, when Chaucer apparently nonchalantly advises that "whoso list it nat yheere" should turn over the leaf and read another tale, he is being ironic: when Chaucer points to the autonomy which the reader possesses but the listener does not, couldn't he also be suggesting that the listener who had merely caught the plot of a tale and didn't like it, or didn't like the beginning and therefore chose to doze through the remainder, can always "chese" to *read* the tale and thus experience the pleasure of the fine points he had missed out on as a listener? In other words, couldn't Chaucer be encouraging the reader also to turn *back* the leaf, i.e., read the text in the manner I call palimpsestic?

Yet while I am concerned with the irony and naughty wit which Chaucer displayed in playing off the old mode of listening to the more intellectually demanding and therefore esthetically more pleasing joy of reading, I will show that even bawdy fabliaux such as the *Miller's Tale* possess what today we call "socially redeeming values," although in the case of this fabliau it might be more correct to speak of *religiously* redeeming values. Kendrick has convincingly argued that "To read for *sentence* enables, not prevents, a covert appreciation of *solas*."[32] What I will suggest is that reading for *solaas* and reading for *sentence* are complementary to each other—or rather, that we should not read the *Canterbury Tales* reductively "for" one or the other but, instead, read the text closely and yet imaginatively, as a natural result of which *both* "solaas" *and* "sentence" will simply come to us.

My concern for the text is precisely the point where I deviate from the Robertsonian approach. A. Leigh DeNeef made the following observation in his 1968 article on "Robertson and the Critics," in an article which actually was rather sympathetic toward Robertson:

> most of the studies which claim to be "Robertsonian" have been most careless . . . [about avoiding the danger of limiting] the significance of a figure too rigidly [to Scriptural exegesis] . . . They have been eager to accept whatever interpretation the exegetical tradition supplies without taking into strict account the requirements of the text itself. This,

however, is not to be condoned, for the critic's purpose is not to impose allegory upon a poem, but rather to demonstrate its presence.[33]

In the works which I will discuss, Chaucer makes moral points, conveys *sentence*, without necessarily composing allegory; he poetically punishes his characters for their wrongdoings without consigning specific allegorical functions to those characters.

In his 1965 article, "Robertsonianism Redivivus," Francis Lee Utley called Robertson's *Preface to Chaucer* "an extended use of the genetic fallacy."[34] While Utley's attack on Robertson and on the latter's stipulation of allegory may have been needlessly harsh in its tone and, as DeNeef would elaborate, on some counts even unjustified, it is precisely because of the genetic fallacy that the Robertsonians tend to downplay or even neglect the value of Chaucer's writings as art. They don't allow themselves the time to enjoy the *solaas* unless the *sentence* reveals itself immediately. As I said a moment ago, the *sentence* will come if we are sufficiently patient—which means that we have to allow the *Canterbury Tales* to affect us palimpsestically-organically. Joerg O. Fichte was putting it succinctly when, in his 1980 book on *Chaucer's "Art Poetical": A Study in Chaucerian Poetics*, he observed that "the Neo-Augustinian model of aesthetics devised by D. W. Robertson . . . effectively ruled out any creative individualism."[35]

While Chaucer's obscenities do "suggest very certain Christian conclusions" as Robertson claimed, certain conclusions may not always express agreement with the Catholic Church's practices or even its doctrine. One of the things that makes trying to explicate Chaucer's creatively individualistic *games* exciting is that after an organic reading of the *Tales* Chaucer's criticisms become evident, especially with regard to gender issues. The possibility that Chaucer may be satirizing, and thus condemning, some of the basic tenets of the Church is a point which has received relatively little attention, probably because Chaucer tried to protect himself by throwing up a smokescreen and attacking blatantly hypocritical ecclesiastics outright.[36]

I have been emphasizing that I will show religiously redeeming values in the fabliau of the *Miller's Tale*. In such an endeavor I obviously will find myself in friendly competition with Thomas Ross, the scholar who not only had the *corage* to write *Chaucer's Bawdy*, a controversial yet groundbreaking work on close-reading Chaucer, but who also is the editor of the magisterial 1983 *Variorum* edition of the *Miller's Tale*.[37] Notwithstanding Jordan's worries about detrimental effects of new readings, I will, *inter alia*, propose "new versions" of what happens in the two window scenes. But since those new versions build on and go considerably beyond what Ross has said, in some cases heartily disagreeing with Ross and in other cases carrying through to their possible conclusions speculations which Ross touched upon but did not pursue, and since those new versions also venture beyond Dinshaw's *Sexual Poetics* in elaborating on Chaucer's ironic use of gender-crossing, I daresay that my discussions of the *Miller's Tale* will not add to the the fog of ennui which according to Jordan is threatening to envelop Chaucer studies. On the contrary, the conclusions I reach about the *Miller's Tale* may have a defogging effect on some readers' view of the *Knight's Tale* as boringly Boethian.

What might further minimize the danger of my study contributing to the aforementioned ennui is precisely that I read the *Miller's Tale* organically and intertextually. It was mainly because of the peculiar function which the cosmic-union motif holds in the *Miller's Tale* that I chose to begin my first chapter with an extensive discussion of that tale, a tale whose very subject matter seems to offer the best opportunity for demonstrating that Chaucer's playful exuberance is earnest. But then, perhaps the Miller's fabliau only *seems* to offer the best opportunity for such a demonstration. After all, wouldn't further pursuit of Robertson's placement of the Prioress among the daughters of Venus[38] offer an opportunity for the *solaas* of discovering that Ross, who in the Introduction of *Chaucer's Bawdy* took pains to distance himself from the Robertsonians since they employed methods similar to his own,[39] may have been correct only in the second half of his obervation that "One does not find bawdiness in Chaucer's Prioress, and one does not expect to"?[40]

The answers to questions like these will be spread out over several chapters of this book. Because I read the *Canterbury Tales* palimpsestically, one particular tale or one particular character will not necessarily receive full treatment in any one chapter but, instead, will be a crucial focus of one chapter and receive additional scrutiny in later chapters. For example, while Chapter III is mainly about the Pardoner, it will provide information about Chaucer's attitude toward the Prioress which I do not provide in Chapter II, a chapter focusing on the portrayal of the Prioress. I chose such an arrangement because in the third chapter I view the portraits of these two ecclesiastics in the light of each other's state of sexuality—but also in the light of information from *Sir Thopas* and that tale's prologue.

In fact, this Introduction, which in its length and because of the interpretive material it offers has been less an "introduction" than it has been an opening chapter, is an example of my methodology in that it has already addressed key aspects of the *Merchant's Tale* which I will elaborate later in my study. I would like to think of my approach as a spiral, overlapping but never circular: as an overlapping spiral which, in addition to providing cross-references both among the chapters and to the General Prologue as well as to other tales, combines into an organic whole what initially might appear to be independent chapters on five individual tales. The organic nature of my study increases in the course of my chapters, with the final chapter returning to the two narratives with whose explication I began my Introduction: the *Merchant's Tale* and the cosmic-union passage in the General Prologue. Thus the spiral completes its largest overlap.

Wouldn't such a spiral offer promise that it could rise above the feared fog of ennui if in a "new reading" I tried to show that Chaucer intended the *Clerk's Tale*, which in the hallowed critical tradition of the Marriage Debate not only extols patient Griselda's marital obedience but also serves to usher in the unhappily married Merchant's apparently misogynistic story, as a feminist joke? And wouldn't it add to our appreciation of the *Canterbury Tales* if we learned that Chaucer even was having a little fun at the expense of the good Parson? If the conclusions which my close-reading of the text leads to will seem extravagant to some Chaucerians, maybe, just maybe, that is because their complacency sometimes needs to be tested. Let us give Chaucer's text an opportunity to speak for itself.

CHAPTER I

This *Queynte Nicholas:*
Poetic Justice, Parody, and Earnest Exuberance

I pleaded at the conclusion of my Introduction, "If the conclusions which my close-reading of the text leads to will seem extravagant to some Chaucerians, maybe, just maybe, that is because their complacency sometimes needs to be tested. Let us give Chaucer's text an opportunity to speak for itself." I will begin this testing with Kendrick's interpretation of the four lines with which the Miller announces the moral of his fabliau:

> An housbonde shall nat been inquisityf
> Of Goddes pryvetee, nor of his wyf.
> So he may fynde Goddes foyson there,
> Of the remnant needeth nat enquere. (I 3163-66)

Kendrick quotes these lines at the beginning of her first chapter, entitled "Reading for *Sentence* versus Reading for *Solas*: A Broadening Example," and comments:

> These lines . . . used to seem dangerous to teach to undergraduates. After I had explained the double meaning of *pryvetee* as "secret intentions" or "private parts" (a euphemism for "sex organs") and pointed out what this meant in terms of a husband's dealings with his wife—not to bother himself about whether he is being cuckolded as long as he is getting enough sex—I would rush on to the next lines before some perverse student had the chance to pose the unseemingly question I was trying to suppress of whether the Miller was making a joke about God's

genitals too: "an housbonde shal nat been inquisityf/Of *goddes pryvetee*, nor of his wyf." . . . *Surely Chaucer could not have intended such a blasphemous innuendo to raise its ugly head? Or could he?*

What of the gigantically grotesque sign that hangs suspended over much of the action of the "Miller's Tale": two round containers and an oblong one, each big enough to hold a person, the "knedyng trogh," "tub," and "kymelyn" (A 3620-21) that the foolish carpenter hangs from the rafters of his house "in pryvetee" (3623)? . . . If the oblong trough were hung parallel to the ground, which it would have to be to serve as a boat, what would this trinity of containers look like from underneath? *Might the carpenter's installation not look like the crude figure of huge male genitals in erection, a burlesque, carnival-esque version of "Goddes pryvetee" . . . ?*[1]

I will answer Kendrick's cautious questions, which I italicized, with an unqualified "yes." Kendrick too in the final analysis answers her own questions with "yes." Yet I think Kendrick complicates the assessment of Chaucerian bawdy by trying to distinguish between a "gentil interpretation" and a "churlish interpretation" of such passages. She refers, in a chapter entitled "The Spirit versus Flesh in Art and Interpretation," to medieval visual representations of Christ's genitalia, representations which presumably were intended as "iconography of the Incarnation"[2] but very easily lent themselves to "churlish" interpretations. Literary artists in turn could simply imitate these churlish interpretations in their writings without running the risk of seeming to mix earnest and game and thus despiritualize the earnest—i.e., literary artists could simply pass the buck to the reader or, as is the case with the *Miller's Tale*, blame any despiritualizing obscenities on the Miller-the-*cherl* and advise the reader, "Turne over the leef." According to Kendrick, such artistic peek-aboo has led to two opposite directions in Chaucer scholarship:

> A long tradition of censorship in Chaucer criticism involves ignoring anything that does not seem sufficiently serious in Chaucer's writing, while demonstratingly praising that which does. . . . Only very gradual-ly have we become willing to acknowledge that Chaucer might play with language upon occasion, that he might take delight in the formal aspects of the tale, in "literature for its own sake," as a game of signification with no moral application, with no higher purpose than *solas*.[3]

I wish to argue against Kendrick's distinction between "gentil" and "churlish" interpretation both *in* and *of* the *Canterbury Tales*, and I will do so in part by showing moral applications in the Miller's fabliau that have been overlooked, one of the moral applications in fact being adumbrated by the Miller's mention of "Goddes pryvetee." I will illustrate how the *solaas* of the formal aspects can be an instrument in achieving *sentence*—and achieving it without allegorizing. I will show Chaucer's spirit of *earnest* exuberance by subjecting the tale to a close textual analysis, to a close organic reading, which the tale has not yet received, notwithstanding Kendrick's dazzling study—and notwithstanding Ross' magisterial *Miller Variorum*.

My close textual analysis will seriously question the validity of Robert Jordan's 1967 assessment of the *Miller's Tale*, an assessment which, as evidenced by Kendrick's remarks about Chaucer taking delight in playing with language, by and large still seems to be shared today: "Thematically barren and morally neutral, the Miller's Tale is an example of inorganic narrative in a relatively 'pure' form . . . what matters is simply the art, the exultation in a master's making . . . [At the end] a kind of miracle has been achieved, but it is primarily an aesthetic achievement, not a moral one."[4] My textual analysis will show that, rather than morally neutral according to Jordan, the *Miller's Tale* is thematically pregnant because it possesses a leitmotif which provides the narrative with a highly organic form that goes beyond the esthetic achievement—so that the exultation in a master's making is an *earnest* exultation.

Any examination of the *Miller's Tale* for *sentence* first has to address a question which Chaucer scholarship never seems to have been very much concerned with, primarily, perhaps, because the plot of a fabliau is not expected to conform to customary norms of justice: does the old carpenter John deserve the fate of being cuckolded by the student boarder who uses a bizarre scheme of deception to achieve his goal? Paul A. Olson has suggested that, as a personification of avarice and as a typical "possessive *jaloux*," the carpenter is "deceived by Nicholas precisely because he is so eager to possess the world after the flood that he forgets the biblical promise that the flood will not be repeated."[5] I submit that Chaucer's presentation of John is more complex than has hitherto been thought. The Miller is making clear what he thinks the carpenter deserves when, prior to telling the story, he advises his audience that John brought his fate upon himself because he did not know what Cato had stipulated for a successful marriage:

> He *knew nat* Catoun, for *his wit was rude*,
> That bad a man sholde wedde his simylitude.
> Men sholde wedden after hire estaat . . . (I 3227-29, italics added)

The reason the Miller gives us for John's downfall is that the carpenter is the typical *senex amans* who marries a woman much younger than himself. However, from Chaucer's stance John's violation of the law of *estaat* is not the full answer. But then, Chaucer is already building into the Miller's own rationale a hint which may eventually lead the alert reader to the real answer: John's mistake is indeed that he lacks the "knowledge" of the pronouncement someone else had made—and Chaucer is using the Miller's pronouncement to lay the foundation for what I will call the tale's "knowledge"-motif.

One of the things which John does not know is that in Genesis God had promised man not to send another flood. Yet John's sin—I use the word *sin* deliberately—lies not so much in his being unaware of the Covenant as in the judgment he had passed earlier when he thought the young scholar had become moonstruck as a result of his endeavors in astrology:

> I thoghte ay wel how that it sholde be!
> Men sholde nat knowe of Goddes pryvetee.
> *Ye, blessed be alwey a lewed man*
> *That noght but oonly his bileve kan!*
> . . . . .
> Me reweth soore of hende Nicholas.
> He shal be rated of his studiyng,
> If that I may, by Jhesus, hevene kyng! (I 3453-64, italics added)

Ross explicates the carpenter's pronouncement concerning his "bileve" as follows: "The Creed ('I believe in one God . . . ') and the Pater Noster were the two indispensable formulas that Christians were supposed to commit to memory." And Ross remarks that "John is proud that he lacks learning."[6] I would like to argue that John's pride in his lack of learning is not the only kind of pride he is guilty of.

When John congratulates himself for being ignorant and expresses pity toward the clerk, the carpenter is claiming to be existentially better off than the well-educated Nicholas, first because he possesses knowledge of the only thing which man needs to know, and second because, in contrast to the clerk, his "bileve" is the *only* thing the old man knows. The carpenter thinks that in the eyes of God, in whom John and, presumably, also the clerk believe, he is a better Christian than the clerk. John, then, is guilty of the deadliest of the Deadly Sins, guilty of *superbia*.

John displays his sin of a holier-than-thou attitude in the scene immediately following his pronouncement on the importance of him knowing "his bileve." First of all, the scene introduces us to John's manner of practicing the Christian religion. He uses a series of memorized formulas, some of them memorized incorrectly or misapplied, as magic charms in an attempt both to protect his house against demons and to help Nicholas out of his trance. There doesn't seem too much that is objectionable about John using those rites, rites which after all had grown out of Christian teachings, although Chaucer's purpose in having John rattle off verses that are much like nursery rhymes[7] is to suggest already that the carpenter's understanding of Christianity may not be as good as he thinks it is. But there is something rather perturbing about what John says to Nicholas when the latter finally comes out of his faked trance:

> atte laste this hende Nicholas
> Gan for to sik soore, and seyde "Allas!
> Shal al the world be lost eftsoones now?"
> This carpenter answerede, "What seystow?

What! *Thynk on God, as we doon, men that swynke.''*
(I 3487-91, italics added)

John does not yet know what Nicholas is planning to announce, but when John believes Nicholas' prediction of a flood more than twice as great as Noah's, John is showing the *he* does not "Thynk on God": John does not "Thynk on" the Biblical promise. Worse yet, John thinks he is a better Christian than Nicholas because, unlike the clerk, the "working man" knows the *only* thing that counts, the memorized Creed—although he does not know the Biblical promise made by Him whom according to John's own announcement the carpenter believes in.

Chaucer, who displays an interest in astrology throughout his work regardless of whether he is the author of the *Astrolabe*, is likely to be more sympathetic toward Nicholas than toward a person who not only takes pride in lacking knowledge but actually claims that only working-class people can be good Christians: "Thynk on God, as we doon, men that swynke." In light of the fact that John is about to show that *he* doesn't "Thynk on God," we interpret John's pronouncement on social-class differences as an additional signal from the poet to point in the direction of John's sinful pride.

John is compounding his sin when, in a judgmental speech in which he even calls upon Jesus to be his witness, he pokes fun at the idea of knowledge gained through formal education and promises that he will scold Nicholas for his studying. Chaucer has John set himself up in this manner for his exposure of being guilty of pride *before* the confrontation which John prays for takes place. While the notion of a man being cuckolded by another man in punishment for claiming to be a better Christian than the other man is hardly consonant with Christian ideas, John's vilification of scholastic knowledge paves the way for the punishment which Chaucer will poetically mete out to him. Chaucer describes John's punishment for his sin of pride even a) before John calls himself blessed for being an unschooled man and vilifies the pursuit of knowledge, and b) before John, through his lack of a proper response to Nicholas' alleged astrological discovery, proves his ignorance of the promise made by Him whom he had professed his belief in. Chaucer foreshadows the carpenter's punishment in the scene where during John's absence *hende Nicholas* unabashedly makes advances at the young wife:

> on a day this hende Nicholas
> Fil with this yonge wyf to rage and pleye,
> Whil that hir housbonde was at Oseneye,
> As clerkes been *ful subtile and ful queynte*;
> And prively he caughte hir *by the queynte* . . .
> (I 3272-76, italics added)

The *queynte/queynte* rhyme, which in the *Miller Variorum* Ross calls "perhaps the most famous example of *rime riche* (or identical rhyme) in Chaucer's work,"[8] has of course received a good deal of critical attention. No one, however, has explained that this famous/infamous rhyme is a theological joke loaded with thematic significance—but then we don't catch the theological significance of the *queynte/queynte* rhyme until we palimpsestically re-read the rhyme in the light of the carpenter's pronouncement on the nature of knowledge. The *queynte* in line 3276 is the contemporary vulgar slang term for the female pudendum. The adjective *queynte* which concludes the preceding line means something like artful, clever, ingenious. Modern English translations usually make no attempt to render the pun, which indicates that the translators ultimately fail to catch Chaucer's point. The adjective *queynte* is cognate with Modern English "ac-quaint." "To become acquainted with" something or somebody means "to get to know" that something or somebody: when Chaucer punningly plays the two words against each other by having Nicholas catch Alison by her *queynte*, Chaucer is introducing into the *Miller's Tale* the idea of a man "knowing" a woman in the Biblical sense. In order to approximate the meaning of Chaucer's pun, I would therefore suggest something like the

following translation: " . . . these clerks are very subtle and know a lot;/
And he privily caught her by the you-know-what.''[9]

Even the Larry Benson who, as mentioned earlier, at the 1984 Chaucer
Congress amused himself and his audience with a presentation on the dangers
of sniffing *queynte* everywhere—the presentation was published in the following year as an article entitled "The 'Queynte' Punnings of Chaucer's
Critics''[10]—could not or did not want to handle the passage about "this hende
Nicholas'' grabbing Alison by the *queynte* when he published the *Riverside
Chaucer* in 1987. As General Editor of that edition, Benson, as he explains in
the Preface, had (together with Patricia L. Eberle) primary responsibility for
the glosses, but he must have pretty much delegated this prickly issue to the
contributor of the Explanatory Notes for the *Miller's Tale*, to Douglas Gray,
because according to the Preface the writers of Explanatory Notes provided
glosses for their parts of Chaucer's text.[11] The glosses explain the *queynte* in
line 3275 as "ingenious, clever,'' and the one in the next line as "elegant,
pleasing (thing); i.e., pudendum.''[12] In the Explanatory Notes Gray comments
on the second *queynte* as follows: "A euphemism, the absolute adjective,
'elegant, pleasing (thing),' used here for the pudendum with a pun on the
obscenity, which was the same in Middle English as in modern speech.''[13]

Chaucer's contemporaries knew of course that the two words in lines
3275 and 3276 were not just homographs but actually were the same word,
with the second being an absolute adjective whose noun referent was so well
known that the noun was eventually dropped, as a result of which the adjective
(which has survived in Modern English "quaint'' in the meaning of exquisite,
pleasing to the connoisseur) came to be used as a noun. Yet even Chaucer's
contemporaries would not have seen any moral significance in the *queynte*
pun-rhyme if the *queynte*-grabbing male hadn't been specifically presented as a
"knowing'' person, as someone with a formal education, whose knowledge the
carpenter would later ridicule vis-à-vis his own. However, once the readers

have caught the various associations radiating from the nucleus of the tale's knowledge motif, they take another look at the *rime riche*, discover the function of that rhyme, and thus become able to see the role which Chaucer's portrayal of a clerk as a *queynte*-chaser plays within the *sentence* of the *Miller's Tale*. Jacqueline de Weever elaborates in her *Chaucer Name Dictionary* on Nicholas as a namesake of the "patron saint of students":[14] I would now like to submit that, when Chaucer three lines before the *queynte* pun refers to the knowledgeable young clerk as "this hende Nicholas," he is insinuating that he is using this fictional amorous young man for lessons to be taught, i.e., knowledge to be conveyed, both to a character within the plot of the *Miller's Tale* and to his readers. Where appropriate in the discussion, I will therefore replace the term *hende Nicholas*, a term almost held dear in Chaucer scholarship, with *queynte Nicholas*.

In his earnest exuberance, then, Chaucer endows the fabliau of the *Miller's Tale* with religiously redeeming values: Chaucer poetically punishes John for claiming that, thanks to the limitations of his knowledge, he is better off than the clerk. The punishment is that Chaucer presents the clerk, whom John makes fun of because of his pursuit of knowledge, as getting to know in the Biblical sense the carpenter's wife—and getting to know her in the Biblical sense because her husband does not know the Biblical promise made by Him whom he proudly professes belief in. Chaucer is setting the stage for such a role on the clerk's part even prior to the identical-rhyme pun when he has the Miller say about Nicholas that "Of deerne love he *koude* and of solaas" (I 3200, italics mine). When Chaucer tells us that the clerk "knows" all about secret love and *solaas*, the poet is preparing us for a tale that will combine "sentence" and "solaas" in the following unique manner: the "solaas" of two of the characters, Nicholas and Alison, will also be part of *the reader's* "solaas" which the poet will employ for the purpose of communicating "sentence."

Chaucer will have Nicholas unknowingly confirm his role in the poet's moral scheme when, in reply to Alison's cautioning words, the clerk assures the woman that he would have used his time poorly, in other words, wasted his education, if he didn't know how to fool a carpenter: "A *clerk* hadde litherly biset his whyle,/But if he *koude* a carpenter bigyle" (I 3300, italics added). In a tale where "knowledge" is the leitmotif which gives the narrative a highly organic form, Chaucer is using *queynte Nicholas* as an agent for punishing John for his sin of pride: while Chaucer is by no means suggesting that he approves of adultery—after all, Nicholas will be punished for his own sin when he gets his posterior burned in the second window scene—in the terms of Chaucer's literary artistry the form of John's punishment fits his crime.[15]

I spoke of the terms of Chaucer's literary artistry because he delineates the punishment already before John commits his act of sin. There is the ironic interaction between the Miller's descriptive statement, "*prively* he caughte her by the queynte" (italics added), and John's criticism of Nicholas' pursuit of knowledge: "Men sholde nat knowe of Goddes *pryvetee*" (italics added). Nicholas had taken the first step toward getting to know John's wife's *pryvetee* of one kind before her husband spoke out against man's attempt to get to know God's *pryvetee* of another kind. The interaction between *prively* and *pryvetee* provides an ironic reminder of the fact that at the very moment of John's pronouncement on what man should not do with respect to God He knows—as well as the story's teller does—not only what the foolish carpenter will do, but also what will happen between Nicholas and Alison.[16] This is not to say that God causes the adultery; rather, in a tale about knowledge and lack thereof—we remember the Miller's early statement, "he knew nat Catoun, for his wit was rude"—we are dealing with *foreknowledge* of an omniscient God. In fact, at this point John is still in a position to control his own fate, but he is relinquishing that control when he commits the sin of pride by claiming to be in a better position with God than Nicholas is.

John knowing about Noah's Flood but not knowing about God's promise could mean that he has totally forgotten about the Covenant, which surely was part of the context in which he first learned about Noah. Even though the carpenter could not read the Latin Vulgate and priests did not preach the actual text of the Bible, which at that time was being treated as a mystery and therefore had not been officially permitted to be translated into English, he must have learned about the Covenant during sermons attached with the mass or at least during his confirmation training. John's once having learned but then having forgotten about God's promise would lend special meaning to Chaucer's presentation of the carpenter as a *senex amans*. For when Nicholas asks him whether he has "nat herd hou saved was Noe," the carpenter answers, "Yis . . . ful yoore ago" (I 3534-37): while the reader will probably assume that in his "ful yoore ago" answer John is referring to the time when the Flood occurred, the poet could be referring to the time, long ago, when John heard about the Flood, which was so long ago that he has forgotten the part about the Covenant. This in turn could suggest that John ceased to attend events of formal religious instruction "ful yoore ago."[17] But then it is part of Chaucer's irony that he also leaves room for the interpretation that John suddenly forgets all about God's promise because he gets carried away by the pride he takes in being a carpenter, a talent which has enabled him to have ready the containers which he believes will be needed to save his own, his wife's, and Nicholas' lives. This would suggest a case of anthropocentric pride, a case of hubris. What at any rate suggests that the carpenter is guilty of anthropocentric pride is the fact that, whereas Noah had been personally instructed by God to build an ark, a mere communication from another human being is enough to get the carpenter to play Noah. Whatever it is that causes

John not to remember the Covenant, he fails to be the outstanding Christian he claims he is.

John is indirectly violating the prohibition he himself had voiced earlier, namely that "Men sholde nat knowe of Goddes pryvetee," when the carpenter allows information given to him by a *human* to get him into Noah's business. Nicholas refers to the mystery plays about Noah's ark in great detail. These mystery plays were performed by the guild thought to be most naturally suited for such plays, by the carpenters' guild, and Noah was often presented as a carpenter. While, as Kelsie B. Harder notes, in the mystery plays "the ark is built according to God's specifications, . . . in the *Miller's Tale* the clerk Nicholas, who gives John the carpenter the specifications to follow, is a shrewd intermediator between God and John."[18] And John is receiving a punishment appropriate for a would-be Noah, appropriate for a would-be Noah who becomes what could be called a parody Noah, when the pride of the ambitious ark builder goes before what literally is a fall: when, burned by Absalom's hot colter, the astrologer who had elevated John to a Noah shouts, "Help! Water! Water! Help, for Goddes herte!" (I 3815), John cuts the ropes holding his kneading tub and his ark crashes to the ground. John breaking an arm in his fall, then, symbolizes the punishment for the breach of the Covenant which John had committed.[19]

Even if John committed the breach *unknowingly*, that is no excuse, as Chaucer makes clear by establishing various associations between various kinds of knowledge on the one hand, and on the other that which Johns claims to be the only thing man needs to know, his "bileve." Since John had at one time heard about God's promise but now no longer knows about it, we are dealing with a case of absence of *Christian belief* alias *faith*. Knowing the story about and accepting, i.e., "believing in," Noah's Flood but not having as part of one's "belief" the Covenant is comparable, perhaps, to knowing about Christ's crucifixion but not His resurrection. As I have discussed,

Chaucer makes it clear that in order to be a good Christian it is not enough to know a couple of memorized formulas. John can recite the Creed all day long, but that won't help him if he does not know about the Covenant which the God he prides himself of believing in had made with man. In fact, Chaucer is satirizing such a simplistic, but not altogether unpopular, notion of what practicing the Christian belief is.

Chaucer satirizes such a notion in particular by having John state that the only thing man needs to know is his "bileve," a word we need to take another look at. All Chaucer editions from Walter Skeat's in 1894 to Constance B. Hieatt's _Miller's Tale_ edition in 1970[20] had explicated _bileve_ as "creed" or, perhaps more explicitly, as "Creed." However, in 1971 John Halverson glossed lines 3455-56 as follows: "Blessed always is the ignorant man who who knows nothing but _his faith_" (italics mine).[21] And in 1977 John H. Fisher glossed _bileve kan_ as " . . . beliefs knows,"[22] a gloss which Fisher would repeat in 1989 in his Second Edition of _The Complete Poetry and Prose of Geoffrey Chaucer_.

Neither Halverson nor Fisher would seem to have been under any obligation to justify their departures from the customary interpretation of _bileve_ as Creed, since both editions are, in Fisher's words, "addressed to the student reader . . . [and] Intended to make Chaucer's text more accessible with a minimum of scholarly interference"[23] (in fact, Halverson's edition is not a complete edition of the _Canterbury Tales_ at all, merely providing summaries of some of the tales). But one might have expected Ross, the Editor of the _Miller Variorum_, who repeatedly cites Fisher's glosses, to address at least Fisher's differing interpretation of what John says he is so glad to know and know only. Neither does the _Riverside Chaucer_ address Fisher's (or, for that matter, Halverson's) deviating interpretation of John's use of the word _bileve_, even though it lists Fisher's 1977 edition as the most recent major edition. In fact, whereas the _Riverside Chaucer_ page glosses offer "creed,"[24] the Glossa-

ry, which refers to line 3456, lists "belief" as the only meaning of
bileve[25]—despite the fact that the Glossary of Robinson's Second Edition, the
acknowledged "model" for the *Riverside Chaucer*,[26] had listed "belief, faith,
creed."[27]   Add to this the fact that the 1979 *Chaucer Glossary*, which had
translated *bileve* as "belief, faith,"[28] referred to three Chaucerian loci but not
to the Miller's line, and that compilers of the *Chaucer Glossary*, including
Douglas Gray, would also be contributors to the *Riverside Chaucer*—and you
don't know *what* to believe.[29]

Could this confusing picture actually be a reflection of the poet's
intent? Perhaps the best illustration of the use of the word *bileve* in the meaning of Creed can be found in William Langland's *Piers Plowman*: "I . . . sat
softly adown and seide my bileues;/And so I babeled on my bedes."[30]   Although Ross makes no reference to it, Langland's description is probably the
best evidence for Ross' claim that when John mentions "his bileve" the carpenter is referring to one of the indispensable formulas that Christians were
supposed to commit to memory. Especially in the light of the magic-charms
scene, we can easily imagine John living up to his perception of himself as an
oustanding Christian by "babbling" bits and pieces he had memorized. I
could even imagine that Chaucer is actually alluding to the scene of a humble
person in *Piers* saying the Rosary in order to contrast that person with the carpenter, who is sanctimoniously contrasting himself with the astrologer who had
dared to pry into God's secrets. In any case, regardless of whether Chaucer is
making an allusion to Langland, John blatantly lacks that which Piers firmly
possessed: *bileve* in the more generic meaning of that word. John does not
know *his faith*, i.e., he does not know his religion, since, as the *Miller's Tale*
emphasizes, the Covenant is part of that religion. Therefore, if John is using
the word in its more generic meaning, he is pretending to knowledge which he
does not possess.

But in that case John's sin would be not only his false claim that he knows his "bileve," not only his taking pride in the fact that that particular knowledge is the only one he possesses, but, more importantly, his claim that the difference between what he knows and doesn't know makes him look better in God's eyes than the clerk's formal knowledge, especially astrology, makes the clerk look. In both cases John is guilty of pride, and in both cases the punishment fits the crime: Nicholas gets to know in the Biblical sense the wife of a man who doesn't know the Biblical promise. However, the second scenario would make John look even worse. John would be basing his existential superiority to the clerk on knowledge which he does not possess, but which he had proudly declared was the only knowledge he had: in the second scenario John ends up a total zero.

If Chaucer had wanted to make clear that John meant the Creed and nothing more generic, the poet could have used the unequivocal term *Crede*, as he would do in the *Canon's Yeoman's Tale*, where he is playing the word *bileve* in its specific meaning of Creed against its synonym *Crede* when he has the alchemy-faking canon assure the credulous priest whom the canon is about to cheat out of his money, "Bileveth this as siker as your Crede" (VIII 1047). If we read the *Canterbury Tales* as an organic work of literature, then the pun in the *Canon's Yeoman's Tale* advises us to re-evaluate Chaucer having the carpenter use the term *bileve* rather than *Crede*. I wish to argue that Chaucer is using the term *bileve* first to cause the same kind of uncertainty or even confusion which I have suggested besets modern critics, and second, and more importantly, to finally convey the idea that knowing, and being able to regurgitate, formulas is not the same as knowing and practicing Christianity.

There may even be a palimpsestic interaction between the two tales. The fact that the Canon and the Yeoman, who are not mentioned in the General Prologue, join the pilgrimage late while it is already in progress has been adduced as evidence that Chaucer added the Canon's Yeoman's story as an afterthought,[31] but the same evidence could be used to argue that Chaucer added it in part for the purpose of informing the earlier tale. At any rate, there is an intriguing parallel between the two tales. The priest in the *Canon's Yeoman's Tale* of course knows his "Crede" alias "bileve," but knowing the Creed does not stop the priest from believing the fake alchemist and buying his supposedly miraculous alchemy powder. Similarly, knowing his "bileve" does not prevent John from being victimized when Nicholas predicts a flood: whatever John meant when he proudly said he knew "his bileve," "knowing" it while not knowing the Biblical promise causes John to *believe* the astrologer's phony prediction.

Once we have witnessed Chaucer pun on the two different meanings of *bileve*, in a fabliau which in part is an audaciously hilarious "game" with the idea of knowledge, we are likely to suspect that the poet is playing a similar wordgame in the passage in which John congratulates himself for being an outstanding Christian. I would therefore like to suggest that we are dealing with a case of both-and irony. Those readers who are aware of the ambiguity will consider the options and come to realize that in either case John is guilty of the sin of pride and is fittingly punished—and that in either case it had been inappropriate for the carpenter to use the heavily loaded term "bileve" in an attempt to present himself as a better Christian than the well-educated Nicholas.[32]

There is yet another direction in which Chaucer's use of both-and irony could be operating: while Chaucer has the carpenter pride himself on knowing only the Creed, the poet is already suggesting that John would be better off if he knew the *entire Christian "bileve"* as it had been taught to him long ago. In fact, this is the direction in which I myself believe Chaucer's both-and irony is operating. But this does not rule out the interpretations I presented earlier: I demonstrate throughout my study that varying interpretations can all coexist, as is appropriate for the consummate ironist. For what Chaucer is trying to tell us about John is that long ago the carpenter was only interested in the sensational or otherwise entertaining Biblical stories he had heard—or perhaps that John may have kept up with his knowledge about his "bileve," about his religion, not through formal instruction but rather by watching the mystery plays from whose crude, non-literary nature Chaucer, as Harder convincingly argues, dissociates himself by fiercely satirizing them.

Chaucer is insinuating something to that effect when he describes how after his fall John tries to tell people the full truth of what had happened but they, interested only in the sensational part of the story as spread by Nicholas and Alison, do not wish to listen to and thus commit to memory John's part of the story:

> For what so that this carpenter answerde,
> It was for noght: *no man his reson herde* . . .
> (I 3843-44, italics added)

Very much like the people who now want to "hear" only about John's preoccupation with and preparations for a second flood but not about the carpenter's reasons for his behavior, many years ago John had not been interested in and therefore rendered subject to oblivion the more intellectually demanding aspects of the story of Noah. John had taken no interest in the idea that, while God did punish mankind by sending a flood, He showed himself to be a *merciful* God by promising mankind not to send another one. By rendering easy prey to oblivion the Christian "bileve" *of* as well as *in* a merciful God, the carpenter hubristically throws away any chance at mercy which the poet might have wanted to give him. Whether or not Chaucer is suggesting that John's ignorance-based hubris is a result of watching and accepting as religious instruction the mystery plays which Chaucer-the-literary-artist so despised, the old carpenter throws away a chance which, as I will elaborate in a Chapter V, Chaucer accords to another sinful character in a tale told by his pilgrims, to the *senex amans* in the *Merchant's Tale*.

John, then, is not giving God a chance. It is therefore poetic justice
that, before John has a chance to make any inquiries about Nicholas' curiosity-
arousing instructions, Nicholas tells him not to ask any questions about God's
secrets:

> Axe not why, for though thou aske me,
> I wol nat tellen Goddes pryvetee.
> Suffiseth thee, but if thy wittes madde,
> To han as greet a grace as Noe hadde. (I 3357-60, italics added)

Especially via the portion which I italicized, Chaucer is alluding to the ancient
Stoics' precept as it had been expressed by Horaces *Carpe diem* poem
(*Carmen* I, 11):

> Tu ne quaesieris, scire nefas, quem mihi, quem tibi,
> finem di dederint . . . nec Babylonios
> Temptaris numeros. ut melius, quidquid erit, pati,
> Seu plures hiemes seu tribuit Iuppiter ultimam . . .
> Do not try to find out—for it is sin to know—which day by the gods'
> decree will be my last, which your last. And do not try astrology.
> How much better it is to accept whatever is in store for us, whether it
> is already our last winter, or whether Jupiter will grant us some more
> winters . . . (1-4, italics added)[33]

The carpenter is violating the precept of the Stoics as formulated by
Horace when John makes provisions for a second flood. The twist is, of
course, that it is not John himself but Nicholas who uses means whereby it
was thought possible to find out the future. The irony is that it is precisely in
order to be able to follow the lesson of Horace's *Carpe diem* poem and "seize
the day" that the astrologer himself echoes Horace's "Tu ne quaesieris" when
Nicholas tells John not to ask any questions, "Axe not why . . . " As Ross,
noting the punning connection between "Goddes pryvetee" ("secrets") and
Alison's "pryvetee" ("private parts"), observes, Nicholas pretends to have
looked into the former while he actually wants to to find out about the
latter[34]—or to combine Horace's terminology with the terms I suggested earlier, to literally "seize" or "catch" and "become acquainted with" that which
"it is sin to know" (that which is "scire nefas"). When Nicholas

"prively . . . caughte her by the queynte," he was catching/seizing the day—or more precisely, if Chaucer is allusively putting Horace's poem to *parodic* use, Nicholas was catching/seizing the *night*.

However, what adds to the moral application, to the religiously redeeming values, of a fabliau about the punishment of an unschooled carpenter who pretends to be a better Christian than someone else because he knows only his Creed is that the punishing agent, an educated young man, is himself punished for pretending to know "Goddes pryvetee," or rather, for using his alleged knowledge of God's will for the sinful purpose of bedding the carpenter's wife.[35] While, as discussed, poetically the carpenter deserves to be cuckolded by the clerk, we must bear in mind that it is as a result of the clerk's pretense to possess the intellectual means with which to find out God's secrets that John commits his sin of pride. It is therefore poetic justice that Nicholas receives his own punishment in the window of the bedroom in which he had just been punishing the carpenter by knowing the latter's wife: Chaucer poetically punishes the clerk for violating two different kinds of "scire nefas." In fact, I now wish to argue that Nicholas too is guilty of pride. As Alfred David has noted in *The Strumpet Muse: Art and Morals in Chaucer's Poetry*,

> Not content with a straightforward seduction, [Nicholas] must turn his sexual triumph into a triumph of his art . . . He enjoys the execution of his plot as much as he enjoys Alisoun, and the chain of circumstances he has set in motion finally proves to be his ruin . . . To be branded in the rear by fire is a punishment worthy of Dante for the false prophet of a second flood.[36]

In a seeming tour de force of esemplastic imagination, Chaucer is intertwining with each other the notions of someone knowing the Creed but not knowing the Biblical promise, of a man Biblically knowing a woman, of man not being allowed to inquire into the (Judaeo-) Christian God's secrets, and, via the allusion to Horace's *Carpe diem* poem, of man not being allowed to inquire into Jupiter's secrets. But how does the notion of what Kendrick calls "the crude figure of huge male genitals in erection, a burlesque, carnivalesque version of 'Goddes pryvetee''' fit into this context of ideas? The sexual notion of ''Goddes pryvetee'' becomes indeed—to use Kendrick's words with whom I disagree at this point—''[a] higher purpose than *solas*,'' i.e., an instance of *earnest* exuberance, when we read it in terms of interaction with the opening lines of the General Prologue, much as I did earlier in my explication of a crucial passage in the *Merchant's Tale*.

Regardless of whether Chaucer is actually using the Oxonian scholar within the plot of the *Miller's Tale* for such a textual interaction when he has Nicholas echo Horace's warning that man should not inquire into Jupiter's secrets, the very idea of a deity sending a flood refers the reader to Chaucer's cosmic-union picture, and thus to the Virgilian picture of Jupiter descending with a fruitful shower into the womb of Mother Earth. It might therefore not be impertinent to look at the following comparisons which Kendrick has made in explicating the Miller's advice, ''An housbonde shal nat been inquisityf/Of Goddes pryvetee, nor *his* wyf'' (Kendrick's italics):

> Whose wife? The pronoun reference is ambiguous . . . When we think of the Miller's advice as an allusion to Joseph and Mary and the Incarnation, and, even more specifically, when we think of visual representations of the Nativity in which Christ and Mary are depicted as *sponsus* and *sponsa*, the proverb turns on us . . . It suggests that God assumed human shape—*like the philandering Jove*—in order to be privy with Mary, cuckolding her husband (who should not be too inquisitive if he knows what is good for him).[37] (The italics in *like the philandering Jove* are mine.)

Kendrick's analogies again are ingenious, but her comparison of an anthropomorphic Christian God to the philandering Jove is actually more helpful than a suggestion of a ''churlish interpretation'' of iconography and re-representation on the part of the literary artist. The notion of God which is insinuated in the Miller's prologue and in his tale is indeed comparable to the notion of an impregnating Jove, i.e., comparable to the *Juppiter descendens* alias rainfall making the soil fertile. In fact, I wish to argue that Chaucer makes the notion of an anthropomorphic God being privy with Mary *allusively analogous* to the notion of the impregnating Jupiter. There is of course the allusively functional contrast that, whereas in the cosmic-union pictures in Virgil and in the General Prologue the respective deities beget life, the rain which Nicholas deceivingly predicts is a force which would, like Noah's Flood, destroy all life on earth. In sexual terms, "Goddes pryvetee" releases an ejaculate so vast that it drowns all living things—an event whose threat is symbolized by the replica of God's phallus-plus-testicles which quite literally hovers over the scene of sinfulness.

The replica foreshadows the Divine threat, a threat posed by a Christian God anthropomorphosed into a Jupiter who punishes the sinners he is angry at with a flood[38]—except that he/He does not need to send a flood to execute the punishment because Chaucer poetically punishes John already *before* any such flood would occur, namely in the theologically meaningful joke of the identical-rhyme *game*. God also does not need to send another flood to punish the clerk, for *queynte Nicholas* receives his punishment during a surprise encounter which he springs on Absalom. For the equally surprising consequences of this encounter ironically cause Nicholas to at least indirectly call upon God (" . . . Water! Help, for Goddes herte!") for a tiny amount of that which in his attempt to deceive John he had predicted would come in the form of a deluge—as "Goddes foyson" coming from "Goddes pryvetee"!

Since in the *Miller's Tale* God does *not* send a deluge, how do the aforementioned heretically gameful associations which Chaucer has established with Noah's Flood help us with our reading of that tale? In an article I quoted from earlier, an article entitled "Chaucer's Use of the Mystery Plays in the *Miller's Tale*," Harder points out numerous allusions to mystery plays about Noah, but does not elaborate on any narrative functions which such allusions might have. The article is persuasive in its claim that "almost point by point the *Miller's Tale* parodies the *popular* literary tradition of Noah's story" (italics added),[39] but it does not add to our understanding of Chaucer's *sophis-*

ticated literary text about the story. I will, however, seize upon Harder's statement that "John quakes for fear that his young wife might be drowned, whereas Noah's chief concern [in the mystery plays] is his age (he is 600 years old)."[40]

Harder seems to be relating the matter of Noah's age to John's statement that he had heard the Noah story "ful yoore ago." I said "seems" because Harder doesn't say whether Chaucer intended this as a parallel, let alone a literary allusion, to the mystery plays' elaborations on Noah's age. I wish to argue that it is an allusion, but then I will have to explain how such a relation helps us interpret Chaucer's text: it helps us understand Chaucer's portrayal of his own parody Noah not only as a *jaloux*, but more specifically as a *senex amans*. Chaucer is introducing the idea that it is because of John's old age that the carpenter fears that his wife may be "drowned": once we are aware of the sexual meaning of Chaucer's rainfall imagery, we know that John, although he never mentions any sex-related concern over his age, fears that his well has dried up and that his young wife, therefore, might be more open to other sources of influence—to the point of possible inundation. We finally have a convergence of Chaucer poetically punishing John for proudly claiming to be an outstanding Christian when he doesn't even know about the Covenant on the one hand, and on the other poetically punishing him as a *senex amans*, i.e., for his violation of the law of *estaat* by marrying someone to whom he would not be able to pay his marital *dette*. Chaucer's use of the theme of the pre-literary Noah mystery plays in a story about a *senex amans* now makes sense. And the fact of John's old age endows with additional irony his boasting statement that he *only* knows his Creed: how well has John "known" his young wife?

I have discussed Nicholas' role as willing and knowledgeable inundator. There is an interaction between the General Prologue's opening lines describing the cosmic union between sky and earth on the one hand, and on the other the form of Nicholas' punishment with regard to which I quoted Alfred David a short while ago: "To be branded in the rear by fire is worthy of Dante for the false prophet of a second flood." The punishment for the false prophet of a second flood is more worthy of Dante than David may have been aware of. For what does it mean that Nicholas' outcry for help from God's earthbound ejaculate occurs in response to Nicholas being punished with a "hoote kultour" (I 3776) put to his rear? I agree with David that Nicholas is over-reaching himself when he feels he must turn his sexual triumph into a triumph of his art, but I view Nicholas' attempt to turn the former into the latter as an integral part of the exuberant *game* which in this fabliau Chaucer is playing with various kinds of "knowledge"—and the form of Nicholas' punishment may well be the high point of Chaucer poetically meting out punishment to his characters in this tale.

First we need to understand why Chaucer has Absalom use a hot colter in his attempt to avenge himself on Alison for having misdirected him to kiss "hir naked ers/Ful savourly, er he were war of this" (I 3734-35). Absalom's intention is to follow up with a befitting parody coitus the parody kiss Alison had granted him. Absalom had interpreted her apparent willingness to exchange kisses with him as a promise of a sexual union, for he had commented to himself:

> I am a lord at alle degrees;
> For after this I hope ther cometh moore . . . (I 3724-25)

Since the *this* which Absalom receives is not exactly what he had expected, he in turn wishes to give Alison a likewise unexpected *moore*, namely the colter of a plow. Absalom, who usually is interpreted merely as a parody of the courteous lover in medieval romance, as a love fool simply to be laughed at, is displaying an appreciable measure of wit when he decides to "plow" Alison in a manner well suited to a woman who directs the man's kissing-stage pursuit to that region of her body which produces material used by the farmer to make the soil fertile.

While nothing sexual is happening in the first window scene—or so it seems at this point of our discussion—the second window scene is indeed a sexual inferno of sorts for knowledgeable Nicholas. Nicholas has been spending almost the entire night in a sexual paradise with Alison when his penchant for demonstrating his intellectual superiority, or at least his "intellectual cleverness,"[41] gets the better of him—as it did when he had caught by the *queynte* an Alison who was more than willing but he decided to apply his intellectual cleverness in response to her caution that he be discreet: "Myn husband is so ful of jalousye/That, but ye wayte wel and been pryvee" (I 3294-95). Alison was mainly playing a teasing game, and the Nicholas who was more than ready to "spille," perhaps even in danger of "raining" into his pants, during his first "acquaintance" with her—

> As clerkes ben ful subtile and ful queynte;
> And he prively caughte hir by the queynte,
> And seyde, "Y-wis, but if ich have my wille,
> For deerne love of thee, lemman, I spille"[42]—

should have taken her to bed right then, with the husband conveniently out of town, but Nicholas decided to put on an astrology show.

In the second window scene Nicholas gets burned when, after having enjoyed himself with Alison, he is not satisfied with his triumph over an extramarital rival for the married *lemman's* attention, but feels a need to improve upon the joke with which Alison had repelled as well as repulsed the rival. Carried away by *both* his sexual *and* his intellectual prowess, Nicholas sticks out his own rear and breaks wind in the face of the rival whom Alison had already blown out of the arena of the mock-courtly contest between the two suitors. The result is that Absalom, who thinks he can now "plow" Alison in a revengefully parodic manner, "plows" Nicholas instead. While any intent to inflict homosexual humiliation would have to be on the part of Nicholas since he wilfully replaces Alison, the person who ends up branded with homosexual humiliation is Nicholas himself. Nicholas is "plowed" in the rear by an Absalom who came back for the *moore* of administering the "hoote kultour" to her. Since Absalom's "hoote kultour" was from the very beginning intended for a parody sex act with Alison, *queynte Nicholas* becomes a homosexual rape victim while the rustic follower of courtly love become a plowman totally gone awry.

Chaucer wants us to contemplate the possible implications of the punishment which Absalom unknowingly manages to inflict upon the "knowledge-able" Nicholas, upon a young man who thinks he can go one better on the woman and takes her place in the window. Let us consider the description of Absalom's reaction to his earlier misdirected kiss:

> "Allas," quod he, "allas, I ne hadde *ybleynt!*"
> His hoote love was coold and al *yqueynt*;
> For fro that tyme that he hadde kist hir ers,
> Of paramours he sette nat a kers,
> For he was heeled of his maladie.
> Ful ofte paramours he gan deffie,
> And weep as dooth a child that is ybete. (I 3753-59, italics added)

The "ybleynt"/"yqueynt" ("turned aside"/"quenched") rhyme contains an ironic pun which suggests just where Absalom should have turned away from, and *perhaps should have turned away from long before this night*, for the rhyme interacts with the earlier pun in the "queynte"/"queynte" rhyme.[43] When the Miller says that Absalom's hot love has been "*al* yqueynt" (italics added), he is first of all suggesting that Absalom's lust has been thoroughly quenched because he did not make it "all the way" to Alison's *queynte* as had been his eventual goal, but, instead, made a different kind of "acquaintance" at an early stage of his pursuit. But the Miller (or at least Chaucer) is also insinuating that Absalom's lust was quenched by her letting Absalom come close enough to her *queynte*—"For *wel he wiste* a womman hath no berd./He felte a thyng al rough and long yherd" (I 3737-38, italics added)—but directing him in such a way that "he wiste" *well* a part of the human anatomy he had no desire to "get to know well," at least not in the manner he came to know it.

Absalom "getting to know" the rear does not of course mean that he will substitute homosexuality for heterosexuality, but there is the ironic twist that the next person Absalom "plows" is a male. On the other hand, there is indeed a substitution that Absalom performs which is perfectly suited to the occasion: cured of his romantic lover's malady,[44] Absalom substitutes a "hoote kultour" for the erstwhile "hoote love" which has now become "coold." This substitution is also logical if we bear in mind that what Alison had done to the hot lover was a form of castration. When Absalom said to himself, "I am a lord at alle degrees;/For after this I hope ther cometh moore," he was speaking of his own male domination, for which the sexual domination he thought he had attained was merely a symbol.[45]

The interpretation that Absalom is cured of his lover's malady is only a surface reading of lines 3753-59. For especially in light of the "allas, I ne hadde ybleynt"/"al yqueynt" rhyme, couldn't Chaucer also be suggesting that Absalom's erstwhile hot love has been so thoroughly quenched that one malady has been replaced by another—i.e., that the lover's malady conventional in the type of medieval romance which the *Miller's Tale* parodies has been replaced by a less coventional "maladie," by an *inability* to feel and physically express "hoote love"? An any rate, whether or not we wish to see an insinuation of Absalom's traumatic experience with Alison leading to sexual impotence, one doesn't have to be overly Freudian to view Alison's misdirection of Absalom's kiss as an act of psychological castration.

Ross seems to have been groping in the direction of some kind of castration on Absalom's part when, in his discussion of the Miller's statement that Absalom, the part-time surgeon and barber, "wel . . . wiste a womman hath no berd," he observed: "There is . . . a belief that some women are provided with a *vagina dentata* (toothed vagina); so far as I know, the folklorists have not brought their science to bear upon this passage.''[46] I am no folklorist, but I would like to submit that there is a *vagina dentata* staring us right in the face. Let us examine the lines immediately following Absalom's misdirected kiss:

> wel he wiste a woman hath no berd.
> He felte a thyng al rough and long yherd,
> And seyde, "Fy! allas! *what have I do?*"
> "Tehee!" quod she, and *clapte the wyndow to*,
> And Absolon gooth forth a sory pas.
> "A berd! A berd!" quod hende Nicholas,
> "By Goddes corpus, this goth faire and weel."
> *This sely Absolon herde every deel*,
> And on his lippe he gan for anger byte,
> And to hymself he seyde, "I shal thee quyte." (I 3737-46, italics added)

When Absalom kisses a mouth that is accompanied by a beard, he is involuntarily performing a gender-reversal. Even if we do not yet consider the gender-role reversal which Alison imposes on Absalom as an act of psychological castration, it certainly becomes one in Absalom's own perception when he is led to believe that another man is aware of and amused by his misdirected sexual advances. And Chaucer is making the castration-idea all but explicit when after the promise of the kiss Absalom first speaks to himself about the ''moore,'' then after the inauspicious kiss queries ''what have I do?'', and finally has his question rhymingly answered by the poet: ''[she] clapte the wyndow to.'' Quite literally looking forward to the ''moore,'' Absalom is symbolically unmanned when Alison slams the window shut on his sexual expectations—that is, symbolically Absalom has been mutilated by a *vagina dentata* of sorts.[47]

Since the *do/to* rhyme is the poet's answer to Absalom's question as to what *Absalom* has done, it could be argued that Absalom has symbolically mutilated himself. At any rate, Absalom has been punished for the phallic pride he was displaying when he designated himself as "a lord at alle degrees."[48] But while there isn't much that Absalom can do to undo the damage inflicted on him, he can punish the female who punished him. What the male who feels psychologically castrated intends to do with the hot colter is to castrate the female—castrate her *physically*, by rendering her incapable of sexual intercourse for a considerable period of time at least. By burning her buttocks, Absalom would render her incapable of having intercourse in what today we call the missionary position, the position prescribed by the Church, although, as I will discuss, Absalom's original intention to sexually disable Alison may have gone farther than skin-deep.

While Absalom's act of "plowing" alias "getting to know" Nicholas may not have caused any sexual impairment to the latter, the form of the punishment fits the crime, as it did in the cases of John proudly claiming to be a better Christian because he only knows the Creed and Absalom hubristically thinking he knew what it took to "get to know" another man's wife. Since *queynte Nicholas* had overreached himself by turning his sexual triumph into a triumph of his art, namely by remaining glued to his chair—when John forced open the door to the room of the allegedly entranced astrologer, Nicholas "sat ay as stille as stoon" (I 3472)—it is only befitting that for a while the knowledgeable clerk will have to pursue his formal studies either standing up or kneeling down. In terms of the tale's religious significance, kneeling down would be an appropriate additional punishment for the namesake of the patron saint of students who had, frivolously but nevertheless hubristically, arrogated the position of intermediator between God and John. Or are we to assume that the clerk's punishment includes continuing any and all pursuits of knowledge in a prone position, which actually would fit Alison just fine—if it means that "ther cometh moore" of plowing?

Students of the *Miller's Tale* have always wondered why, while John, Absalom, and Nicholas get hurt in one way or another, Alison gets off scot-

free. I wish to argue that Alison gets off scot-free because Chaucer is presenting her as the dominant female, not just as a dominating wife of the type
which is portrayed as well as embodied by the Wife of Bath, not just as a
dominating lover, but as the *Ur*-female. In this role as a representative of
creative energy, perhaps we could say as a representative of the life force,
Alison is invulnerable. Even the hot colter of a plow is unsuccessful in violating this Mother Earth.[49] Alison is the stable figure in an at least nominally
male-dominated world whose instability is symbolized by misdirected kisses as
well as misdirected colters, in a world which is finally symbolized by the
misdirection of the carpenter who does not even know that God had promised
not to "descend" with another flood.[50]

The only rain-like "descent" taking place in the *Miller's Tale* finds a
more than matching vessel in Alison, who will oblige as a field to be plowed
and rained on every time Nicholas is ready to "spille." But then, as Edward
C. Schweitzer has noted, it is precisely in accordance with Boethius'
Consolatio Philosophiae that, while Absalom, Nicholas, and John are made to
suffer, "Alisoun escapes unscathed. She, after all, is the good they have
chosen, as innocent in herself as gold or rich food or drink. The choice, not
the object chosen, is punished."[51] What makes this *Ur*-female innnocent in
herself, however, is the fact that in the *Miller's Tale* "Women have been
assigned the role of physical creation [and that] Alison's animal nature, her
lack of verbal existence, emphasize[s] that her importance is primarily biological."[52] And it will be necessary to bear in mind Alison's importance as the
chosen good when we deal with the adulteress in another *senex amans* tale,
with May: will we find January's wife innnocent in herself?

As *Ur*-female, Alison plays an important role in Chaucer's treatment of
the theme of justice. Chaucer is underscoring this role by means of yet another
one of those famous/infamous rhymes when he describes the second window
scene. Absalom offers Alison a ring if she will give him another kiss:

> " . . . This wol I yeve thee, if thou me *kisse*."
> This Nicholas was risen for to *pisse*,
> And thoughte he wolde amenden al the jape,
> He sholde kisse his ers er that he scape. (I 3797-3800, italics added)

It is simply doing injustice to the organic unity of Chaucer's work of art to argue as Robert Jordan does: "The electrifying effect of this rhyme is due not simply to the extreme semantic antipathy between the two words but to the suddennness with which this antipathy is invoked and the total contextual contrast borne by the words. *Stark collocation is possible within the mode of Chaucer's art*" (italics mine).[53] Why did Jordan merely decribe this artistic device as "possible" in Chaucer? Nonorganic readings such as Jordan's become self-mutilating when they ignore the possibility that the artist may be using stark collocation for the purpose of pointing to a thematic intent.

In a work of literature which satirizes the sin of pride in its various manifestations and presents characters who try to outwit or outdo each other, a female has just outstripped a male who thought he could commit her to "moore" by planting a kiss on her. While Nicholas gets a laugh out of Alison's victory over Absalom, Nicholas wants to improve upon the kissing-joke with which the female has sexually humiliated the male: Chaucer uses the *kisse/pisse* rhyme to indicate that Nicholas intends to top Alison's kissing-joke in a manner which not only outdoes Alison, but which also enables a male to sexually degrade another male by means of homosexual humiliation. Nicholas intends to top Alison's "jape" before Absalom can, as Nicholas knows he eventually will, totally "scape" from the sorry scene. On the other hand, in terms of the plot of the story Absalom intends to improve upon Alison's joke, namely by upping the ante and bringing to the scene the hot colter of a plow.

Whether or not we wish to regard the manner in which Chaucer uses an *Ur*-female to have Absalom unknowingly upstage Nicholas as morally redeeming, the poet makes it clear that Nicholas is, like Absalom at the beginning of the first window scene, guilty of phallic pride. Chaucer is giving expression to that idea precisely through the stark collocation of the _kisse/pisse_ rhyme. When Chaucer first has Alison humiliate Absalom by making him kiss her "nether ye" (I 3244), then makes a graphic reference to Nicholas' penis ("pisse"), and immediately thereafter presents Nicholas as trying to top the kissing-joke Alison had played on Absalom, Chaucer is introducing the idea that the reason Nicholas feels he can "amenden on the jape" is that his appendage gives him an edge over Alison. Since Nicholas expresses his phallic pride vis-à-vis the woman in an act which involves homosexual humiliation of another male—the notion of homosexual humiliation is reinforced by the _kisse/pisse_ rhyme, where the word _kisse_ is spoken to a woman by the male whom Nicholas will try to humiliate—it is poetic justice that the _queynte_-chaser Nicholas is "plowed" by the man whom he is trying to humiliate. As Carolyn Dinshaw has noted, "literary activity has a gendered structure," and "Some of the richness of . . . the denouement of the _Miller's Tale_ lies in its playful reversal of [a model of gendered hermeneutics] so that the feminized Absolon brands with a hot poker—'writes' on—the naked body of the clerk Nicholas."[54] Appropriately for a rustic disciple of courtly love, Absalom performs his "writing" on the learned Nicholas with the _stilus_ of a plow.[55]

As Eric Partridge notes in _Shakespeare's Bawdy_, the slang meaning of _to plough_—"[Caesar] plough'd [Cleopatra], and she cropt"—goes as far back as Lucretius.[56] I purposely refer to Shakespeare's plowing-and-cropping image first before addressing what Chaucerians have said about Absalom using a hot colter. Roy Peter Clark has remarked in an article on "Squeamishness and Exorcism in Chaucer's _Miller's Tale_" that posterior-kissing (in the first window scene) and breaking wind (in the second window scene) associate Absalom with the demonic, and that one way to exorcise demons was the famous flatulent stratagem which Luther would advocate and use in fighting the devil: "Nicholas employs the blinding thunder of anal wind to purge himself and Alison of their sequeamish intruder. _Absolon responds by thrusting_ *the hot iron up Nicholas' arse*, an act of symbolic sodomy, given the blatant effeminacy of Absolon. This symbolic buggery finally links Absolon with the devil" (italics mine).[57] Interesting though the exorcism-plus-sodomy interpretation may be, Absalom's hot-colter assault is *not* in "response" to what Nicholas does. What is being ignored or neglected here is that the intended target of the colter is Alison,[58] and that devoting some of our critical attention to the misdirectedness of the "plowing" might tell us something about Alison's role in the tale.

Ross, who in his *Miller Variorum* has a lot to say about the phallic symbolism of the plow in this tale,[59] quotes Clark's observation but does not comment on Clark's apparent neglect of the second misdirection.[60] In fact, it might irk some readers that Ross occasionally treats in a cavalier fashion errors or oversights in the critical opinions he cites when those critical opinions can serve to buttress his own interpretations. A case in point is Clark's buggery-interpretation which suits Ross' own. Ross argues that "the *cultour* enters the anus but at the same time, and unavoidably, burns the *toute*, or rump."[61] While there is nothing in the text to warrant Ross' anal-penetration reading—besides, after an *in ano* cauterization,[62] would Nicholas be able to publicly celebrate with Alison John's immediately following disgraceful 'fall'?—it would seem more plausible that Absalom initially intended to apply the colter vaginally but then, blown off course if not exorcised, takes a hasty swing in the general direction.[63]

What is more important for our discussion of the window scenes is that Ross interprets Absalom's "allas, I ne hadde ybleynt" to mean the exact opposite of what had been the critical consensus. Ross offers this reading: "Absolon evidently means, 'If only I had not jumped back'—that is, if he remained with his lips pressed to Alison's hole, he might have taken immediate vengeance (what exactly, we need not inquire: it is Absolon's *pryvetee*)."[64] I submit that those of us who, unlike Ross, have been reading

Absalom's exclamation to mean that he wishes he _had_ turned away from Alison have not been misconstruing Absalom's grammar.

In order to be able to accept Ross' reading of Absalom's syntax, one would have to treat the "I ne hadde ybleynt" as an irrealis-clause in which Absalom expresses the contrary-to-fact wish that he had not turned away. But then, I think one could do so without feeling too uncomfortable. When first confronted with Ross' reading, or more precisely with Ross' translation, "If _only_ I had not jumped back," the immediate objection probably is that there is no _only_ in Absalom's exclamation. But as a native speaker of German, I sometimes try to read Middle English as if it were German because much of what distinguishes Middle English from Modern English has survived in Modern German, in terms of grammar and syntax as well as vocabulary. If you translate "allas, I ne hadde ybleynt" into a German sentence whiçh would reproduce Ross' reading, you get something like this: "schade, _hätte_ ich mich (nur) nicht weggedreht." This means literally "what a pity, _had_ I (only) not turned away." The German sentence suggests not only that _hadde_ could be a subjunctive in an irrealis-clause,[65] but also that Ross' addition in "If _only_ I had not jumped back" perhaps was not needed in Middle English since the _nur_ is not needed in the German sentence.

J. Kerkhof's _Studies in the Language of Chaucer_ adduces several "instances of the irrealis in exclamatory sentences."[66] While Kerkhof's study does not furnish examples of irrealis-clauses introduced by an _allas_—neither does the _Middle English Dictionary_, which lists declarative sentences where an _allas_ introduces _that_-clauses, and the _Chaucer Concordance_ doesn't provide any help in that direction either—it lists of course exclamatory irrealis-sentences that begin with _God wolde_. The exclamation _God wolde_ (meaning God had _not_ wanted for something to happen and that something didn't happen) and _allas_ are the same insofar as they convey the same idea, the idea of regret, even if they are not syntactically interchangeable. And Ross' reading that

Absalom wishes he had not jumped back but, instead, kept his lips pressed to Alison's hole and avenged himself immediately becomes plausible in light of the preceding lines, where Absalom, already on his way to the blacksmith, says to himself that he would rather be avenged than possess the entire town:

> "Allas!
> My soule betake I unto Sathanas!
> But me were levere than al this town," quod he,
> "Of this despit awreken for to be.
> Allas," quod he, "allas, I ne hadde ybleynt." (I 3748-53)

Note the closeness of the "allas, I ne hadde ybleynt" to the "awreken for to be," which is in the passive voice: if Absalom had avenged himself immdiately, there would now be no need for him to consign his soul to the devil and seek help from a blacksmith, in whom, as Ross has shown, Absalom "does indeed meet with a type of devil."[67] Ross' reading of Absalom's exclamation, then, does make sense. Unfortunately, *how* Ross arrived at an interpretation diametrically opposed to the standard reading, a reading which, in a *variorum* edition of all places, he doesn't even mention, is his own "pryvetee."

That Ross' interpretation makes sense doesn't necessarily mean that it catches the meaning which Chaucer intended. On the other hand, it could be argued that Chaucer is being deliberately ambiguous and wants the reader to contemplate *both* meanings as a possibility. When Chaucer has the Miller interrupt Absalom's interior monologue almost at the beginning of the line by inserting the little phrase *quod he*, the poet is creating a caesura which could be intended to warn us to read the next few words very carefully. The "quod he" could more specifically be intended to distance both the poet and the teller from the speaker of the next five words because there will be something strange about those five words. Even if we opt for what I have called the standard interpretation of "allas, I ne hadde ybleynt," Absalom's use of the pluperfect seems curious: just prior to which event or at what point does Absalom now think he should have turned away? If Chaucer indeed intended

Absalom's syntax to be confusing or at least open to interpretation, then the young lover's utterance is meant to illustrate linguistically the state of confusion caused by that which he had "Ful savourly" touched orally. The all-important question for a conscientious scholar is: "*What if* Ross is right?" I will therefore 'inquire' more deeply into the intriguing possibilities which Ross' reading has raised.

There has always been some disagreement over whether *ybleynt* derives from *blenchen* (for which the *MED*, citing Absalom's line, gives "To avoid, evade, abstain; elude, escape") or *blinnen*, which means "to abstain."[68] As will become clear shortly, "abstain" would be outrageously comical if we accept Ross' reading of Absalom's syntax.[69] Ross has, somewhat coyly, observed that "There may be some question about which hole Alison projected, one having more 'beard' than the other."[70] Ross could have made his case for an ambiguity concerning Alison's projected hole much stronger if he had adduced evidence from historical linguistics, as he had begun to do in 1972 in *Chaucer's Bawdy*, where under the entry *ers* he had first observed, "In England this continues to be 'arse,' though in America it is . . . 'ass,'" which provides puns with the beast of burden," and then, specifically referring to the *MED* concluded: "*Piers Plowman* . . . speaks of 'an hore of hure ers-wynnynge' (a whore, from her arse-winning—arse-gain)."[71] Ross did not mention that the *MED* citation from *Piers Plowman* is immediately preceded by this entry: "The vulva; *[ars] winning*, money obtained by prostitution" (the *MED* lists the word *ers* under the heading of that word's alternate version, *ars*).

In *Chaucer's Bawdy*, Ross had also referred to the *Oxford English Dictionary*'s listings under *arse*, but apparently Ross had chosen to discount the *OED*'s cross-reference to *ass*, under which the *OED* lists: "Now chiefly *U.S.* [vulgar and dial(ect) sp(elling) and pronunc(iation) of ARSE] . . . Sexual gratification. Also a woman or women, regarded as an object of affording this.''[72] Perhaps the *OED*'s definition of the "Now chiefly *U.S.*" term *ass* as sexual gratification is more accurate than the *MED* offering of *vulva*, which may be somewhat too specifically anatomical. However, while the sexual connotation has not survived in British English,[73] the very fact that the sexual connotation has survived in American English, which is less removed from older developmental stages of the English language than British English is, strongly suggests that the Middle English word may have had a somewhat more specifically anatomical meaning than William Langland's compound noun *ers-wynnynge*. That Langland was punning with the notion of a whore making money by lying on her backside becomes clear from the sentence which the *MED* quotes from *Piers Plowman*: "For an hore of hure erswynnynge may hardiloker tythe than an *erraunt* vsvrer" (emphasis mine): lying down, the whore makes more money than does a money-lender who spends his time busily traveling the road. At any rate, what is important for our interpretation of Chaucer saying that Absalom kisses Alison's *ers* is that the American idiom "chasing ass" obviously does not refer to a woman's posterior.[74]

In fact, I now wish to argue that the consummate ironist Chaucer is toying with his readers in the narrative movement within the description of the kissing scene. He first leads his readers to believe that Absolon kisses Alison's posterior, but then he mentions the "berd" in order to force his readers to reconsider their first impression:

> at the wyndow out she putte hir hole,
> And Absolon, hym fil no bet ne wers,
> But with his mouth he kiste hir naked ers
> Ful savourly, er he were war of this.
> Abak he stirte, and he thoghte it was amys,
> For wel he wiste a womman hath no berd.
> He felte a thyng al rough and long yherd,
> And seyde, "Fy! allas! what have I do?" (I 3732-39)

When Chaucer writes, "[Absolon] felte a thyng *al rough* and long yherd" (italics added), evidently the poet isn't talking about the softness of the part-time barber's *hands* to which Alison's pubic hair feels "al rough": Chaucer is talking about Absalom's face. And when in the concluding lines the Miller states that Absalom has kissed Alison's "nether ye," this could also be a reference to a slightly more frontally located aperture if the poet wants the reader to associate that statement with the earlier description of Alison as possessing a "likerous ye" (I 3244): the lecherous eye would be naturally matched by a lecherous nether eye. The consummate ironist is leaving enough room for the interpretation that we could be dealing with a case of involuntary quasi- or at least near-cunnilingus: such a case actually would seem to be the best explanation of why before the second window encounter Absalom replaces his tainted lips with the shaft of a plow.

Near-cunnilingus is precisely what Nicholas thinks has happened when he exclaims, "A berd! A berd! . . . this goth faire and weel!", in lines 3742-43. It has of course been noted that "berd" can mean trick or deception (as Ross notes, "to make someone's beard" meant to make a fool of someone[75]). Thus Nicholas, whom Alison had told in a whisper to be quiet and enjoy what she was about to do—"Now hust, and thou shalt laughen al thy fille" (I 3722)—could simply be rejoycing over Alison's trick and may not even have thought of pubic hair at all, but then we have Ross' observation: "There is an obvious, and not very subtle, pun with *berd* [in the earlier line mentioning Absolon's thought about a beard]. Absolon thinks to himself *a womman hath no berd*, which, of course, Nicholas could not have heard: the outrageously implausible coincidence makes the joke funnier perhaps."[76] In this coincidence the pun presumably is by the teller or the poet, but not by Nicholas himself.

I would argue, however, that this is not at all an implausible coincidence. In an adroit narrative movement Chaucer presents a Nicholas who had overheard Absalom's request for and Alison's apparently complying promise of a kiss, as well as Absalom's "What have I do?" Whatever Alison had planned to do in order to make Nicholas laugh, when Nicholas hears Absalom's shock-displaying question, he knows her plan must have worked and he exclaims "A berd!" By the word *berd* Nicholas means trick, but as soon as he has uttered the word the clerk, whose intellectual curiosity must have caused him to try to figure out how Alison could turn a kissing scene into a laughing matter, and possibly caused him to use his imagination and try to put himself into Absalom's position, realizes that he may unknowingly have created a pun by hitting the nail on the head. Nicholas therefore repeats the word "berd," but this time in its literal sense. When Chaucer has 'queynte Nicholas' *unknowingly* create the trick-and-beard pun, the poet is not only including the clerk's reaction to Alison's "jape" on Absalom in his ironic treatment of the *Miller's Tale*'s "knowledge" leitmotif, but more specifically Chaucer is also ironically foreshadowing the "berd"-alias-trick which will backfire in more ways than one when Nicholas quite literally overreaches himself by trying to improve upon the woman's own "berd"-alias-trick.[77]

While the narrative movement in what Ross sees as an outrageously implausible coincidence perhaps is not in itself sufficient to suggest that oral-vaginal contact has occurred in the Absalom-Alison encounter, the lines that follow could shed some light on what Chaucer is trying to communicate:

> "A berd! A berd!" quod hende Nicholas,
> "By Goddes corpus, this goth faire and weel."
> This sely Absolon herde every deel,
> And *on his lippe he gan* for anger *byte*,
> And to hymself he seyde, "I shal thee *quyte*."
>   (I 3743-46, italics added).

Note the *byte*/*quyte* rhyme—another stark-collocation rhyme?—in a couplet which describes Absalom as biting his lower lip, which especially in a situation involving a kiss obviously would have to be his lower lip. If Chaucer is indeed insinuating that Absalom kisses Alison's pudendum, Absalom could have "quyted" himself, i.e., Absalom could have got even with Alison, immediately if only he had not "abstained" from biting into that which Absalom already had his lips on. Chaucer would be slyly insinuating that Absalom would not have to bite his lower lip in anger now if, in a *vagina dentata* reversal, he had avenged himself on the psychologically castrating, albeit literally toothless, *vagina* with his own teeth and bitten into the lower lips alias labia which had touched his own lips.

In fact, the part-time barber and surgeon Absalon could have struck a mighty blow for his profession by taking a mouthful of the beard which was within shearing distance of his incisors. At any rate, once Absalom had "Ful savourly" begun to taste, to "abstain" was exactly the wrong thing for him to do. The part-time barber Absalom could have performed a gender-reversed Delilah trick on the woman who had cut *him* down: the part-time barber could have rendered Alison physically incapable of intercourse in revenge for her psychological castration of him.

I quoted earlier Dinshaw's observation that "some of the richness of the . . . denouement of the *Miller's Tale* lies in its playful reversal of [a model of gendered hermeneutics] so that the feminized Absolon brands with a hot poker . . . the naked body of the clerk Nicholas." Venturing beyond Dinshaw's hermeneutics, I wish to argue that Chaucer is introducing the *idea* of a playful reversal of a mode of gendered hermeneutics which is even more comical than the plot denouement in which the feminized Absalom brands Nicholas. That is to say, in Chaucer's characterization of Absalom we are dealing with a case of gender-crossing which introduces the notion of a *male* "vagina dentata"—so that we are presented with an an encounter between a female *vagina dentata* and a male one. Or, more precisely since Absalom "abstains" from doing that which he is in a perfect position to do, Chaucer presents us with a case of gender-crossing in which a male loses out to the female because he stops at being a *would-be* "vagina dentata"—that is, because the male fails to complete the act of gender-crossing which for a moment he had contemplated performing.

Chaucer, then, has endowed the *Miller's Tale* with the additional irony that the poet's *insinuation* of what could have happened in the scene of the misdirected kiss is even more comical than what he *actually describes* as happening, both in the scene presently under discussion and in the second window scene where Absalom allows himself to be misdirected into sparing the woman he intends to avenge himself on. As a matter of fact, Chaucer's insinuation of what could have happened but didn't happen in either window scene gains further in comic effect if we bear in mind that we are dealing with a gender power-struggle, a gender-role battle which is started by a male who prematurely claims a victory. Absalom is celebrating victory in the gender-role battle when, in response to Alison's promise to kiss him, Absalom, ironically kneeling down to receive the kiss, says to himself:

> I am a lord at alle degrees,
> For after this I hope ther cometh moore.
> Lemman, thy grace, and sweete brid, thyn oore!'' (I 3724-26)

I noted earlier that, when Absalom says, "I am a lord at alle degrees," he is claiming that sexually he has control over Alison: the *moore* which he expects to follow the promised kiss is sexual intercourse. Absalom claims he is close to obtaining Alison's "grace." Absalom's statement literally means of course that he thinks he is about to obtain Alison's favor. But since, as Ross noted in *Chaucer's Bawdy*, the precursors of Modern English *grace* and *grass*, respectively, "were both homographs and near homophones in Chaucer's time,"[78] Absalom's statement about Alison's "grace" also contains a pun which is not only sexual but indecently sexist: Absalom thinks he now has Alison by the "bottom grass" a.k.a. "beard."[79] It therefore is poetic justice that Alison tricks Absalom into a type of contact with her "berd" which this "lord at alle degrees" would not have expected.

Regardless of whether Chaucer wants us to assume that Absalom is making the sexist joke involving "grace" and bottom grass *consciously*, Absalom's "I am a lord at alle degrees . . . there cometh moore" speech indeed is indecently sexist: as noted, the speech is a case of phallic pride or, if you will, a case of phallic hubris. There is the ironic twist, however, that Chaucer puts this phallic-hubris speech into the mouth of what in her gender-hermeneutics argument Dinshaw calls a deliberately and thematically "feminized" character, Absalom. The strongest twist in that ironic development, an ironic development in whose understanding Thomas Ross would seem to have anticipated Carolyn Dinshaw's hermeneutics by about seventeen years, is that Chaucer presents the mock courtly-lover Absalom as having a perfect opportunity to be a male *vagina dentata* but "abstaining" from taking advantage of that opportunity.

Chaucer's presentation of gender-crossing actually may have been a little more complex than some modern literary critics would have us believe. For isn't it possible that the consummate ironist Chaucer portrays the "feminized [Absolon]" as a barber because by cutting *men's* hair the effeminate and "feminized" Absalom could be a Delilah? In that case, Chaucer's presentation of gender-crossing would give us a mock-Samson who exchanged gender-roles not only with Delilah, but at the same time also with Alison. For in a symbolic sense Chaucer presents the trick which Alison plays on Absalom as a kind of Delilah act. Or more precisely, Chaucer presents Alison as as a barber who symbolically puts the scissors to Absalom's hair. In the scenario which I have suggested for the first window scene, Alison places Absalom's head between her buttocks which extend into her thighs—so that her buttocks-and-thighs for a moment become an iconographical representation of a gigantic

pair of scissors encompassing in its entirety Absalom's abundant coiffure, a
coiffure which Chaucer describes in detail:

> Crul was his heer, and as the gold it shoon,
> Ful streight and evene lay his joly shode.   (3314-16)

In other words, in Chaucer's presentation of gender-crossing not only does
Absalom take on Alison's gender-role as a female, but Alison also takes on
Absalom's gender-role as a male whose job it is to cut men's hair. Not only
is Alison a *vagina dentata*, but symbolically she also wields the threatening
metal of the scissors—which is the reason Chaucer presents Absalom, the
failed *vagina dentata*, as arming himself with a piece of iron for the expected
rematch in his gender-role battle with Alison's *ers*.

Yet Alison's *ers* possesses even more power than I have suggested so
far, for I have yet to discuss the symbolic significance that the name Absalom
has for our understanding of the *Miller's Tale*. I argued earlier that Alison is
spared the carefully planned revenge because she is a Mother Earth figure who
is invulnerable even to the hot colter of a plow with which Absalom returns to
to the window. I would now argue that already in the first window scene
Alison symbolizes Mother Nature in the sense that, in his description of what
Alison's *ers*-plus-thighs do to Absalom Chaucer is making allusively operative
the story of David's son Absalom as recounted in II Kings 14-18. That Biblical passage describes how Absalom, whose rebellion against his king and
father had failed, tries to flee on the back of a mule but meets his fate when
his gorgeous hairs get caught in the branches of an oak tree.[80] That is, Chaucer is allusively endowing the *ers*-and-thighs of the woman who psychologically castrates the parish clerk, perhaps even drives him to the "maladie" of
impotence, with the power of the oak tree which led to the death of the Biblical Absalom. Like the Biblical character, Chaucer's Absalom deserves his
fate, for he too is guilty of rebellion. His attempt at adultery is of course an
act of rebellion against the sacrament of marriage, but, like King David's son,

the parish clerk is guilty of engaging in a special kind of socio-political power struggle: when Absalom proclaims himself to be "a lord at alle degrees," he is arrogating a position of mastery over a female which he does not possess.

Since the rebellion which Absalom initiates is a gender power-struggle involving sexual control, it is only appropriate that Chaucer is allusively endowing Alison's *ers*-and-thighs also with the phallic symbolism which ancient fertility ritual had vested in trees—e.g., the Priapic symbolism which Chaucer, as I will discuss in my final chapter, would elaborate in the pear-tree episode in the *Merchant's Tale*, where the tree which enables *May* and Damian to copulate is a carry-over from phallic fertility rituals residues of which have survived in the *Maypole*. In fact, Chaucer had already gender-crossingly endowed Alison with a phallic function in his early descriptions of Alison:

> She was moore blisful on to see
> Than is the newe *pere-jonette tree* . . .
> . . . . .
> Wynsynge she was, as is a joly *colt*,
> Long as a mast, and *upright as a bolt*.
> (3247-48 and 3263-64, italics added)

If we read the *Canterbury Tales* palimpsestically, we realize that Chaucer is comparing the Alison of the *Miller's Tale* to a pear-tree for the specific purpose of associating her with the phallicism of the pear tree in the *Merchant's Tale*. And Chaucer is doing so in a context in which he compares the young woman not only to a young *male* horse but also to a "Long . . . mast" and to the "upright . . . bolt," i.e., to the dart of a crossbow[81]—in a double-comparison where the seemingly innocuous *colt/bolt* rhyme serves to underscore the the phallic role which Chaucer assigns to Alison.

After Chaucer has had Alison's *ers* gender-crossingly out-phallicize the male gender-supremacist, Absalom consigns his soul to the devil in his attempt to avenge himself upon the *vagina dentata* who had defeated him. Absalom, so to speak, "steels himself" for his expected second encounter with the

"ers"-power of a Mother Earth by asking a satanic Vulcan figure to arm him
with one of the archetypally strongest phalluses there are: with the colter with
which to "plow" alias "swyve" the earth. Unfortunately for Absalom, the
power of the plow becomes misdirected when Absalom succeeds in plowing
Nicholas' *ers* instead of Alison's. As discussed, the misdirection in the second
window scene occurs because a male feels a need to prove his intellectual
superiority to the female with whom he is having a mutually consented-upon
sexual relationship by trying to improve on the joke which *the female* had
played on Nicholas' fellow male and rival for her "grace":

> [Nicholas] thoughte he wolde amenden al the jape,
> [Absolon] sholde kiss his ers er that he scape.

Being, like Absalom, a male supremacist himself, Nicholas is punished when
he insists that his *ers*-power can go one better on Alison's. Chaucer's point in
the second window scene, then, is that *hende Nicholas* too overplays his hand
in a gender power-struggle which he himself had initiated, as a result of which
Nicholas becomes another instance of Chaucer's ironic use of gender-crossing.

In the last few pages I have not been trying to out-Ross Ross, nor have
I been trying to "amenden al the jape." Rather, I have been pursuing some
of the suggestions which a prestigious *and* creatively imaginative Chaucer
scholar and the editor of the *Variorum* Edition of the *Miller's Tale* has thrown
out, but not carried to what might have been their logical conclusions; and I
have tried to place the outgrowths of those suggestions in the context of what I
consider the tale's moral significance. I take of course full responsibility for
my own conclusions, but I ask the reader to extend to me the same favor that I
have extended to Ross, i.e., to ask himself or herself, "What if?" What if
Ross' reading of Absalom's syntax *is* right, or more precisely for a discussion
of a mercurial ironist, what if Ross' reading is *also* right? I have a feeling
that Ross' reading *is* also right, and the reasons for that feeling now are no
longer my "pryvetee."

There is, however, another "pryvetee" which I would like to share, but share only in the form of a hypothesis. This hypothesis is based on the premise that Chaucer is indeed using Absalom's "allas, I ne hadde ybleynt" with both meanings simultaneously possible. I think I have quite thoroughly, for some tastes perhaps too thoroughly, discussed the implications which offer themselves if Ross' reading of Absalom's syntax is right. The situation gets even more unpalatable when we "inquire" a little more closely into the pluperfect whose use by Absalom I noted earlier seemed so curious that I raised the following question: just prior to which event or what point does Absalom now think he should have turned away? I will tentatively suggest that there was a point during the first window scene at which Absalom felt an impulse to turn away from Alison and he now, while he is on his way to the blacksmith, wishes he had followed that impulse.

Douglas Gray has made the following observation concerning the window episode in the Explanatory Notes in the *Riverside Chaucer*:

> Chaucer is unique among early tellers of the story in having the woman execute the trick; he also intensifies the affront to Absolon by *stressing his sensitivity to smells* and sounds (I, 3337-38). The episode, and particularly the roles of [the blacksmith] Gervase and of the fart, has been the subject of some absurdly earnest symbolic and moralizing criticism.[82] (italics added)

In the portion I italicized Gray is referring to the passage where the Miller advises his audience that Absalom is squeamish about farting. I agree with Gray that too much has been read into the farting episode.[83] In fact, I would argue that the farting episode in the second window scene is a smokescreen of sorts in the sense that the announcement of Absalom's squeamishness about farting fulfills a function different from the one Gray and others have attributed to that announcement. That function, I submit, reveals itself to an organic reading. Let us examine the context in which the announcement is made, a context which introduces Absalom as a party-goer and womanizer:

In al the toun nas brewhous ne taverne
That he ne visited with solas,
Ther any gaylard tappestere was.
But sooth to seyn, he was somdeel squaymous
Of farting, and of speche dangerous.
This Absolon, that jolif was and gay,
Gooth with a *cencer* on the haliday,
Sensynge the wyves of the parisshe faste;
And many a lovely look on hem he caste,
And namely on this carpenteris wyf. (I 3334-43, italics added)

Why does Chaucer announce Absalom's squeamishness about farting immediately after mentioning that Absalom enjoys the company of merry barmaids?
And why does Chaucer subsequently say that Absalom eagerly perfumes the
parish wives with incense, and then that he casts many a loving look on the
Alison whom he has just been censing? Isn't Chaucer establishing some kind
of association between Absalom's sensitivity to and preoccupation with smells
on the one hand, and on the other Absalom's preoccupation with women?

If the answer to my last question is yes, we may have solved the mystery of the *pryvetee* of Absalom's use of the pluperfect: as Absalom, who had
sweetened his own breath for the expected kiss, is getting close to what he
thinks is Alison's face, he catches a whiff that is quite different from the smell
of the woman whom he had censed earlier[84]—and his first impulse is to turn
away. He resists that impulse, however, and on the way to Gervase he will
review the entire situation and, in the non-Rossian reading, reproach himself
for not having followed the impulse he had felt before he "Ful savourly"
planted a kiss on whatever it was that he kissed, meaning: "I kissed her
because, *allas, I had not turned away* when I noticed that smell."

If Chaucer deliberately wrote Absalom's exclamation in such a way as
to make both readings possible, he was using both-and irony to convey two
meanings which actually can operate synergistally and complement each other
in a work of literature that possesses an organic unity. The non-Rossian self-
reproach eventually has the same implications for our understanding of Absa-

lom's "private" feelings, since in either case his feelings are directly related to Alison's *queynte*. Absalom smelt something he had not expected (but he failed to act upon that smell) because Alison had been swyving all night, and Nicholas presumably has enjoyed a *descensus* or two: a palimpsestic reading can relate the misdirected kiss to the cosmic-union picture in the opening lines of the General Prologue and to *Goddes pryvetee*—and thus even to the story of Noah's Flood, the story whose theological significance constitutes the basis for much of the *sentence* of the *Miller's Tale*.

After emphasizing the point that the *Canterbury Tales* possesses an organic unity, it might not be impertinent to return to the point where I first raised objections to Lindahl's approach, i.e., to the point where I objected to his misrepresentation of Chaucer's text to make it fit his folk-mode thesis: the misattribution in Lindahl's pronouncements on the prologue of the *Miller's Tale*. Lindahl attempts to read the *Miller's Tale* as a *Schwank*, i.e., as a manifestation of folk humor, rather than as a fabliau, because he sees in it a typical example of how "the dupe reflects the personality of the teller's foe."[85] In Lindahl's view, the Miller's story about a duped carpenter is a *Schwank* rather than a fabliau since it is directed at the Reeve, a fellow pilgrim and former carpenter, and thus constitutes social interaction. Stevens comments on Lindahl's *Schwank* reading: "the new classification . . . introduces problems. For example, we have to search elsewhere to account for the more overt literary features. Thus, while Lindahl's analysis highlights the use of the Miller's Tale to embarrass the Reeve, and shows us how John is the typical victim character of the *Schwank*, it virtually says nothing about Alisoun and Absolon, or about the parody of [theological lore]."[86] I will add that besides neglecting to address the literary function of the mock-courtly Nicholas-Alison-Absalom triangle, a triangle which I have demonstrated to be an integral part of the *Miller's Tale's* moral significance, Lindahl's folk-humor analysis ignores the religious function that the duping of John at the hands of *queynte*

Nicholas holds in a story which is about various kinds of knowledge and lack thereof—a story in which *solaas* is surprisingly well matched by *sentence*.

The *solaas* and the *sentence* are particularly well matched insofar as the duping of the carpenter, who is a colleague of the teller's foe, a colleague of the Reeve, is presented in a form that parodies theological lore. I have said quite a bit about Chaucer's parodic treatment of the theological lore of Noah's Flood, but I have by no means finished my discussion of the deluge from "Goddes pryvetee." A notion not only of the monotheistic Christian God as ejaculating but actually of Him as using His ejaculate as a means for destroying mankind is perhaps the culmination of Chaucer's heretically parodic manipulations of Christian ideas. If it is permissible to play on one of Kendrick's rhetorical questions, quoted earlier, about what Chaucer could be doing in the "trinity of containers" as seen from underneath: Surely, Chaucer could not have intended such a blasphemous innuendo about the Creator; or could he? The answer to my question lies in suggesting that we close-read Chaucer's text, or more precisely, in suggesting that we read the *Canterbury Tales* palimpsestically, i.e., read individual tales not only for possible interaction among each other—as oral "games" which Chaucer stages to have the respective tellers "quyte" one another—but also read the tales plus their interactive significance as both informing and being informed by the poet's framing description of the pilgrimage, especially by the General Prologue.

In the idea of the monotheistic God as ejaculating, Chaucer is merely putting to comical use the contemporary teaching of the story of Noah's Flood, a teaching according to which the Flood was man's punishment for the particular sin of lechery. As one critic has noted, "there is a theological joke, for we are told in *The Parson's Tale* (839) that 'by the synne of leccherie God dreynte al the world at the diluge,' and here is Nicholas inventing a second deluge as a means to lechery."[87] However, there may be more than the additional irony, which I mentioned earlier, of Nicholas having to call on God for water, for Chaucer may also be introducing an audaciously comical interaction between the Parson's words and the notion of the destruction of the world by a special kind of "Goddes foyson." If we read the preposition _by_ not merely in the meaning of "because of" but in the meaning of "by means of," God's sending of the Flood was an act of lechery similar to the one which the Parson will describe as follows: "another synne aperteneth to leccherie, that comth in slepyinge, and this synne cometh ofte to hem that been maydenes, and eek to hem that been corrupt; and this synne men clepen polucioun" (X 912).

If we assume that in the section of the _Parson's Tale_ which deals with lechery Chaucer did indeed intend a comical interaction between the Parson's discussion of the "synne" of nocturnal emission and of Noah's Flood which God sent to punish mankind for the "synne of leccherie," such an intent would lend special meaning to Chaucer's presentation of Noah's Flood as a gigantic ejaculation by God. Or more precisely, through the _Canterbury Tales'_ palimpsestic mode of existence, Chaucer would be establishing a self-allusion from the early _Miller's Tale_ to the much later _Parson's Tale_ that would indeed necessitate a retraction by Chaucer not only of his secular writings in general, but a retraction in particular of those tales "that sownen into synne" (X 1085)—a retraction going far beyond the recantation convention. Such a self-allusion would of course have the function of pointing to the following contrasts. God's gigantic ejaculation, while it is a punishment for man's sin of perverting his originally pure sexuality, could not be viewed as an act of sin. But such an allusive connection would nevertheless taint God's act of punishment with the very same sin that this act was punishing. The form of the punishment inflicted by an anthropomorphic God would be tainted because, according to St. Augustine, as a result of Original Sin human sexuality became forever tainted with sin, as opposed to the _sanctum gaudium_ which the sex act would be had it not been for man's Fall (_The City of God_, XIV, 26).

I will discuss some of the specifics of Augustinian sexual theology in a moment; suffice it for now to note that, in order for Mary to be able to give birth to the Savior, she had to be free from Original Sin. Chaucer may well be putting to comical use such a need on part of the Second Eve and introducing as an ideological equivalent the notion of God's gigantic ejaculation—not of course as an act of "synne," but nevertheless as having been tainted by Original Sin *as well as* by the sexual sinfulness of Adam's and Eve's descendants whom He is punishing with the Flood. In fact, there does exist a passage in the *Canterbury Tales* which introduces the notion of God's ejaculation more directly than does the comic "trinity of containers" which Kendrick perceives in the *Miller's Tale* or even the association which I perceive with Jupiter's *descensus*, and perhaps significantly that passage is in a tale told by another member of the clergy.

Chaucer is treating us to an exuberant variation on the cosmic-union theme, to a heretically exuberant theological joke, when he has the Monk, in his otherwise boring stories of the *de casibus virorum illustrium* type, remark about God's creation of Adam:

> Loo Adam, in the feeld of Damyssene
> With Goddes owene fynger wroght was he,
> And nat bigeten of mannes sperme unclene. (VII 2006-2008)

These lines contain a bawdy innuendo. Chaucer has the Monk establish a contrast between postlapsarian humans who are begotten of man's *unclean* sperm, and Adam who was begotten by *Divine* and *clean* machinery, but, according to the statement of the double entendre, nevertheless by sperm: in an exuberant theological joke Chaucer has the Monk, consciously or unconsciously, give away his method of coping with the restraints of celibacy and, perhaps, his own remedy for nocturnal emission. Unlike Virgil's Jupiter who with fruitful showers descends into the womb of Mother Earth, the God in Judaeo-Christian monotheism does not have a female partner. Therefore the

union that begets Adam, the cosmic union between God and Earth, occurs
"with Goddes owene fynger." Northrop Frye, in reference to a different
context, has remarked: "Egyptian mythology begins with a God who creates
the world by masturbation—a logical enough way of symbolizing the process
of creation *de Deo*, but not one we should expect to find in . . . the Old Testament."[88] Chaucer has put into the Old Testament the unexpected, through the
centrifugal vectors of his allusion:[89] in an audacious theological *game* Chaucer has endowed the Genesis account of the creation of man out of dust with a
new element.

Or put differently, when Chaucer has the Monk say that Adam was
"nat bigeten of mannes sperme unclene," our poet is playing a hilariously
heretical joke with the contemporary teaching, expressed for example in Innocent III's *De miseria condicionis humanae*, that "Formatus est homo . . . de
spurcissimo spermate":[90] it is one thing for a theologian to say that man is
made of unclean sperm, that unlike Mary's conception of Jesus by the Holy
Spirit the human act of propagation involves an element that is unclean, and it
is another for a poet to include a contrasting reference to God's *formatio* of
Adam in a sentence about the role of sperm in human propagation. I would in
fact argue that Chaucer is parodically playing Innocent's illustration of the
miserable state of man against God's command that man should increase and
multiply ("crescite et multiplicamini," Genesis 1:28[91]), as well as against the
account of man's creation: in the Monk's account Chaucer is providing us
with a heretical answer to the fundamental question of the origin of man.

I am not yet saying, as I will be later in this study, that Chaucer is
parodying Innocent III in order to attack certain teachings as well as practices
of the Church, e. g., the doctrine, vigourously espoused by Pope Innocent III,
that the use of genitalia during the human reproductive act is a dire result of
Original Sin, as well as the practices of imposing celibacy on members of the
clergy and the selling of papal indulgences. Such interpretations will eventual-

ly and gradually develop from my palimpsestic examination of the *Canterbury Tales*. But we are headed in that direction once we realize that Chaucer is in a bold allusive transaction playing the creation story in Genesis against the myth of the *Juppiter descendens*. Chaucer plays a theological *game* by "churlishly" interpreting Genesis in the light of the blatantly physical aspects in Graeco-Roman mythology which had become an integral part of what we call the Classical/Christian Tradition. Of course Chaucer's amalgamation of the more spiritually oriented Christian Tradition and the more physically oriented Classical Tradition is an act of walking a tightrope. As Kendrick puts it in her discussion of the sexual innuendoes in the *Miller's Tale*, "paradoxically, that art which appeals most strongly to the senses may finally be most challenging to the intellect, which seeks to control the emotional response. Good art is always a dangerous game."[92]

Chaucer's theological *game* is even more dangerous if we can assume, as I now wish to argue is the case, that it is for parodic purposes that Chaucer has the Parson make the statement as to why and how God punished Noah's contemporaries. The poet wishes to play the Parson's statement—"by the synne of leccherie God dreynte al the world at the diluge"—against the Monk's statement concerning God's creation of Adam and thus insinuate the following innuendo: the God who used masturbation to create man used the same technique excessively to kill off His creation. Or put differently: when the creation which God had wrought with His "owene fynger" grew out of hand, He used the very same hand with which He had created man also to destroy him—in an occurrence of "polucioun" quite different from the *polucioun* which the Parson is talking about.

The fact that the occurrence of God's "polucioun" is different from that to which the Parson is referring makes Chaucer's theological *game* meaningful. It makes the *game* meaningful because it describes the punishment which God inflicted on Noah's contemporaries for the latters' sinful sexuality precisely in the terms of Augustinian sexual theology. As the Parson notes, nocturnal emission "cometh ofte to hem that been maydenes, and eek to hem that been corrupt," i.e., it is something *involuntary* that can happen to the sexually innocent just as it happens to the sexually corrupt. Nocturnal emission is a manifestation of man's postlapsarian sexuality as characterized by St. Augustine. Man's Original Sin was disobedience to God, man's master, and according to St. Augustine man was as a consequence punished by losing authority over his own subordinates, i.e., his flesh:

> per iustitiam dominantis Dei, cui subditi servire noluimus, caro nostra nobis, quae subdita fuerat, non serviendo molesta [est].
> through the justice of God, who is our master and to whom we his subjects refused service, our flesh, which had been subject to us, is troublesome by its insubordination. (*The City of God*, XIV, 15)

As postlapsarians we are subject to a phenomenon which according to St. Augustine did not exist in man before the Fall, i.e., we are subject to lust a.k.a. "leccherie," so that even the "maydenes" among us are subject to what we commonly call wet dreams. By contrast—and Chaucer here is playing the Parson's statement on why and how God punished Noah's contemporaries against St. Augustine's theories, theories on which the Parson's pronouncement on a certain type of "leccherie" is based—God has mastery over His own ejaculation, both in creating man and in destroying him. When man again disobeys God, he ironically is doing so in a manner which is a direct result of the punishment man had received for his initial act of disobedience: man is sinning because he had lost mastery over his subjects. This time God punishes his subjects by, so to speak, taking matters into His own hands.

There is no *pryvetee* left, it seems. With a helping hand from St. Augustine and Chaucer's own Parson, we can even figure out some of the things that must have gone on with *this hende Nicholas* between the time he grabbed Alison by the *queynte* and the night he was allowed to "rain" on her: after all, Nicholas had to pay the price for being postlapsarian. I firmly believe that this notion, which Chaucer insinuates through the organic mode of his artistry, is religiously redeeming. But why couldn't Robertson, who was thoroughly involved with Augustinian theology, have discovered it? Therefore, "Blameth nat me" if I have written a risqué chapter about a gamy tale. And I promise not to add a risqué chapter on the *Knight's Tale*, but since Chaucer wrote the fabliau of the *Miller's Tale* expressly as a parodic foil for a courtly romance, I am faced with the following question: do the conclusions I have reached about the *Miller's Tale* in any way affect our reading of the *Knight's Tale*?

I earlier quoted a critic who noted about the *Miller's Tale*, "there is a theological joke, for we are told in *The Parson's Tale* (839) that 'by the synne of leccherie God dreynte al the world at the diluge,' and here is Nicholas inventing a second deluge as a means to lechery"; and I used the Parson's pronouncements about the Flood to show that the Augustinian argument concerning pre- and postlapsarian sexuality is an integral part of both the *solaas* and the *sentence* of the fabliau which Chaucer puts in the mouth of the Miller-the-*cherl*. Once we have discovered the Augustinian elements in what Chaucer intended as a parodic response to a story about courtly love, we begin to wonder whether Chaucer may not palimpsestically have brought Augustinian sexology to bear on a poem which, while its plot is about idealizing love, the lovers involved are postlapsarian. Once Chaucer has had the Parson elaborate on the "synne" of nocturnal emission which "cometh ofte to hem that been maydenes, and eek to hem that been corrupt," are we able *not* to suspect that Palamon and Arcite are subject to the sin of involuntary "polucioun"—if not the voluntary self-pollution which Chaucer has the Monk unwittingly confess to? After all, they are young men desperately in love with a woman they can only catch glimpses of while imprisoned in the tower.

While Palamon continues his pining in the tower from which he has a chance to see Emily from a distance, Arcite, who has been set free on the condition that he never returns to Athens, feels that the imprisoned Palamon is much better off. But there is hope for Arcite, for Mercury encourages him to return to Athens:

> Upon a nyght in sleep as he hym leyde,
> Hym thoughte how that the wynged god Mercurie
> Biforn him stood and bad him to be murie.
> His slepy yerde in hond he bar uprighte . . .
> And seyde hym thus: *"To Atthenes shaltou wende;*
> *There is thee shapen of thy wo an ende."*
> *And with that word Arcite wook and sterte.*
> "Now trewely, hou soore that me smerte,"
> Quod he, "To Atthenes right now wol I fare . . . "
>   (I 1384-95, italics added)

Here Chaucer is alluding to the famous context in Virgil's Fourth *Aeneid* where Mercury visits Aeneas to admonish him to pursue his *fatum Romanum* and move on to Italy, where the king's daughter is destined to become his wife and beget with him the Roman race. Actually, Mercury pays the lingering Aeneas *two* visits in quick succession. The second visit, during which Mercury appears in Aeneas' dream and admonishes him so vehemently that Aeneas is startled out of his sleep, is the scene which Chaucer is verbally echoing,[93] but the *entire* description of Mercury's visit to Carthage (*Aeneid*, IV, 256-80 and 557-72) is allusively functional in Chaucer's lines: the primary parallel is between Chaucer's Mercury calling on Arcite to go to Athens to pursue Emily and Virgil's Mercury calling on Aeneas to go to Italy in pursuit of Lavinia.

In both dreams Mercury urges the man do renounce his do-nothing attitude; Arcite will eventually have to fight for Emily just as Aeneas will for Lavinia. In fact, since Arcite's journey to Athens and Aeneas' journey to Italy are allusively connected, I will now argue that Mercury's prophecy concerning the end of Arcite's woe ("Ther is thee shapen of thy wo an ende") makes allusively operative a line from the context describing Aeneas' arrival in the country where he will have to fight for the woman. The arrival marks the end of the troubles to which at Mercury's advice Aeneas had again subjected him-

self: "ea vox audita laborum/prima tulit finem" ("[Ascanius'] remark signi-
fied the beginning of the end of the troubles," *Aeneid*, VII, 117-18).
Ascanius' words mark the fulfilling of a prophecy by Aeneas' father Anchises.
The prophecy, which Aeneas repeats in the subsequent lines, concerns the end
of the journey. Through the allusion to Aeneas' fated journey, Chaucer establishes a correspondence between Arcite's *thurghfare ful of wo* and Aeneas'
fatum Romanum, thus importing into the present context the idea of life as a
journey just as Aegeus will express it after Arcite's fatal accident:

> This world nys but a thurghfare ful of wo,
> And we been pilgrymes, passynge to and fro.
> Deeth is an ende of every wordly soore. (I 2847-49)

We are dealing with a case of Chaucerian double-irony in Mercury's admoni-
tion to Arcite, "Ther is thee shapen of thy wo an ende." Whereas in Italy
Aeneas' own *thurghfare ful of wo* will come to an end when he finally wins
the war against Turnus and gets to marry his destined wife Lavinia, Arcite's
painful lovesickness will end because his life will end. It is all the more ironic
that Arcite's life will end after he has defeated Palamon in the tournament for
Emily's hand in marriage, only to be deprived of his prize when he falls off
his panicking horse and and is fatally injured.

I elaborate elsewhere how through Virgilian allusions Chaucer makes
the *Aeneid* part of the *Knight's Tale's* mode of existence in order to highlight
the eventual contrast between Aeneas' successful life-journey, which is guided
by *pietas* and the *labor* that *pietas* requires, and Arcite's life-journey which,
like the life of Aeneas' opponent Turnus, is guided by *amor*.[94] At present I
am more interested in how, in his presentation of Arcite's *thurgfare ful of wo*
as guided by *amor*, Chaucer matches *sentence* and *solaas*. I would like to
suggest that Chaucer combines these two elements by palimpsestically using
the description of Arcite's dream to parody the Parson.

Ross has said about the _Parson's Tale_ that "it reveals (to some readers, including this one) a morbid concern with, and a misunderstanding of, sex."[95] It therefore may come as a surprise that, after Ross has suggested under the heading _yerde_ that "there are a few passages in which 'penis' may be the meaning," he proceeds to make the following observations about Arcite's dream:

> [Arcite] is described as suffering from lovesickness . . . he has a vision of the god Mercury, who "biforn hym stood and bad hym to be murie." Then Chaucer continues, "His slepy yerde in hond he bar upright," and leaves the "his" (Mercury's? [Arcite's]?) ambiguous . . . one wonders if there would not be a titter in the audience when they heard this line read. Some think that the tale needs a little comic relief; perhaps it is here, though _it would not seem particularly appropriate in this passage._[96] (italics mine)

To me, the comic relief is _very_ appropriate in this _Knight's Tale_ passage. Ross was on the right track, but he did not follow through his initial hunch that in his ambiguous phrasing Chaucer was indeed suggesting that Mercury had caught the supposedly sleeping Arcite engaged in an act of masturbation. Chaucer's presentation of a courtly lover as masturbating is the poet's parodic response to the Parson's unnecessarily harsh pronouncements on nocturnal emission being a _synne_: since the lovesick Arcite is subject to involuntary emissions anyway, no matter how pure he may be in his heart, he might as well go ahead and experience a "polucioun" that is voluntary.

Arcite is all the more justified in becoming what the Parson calls "corrupt" and putting his _yerde_ to personal use since there is the dramatic irony that, as the reader knows, Arcite will not be allowed to unite with Emily in a marital union. That is, fate prevents Arcite from making love with a woman who he thinks Mercury is promising will terminate his "wo." Especially in the light of the Parson's massive attack, four times within four lines, on "the shameful membres of man," "the horrible swollen membres, that _semeth lik the maladie of hirnia_," "the wrecched swollen membres," and the "shameful privee membres'' (I 421-24, italics added), Arcite's "wo" may well be the following malady. It could be the pain caused by the "maladie" of some kind of priapism—why do we think the Arcite whom Mercury interrupts in his autoeroticism says he will immediately hit the road to Athens, "hou soore that me smerte''?—i.e., the pain that results from a "synne" which, in accordance with St. Augustine's teachings, can be just as involuntary[97] as nocturnal emission.

At any rate, what is important is that Chaucer parodies the Parson not only in the *Miller's Tale* by playing the Parson's pronouncements about the Flood against Augustinian theology, but also in the *Knight's Tale*. In fact, what endows the *sentence* of the Boethian *contemptus mundi* in the Knight's story with a measure of *solaas* is that Chaucer represents the arbitrariness and the unpredictability of the Wheel of Fortune in the terms of the arbitrariness and unpredictability which Augustinian theology assigns to postlapsarian sexuality.

CHAPTER II

The Prioress' *Pryvetee:*
Gender Issues and Anti-Semitism

I quoted in my first chapter an observation which Kendrick makes in her discussion of the sexual innuendoes in the *Miller's Tale*: "paradoxically, that art which appeals most strongly to the senses may finally be most challenging to the intellect, which seeks to control the emotional response. Good art is always a dangerous game." I will now raise the following question: if Chaucer's good art is a dangerous game, wouldn't it follow that teaching the appreciation of his art can be likewise a dangerous game?

Kendrick is making a suggestion in that direction when she mentions the possibility of "some perverse student" asking an unseemly question about the meaning of "Goddes pryvetee." I respectfully submit that some of our own colleagues have helped make teaching our students the appreciation of Chaucer's art a dangerous game by ignoring in one of the *Canterbury Tales* that kind of art which appeals most strongly to the senses. A 1989 issue of the *CEA Forum*, a journal which, as its name indicates (a forum for the "College English Association"), is dedicated to the teaching of literature rather than to scholarship/literary criticism per se, carried an article by Albert C. Salzberg entitled "A Jew Teaches Western Literature."[1] Salzberg begins his contribution by pointing out that the selections in the main anthologies used in Western World Literature courses offered at North American colleges and universities, the Norton and Macmillan anthologies, "clearly suggest a Christian point of view," and that "for whatever reason, possibly careless omission, the Jewish contribution to Western culture is underrepresented."[2] I wholeheartedly agree with some of Salzberg's objections, such as the labeling of early Biblical excerpts as Old Testament without any recognition of the Torah.[3] I am, however, bothered by what he has to say about Chaucer:

> A kind of generic anti-semitism pervaded [the Middle Ages] . . . Perhaps the most sophisticated and otherwise delightful of medieval authors, Geoffrey Chaucer, gives to his Madame Eglentyne a vicious tale ([the *Prioress's Tale*,] *thankfully not chosen for inclusion* in either [the Norton or Macmillan] anthology) of a Jewish blood ritual. Embarrassed scholars today *try to soften the impact of the tale* by emphasizing the story's hymn to the Virgin and explaining the treatment of the Jews on the basis of the medieval crusade spirit that lumped all non-Christians together . . . However one tries to explain the *unpleasantness* of the *Prioress' Tale*, the wicked Jew, using Christian blood in his Passover matzo, is a stereotype of the age, which Chaucer . . . employs.[4] (italics mine)

I wish to argue that both Salzberg and the apologists to whom Salzberg refers fail to realize that Chaucer deliberately made the *Prioress' Tale*, in Salzberg's phrase, "unpleasant," by appealing most strongly to the senses. I for one am not an embarrassed scholar, or embarrassed scholar-teacher, who tries to "soften the impact" of the *Prioress' Tale*, an impact which in my reading includes the Prioress' Prologue. On the contrary, it is partly *because of* its impact that I teach that tale in all of the classes in which I cover Chaucer—because of several sensuous "unpleasantnesses" in the tale which have gone unnoticed as sensuous or at least have not been subjected to scholarly-critical discussion in print. Most students' initial reaction to the *Prioress' Tale* is indeed that it is vehemently anti-Semitic, but when I ask them to ponder, especially in light of the satiric portrayal which in the General Prologue Chaucer gives us of several other ecclesiastics, whether the poet himself displays anti-Semitism, I get the following critical, albeit still tentative, response: in his description of the Prioress in the General Prologue Chaucer could be satirically presenting her as a hypocrite since she wears jewelry and displays her fine forehead, i.e., behaves in a manner which befits a woman trying to appeal to the opposite sex rather than in a manner befitting a nun.

Thus, apparently, an assessment of the Prioress and her tale need not, as our present-day sensitivity to racism would seem to dictate, begin with the question of anti-Semitism. But then, Paull F. Baum, whom Beverly Boyd places "Among the more irreverent scholars [of the *Prioress' Tale*]" in her 1987 *Variorum Edition* of that tale,[5] may have been underestimating the reverence of his own colleagues when in 1958 he remarked that Chaucer wrote the *Prioress' Tale* "with his usual keen sense of the ridiculous and a twinkle which he trusted each of us to catch." And Baum may have been overestimating his colleagues' alertness to raillery when he went on to say that the tale "matches the reverent raillery of our first introduction to the Prioress [in the General Prologue]."[6] Baum was preaching to a dynasty of scholars who simplemindedly and piously refused to see the sensuous elements in what on the surface Chaucer is presenting as a saint's tale/miracle story. These scholars are guilty of what I will call the apologetic fallacy[7]—and I deliberately used the present tense *are* instead of the past because I will later quote from a 1992 article on Chaucer's portrayal of the Prioress.

Perhaps the most revealing example of the apologetic fallacy in *Prioress' Tale* criticism is Edward H. Kelly's 1969 article, which is still being cited as an authoritative study, entitled "By Mouth of Innocentz: The Prioress Vindicated."[8] After opening his article with the statement,

> Recent readings of the *Prioress's Tale* tend to fall into two common categories. The first views it as devoutly religious despite the womanly wordliness in Madame Eglentyne's description in the [General Prologue]; *the other finds the tale vicious and hypocritical but entirely consistent with the nature of the teller established in the General Prologue,*

Kelly pronounced this hermeneutical judgment:

> Those who see the appropriateness of the tale to the teller frequently
> stress her clerical failings apparently *without appreciating* the earnest,
> heartfelt religion revealed in her story of the Virgin miracle or *the
> poetic artistry of the tale itself.*[9] (italics mine)

The messages conveyed by the two separate portions which I italicized in the
indented quotations exemplify the simplemindedness or piety of some of the
Prioress' vindicators. I would have been able to spare Chaucer scholarship a
lengthy discussion, spread over two chapters, of Chaucer's portrayal of the
Prioress, if my own view of her tale as vicious and hypocritical had rendered
me unable to appreciate the poetic artistry of the tale itself. Does our ability
to appreciate Chaucer's artistry depend on our appreciation of the revelation of
the Prioress' religion as "earnest" and "heartfelt"? Prithee, what if Chaucer
did intend to satirize the tone as well as purpose of the Prioress' devotional
story, or at least was deliberately writing the tale in a manner which left room
for such an interpretation? Kelly is putting Chaucer's readers in a double-
bind. I imagine that such "heartfelt" scholarly-critical arguments about the
Prioress' religion could elicit responses like Salzberg's more easily than does
Chaucer's work of art (Salzberg doesn't mention Kelly's study).

Kelly is repeating the apologetic fallacy when he tries to vindicate the
Prioress from the charge of anti-Semitism by arguing: "had she slandered
Turks or Mongolians, modern critical hackles would not rise *at the expense of
missing exquisite poetic artistry* which unites character of teller to tale told,
through faultless use of diction, detail, and unerring poetic tone" (italics
mine).[10] Again, what has our appreciation of Chaucer's poetic artistry got to
do with the question of the Prioress' possible anti-Semitism? Are certain
critics trying to defend the Prioress, or do they feel they need to defend
Chaucer?

Vindication attempts can lead apologists to the sin of misrepresenting or
at least misreading Chaucer's text. Kelly contends: "scholars who label the

Prioress anti-Semite neglect close reading of the *General Prologue* and tale as well, failing to note, for instance, that her story is set in 'Asye,' where both Jew and Christian are alien, and that it is neither the Christians nor the Prioress who punishes the murderers, but the 'provost' of the land."[11] Let us therefore do a "close reading" of the lines about the provost of the land in Asia. After the discovery of the child's body, the Christian community

> hastily . . . for the provost sente;
> He cam anon withouten tariyng,
> And *herieth Crist that is hevene kyng,*
> *And eek his mooder, honour of mankynde,*
> And after that the Jewes leet he bynde. (VII 616-20, italics added)

When in a story which pits Jews against Christians the provost praises Christ and Mary before he arrests the Jews and has them punished, the provost is being identified as Christian. Thus Kelly's argument which exempts any and all Christians from involvement in the punishment process is at best sophistry and at worst a misrepresentation of Chaucer's text.

It could of course be argued that the Prioress gets carried away by her Christian militantism and merely attributes to a non-Christian provost the praise of Christ and Mary, but if that is Kelly's reading he should have indicated such an an important distinction. After all, as Boyd would point out in her *Prioress Variorum*, "the provost does not forget to offer praise to Christ and his mother before exercising his legal authority" and "the hasty entrance of the provost [may be] a characteristic bit of Chaucerian irony undermining the travesty of justice that takes place."[12] Kelly's study, then, disqualifies itself because of its "heartfelt" tendentiousness—and so do numerous other studies which display, although at times in somewhat different ways, a "heartfelt" need to defend Chaucer by defending the Prioress. I therefore find it regrettable that the *Prioress Variorum*, which cites Kelly on several occasions and seems to sanction Kelly's entire argument by practically summarizing it,[13] fails to caution students of the *Prioress' Tale* by not pointing out the glaring mistake I have just noted—and, more generally, by not questioning Kelly's verdict on which school of thought is incapable of appreciating Chaucer artistry in the tale.[14] But let us return to what I earlier said about students in the classroom suggesting that Chaucer could be presenting the Prioress as a hypocrite.

Once questions about the Prioress' sincerity concerning her vocation have been raised, we have to confront the fact that the sweet disposition attributed to the Prioress in the General Prologue is inconsonant with her tale: how can a person whose feelings are so tender that she weeps over the suffering or dying of animals tell such a ghastly story? Does the Prioress *have* to elaborate on the unsavory circumstances of the disposal of the boy's body, namely his being thrown into a privy where the Jews purge their entrails?[15] Once we have come to suspect in this supposedly tender-hearted nun an interest in unpalatable descriptions, she begins to appear as anything but what one would expect a nun to be, especially when she treats her audience to the following description of the punishment of the Jews:

> With torment and with shamful deeth echon,
> This provost dooth thise Jewes for to sterve
> That of this mordre wiste, and that anon.
> He nolde no swich cursednesse observe.
> "Yvele shal have that yvele wol deserve";
> Therfore with wilde hors he dide hem drawe,
> And after that he heng hem by the lawe. (VII 628-34)

It could perhaps be argued that the eagerness with which the Prioress describes the torturing and execution of the Jews and her apparently relishing of that description make her a sadist. At any rate, her being "charitable . . . and pitous" (I 143) toward animals whose suffering makes her weep whereas she applauds the torturing of the Jews ("Yvele shal have that yvele wol deserve") suggests that in her assessment Jews are lower than animals, are even less than *Untermenschen* as the Nazis would officially label Jews more than five centuries later.

The Prioress has indeed been accused of sadism; Florence H. Ridley observed in her 1965 study on *The Prioress and Her Critics:*

> The judgment of Maurice Cohen [in his 1962 article, "Chaucer's Prioress and Her Tale: A Study of Anal Character and Anti-Semitism,"] caps the climax [of the "hard reading" of the tale]—or at least one may hope so. According to this critic [i.e., Cohen] Chaucer has the Prioress "choose for the story what is in effect a paradigmatic and sadistic—and anti-Semitic—fantasy." . . . [Chaucer] has intentionally "steeped the Prioress and her tale in anal and sadistic symbolism, illustrating Freud's formulations on the sadomasochistic, sexually ambiguous characteristics of anal eroticism." . . . *Criticism such as this is warped.* Only the most determined efforts to magnify the anti-Semitism of "The Prioress's Tale" and turn its teller into a monster can completely negate *all her pity and love*, and can completely set aside the devotional purpose and tone of her story.[16] (italics mine)

While I disagree with Ridley's apparently sweeping rejection of *any* application of psychoanalytic approaches to interpreting the tale—"Criticism such as this is warped"[17]—I consider her 1965 monograph still the strongest case against what she called the "hard reading" and the "hard critics" of the *Prioress' Tale.*[18] I will therefore cite a good amount of material from that study, as well as from Ridley's 1987 contributions to the Explanatory Notes in the *Riverside Chaucer* which clearly suggest that she has not softened toward the "hard" critics or become any harder toward the Prioress. In fact, I believe Salzberg might have been able to further harden his own criticism had he tried to refute Ridley's defense of the Prioress, but in referring to the tale's apologists he does not even mention Ridley. The main problem with Ridley's approach as I see it is that she reads the *Prioress' Tale* exclusively—perhaps I should say uncritically—as a saint's tale, i.e., as a tale in which the teller simply expresses his or her simple faith in an almost prayer-like fashion, as, in Ridley's own words, a "display of naiveté, ignorance, blind, vehement devotion."[19] Ridley seems to be trying to empathize into the Prioress when, for my personal taste protesting too much, she dramatically speaks of "all her pity and love"—*what* pity and love, it has rightfully been asked,[20]—also when she she resorts to interpreting the Prioress as "simpleminded"[21] and claims: "The content, which of course does not offer much to engage the mind, being only an expression of the most childlike faith, is a perfect reflection of the Prioress's limited mentality."[22]

When Chaucer assigns to one of his better-educated pilgrims a seemingly limited mentality, we are being called upon to suspect that the consummate ironist and sophisticated artist may be playing a "game." The game which I wish to argue Chaucer is playing is one that involves a curious combination of anti-Semitism and sexual ambiguity. Ridley is absolutely right when she observes that, given the anti-Semitic *Zeitgeist*, especially in the Church which often condemned the Jews as infidels and even as Christ-killers,[23] "it would have been most unlikely for a fourteenth-century poet to satirize a nun and a legend of the Virgin *in order to attack anti-Semitism*" (italics added).[24] As I hope my study will show, attacking anti-Semitism is not Chaucer's main intent: such an attack is merely ancillary to an attack of a much broader nature. From the poet's stance the *Prioress' Tale*, whose prologue I will treat as an integral part of the tale,[25] is not an anti-Semitic story but, instead, a story which is *about* anti-Semitism.

The *Prioress' Tale* possesses a particular element of dissociating irony whose permeating nature has never been fully addressed. The perpetual tempest in a teapot over the desirability of the tale in our curricula may well be the result of an inability or unwillingness on the part of many a scholar-teacher, in the camps of both the apologetic fallacy and what I will call the anti-Semitism fallacy of those who deplore Chaucer's having written the *Prioress' Tale* at all, to read Chaucer's text closely and—in spite of Robert Jordan's assessment of Chaucer's art—*organically*. Let us, for example, examine the Prioress' prologue, in which she praises God with the following lines:

> "O Lord, oure Lord, thy name how merveillous
> Is in this large world ysprad—*quod she*—
> For noght oonly thy laude precious

> Parfourned is by men of dignitee,
> But by the mouth of children thy bountee
> Parfourned is, for on the brest soukynge
> Somtyme shewen they thyn heriyinge.'' (VII 453-59, italics added)

In the Introduction I cited Ross' comment that ''One does not find bawdiness in Chaucer's Prioress, and one does not expect to.'' Prior to quoting lines 457-59 Ross continues his observation: ''But the passage in which she praises little children who can laud the Blessed Virgin in strange ways, even though infants, strikes me as 'obscene' in some special sense.''[26] Unfortunately, Ross does not tell us what that ''special sense'' is. In the prologue to a tale celebrating the Virgin Mother, this picture appears indeed out of place. Perhaps it could be called, to use Kendrick's term, a ''churlish interpretation'' of visual representations of the suckling Jesus child[27]—but on the Prioress' rather than Chaucer's part.

Edward I. Condren observes in a 1989 article entitled ''The Prioress: A Legend of Spirit, a Life of Flesh'':

> [The Prioress] begins with a simple paradox: lofty praise comes not only from the mighty but from humble children too. However, the praise ''by the mouth of children'' influences the thought to develop very differently. Presumably intended as a simple image of helpless innocence, in contrast with ''men of dignitee,'' the phrase acquires much more importance when ''mouth'' is gratuitously put to breast. The notion of helplessness, toward which the stanza seemed to be moving, is lost behind the more complicated figure of an infant sucking. That tableau becomes even more complex when the curious qualifier ''somtyme'' suggests that praise depends on some aspect of the sucking, not on the innocence . . . the stanza's conclusion suprises us by reducing those imagined children to suckling infants.[28]

While Condren does call the stanza's surprising movement from innocent to suckling gratuitous, he does not consider that development ironic; on the contrary, Condren interprets the movement to physicality as part of the saint's-tale celebration of the Incarnation. Condren's ingeniously developed argument is persuasive—so long as we read the *Prioress' Tale* as a saint's tale and nothing else. In my view, Chaucer is introducing an ironic stance when, after the

Prioress' statement *that* the Lord's marvelous name is spread through this wide world and before her description of *how* the spreading is done, the poet inserts the little phrase "quod she": two lines into the Prioress' hymn to the Virgin Mother the poet is distancing himself from what the Prioress is about to say. In the hymn's first stanzas, Chaucer is distancing himself from the Prioress' reduction of the imagined praising-and-praying children to sucking infants.

The surprising development within the first stanza reveals the Prioress' own desire: she yearns for a child. However, since she is vowed to celibacy, she wishes for some kind of Immaculate Conception. Such a conception would be "immaculate" not of course in the sense of that of Mary who had to be exempt from Original Sin before she was impregnated; the Prioress' child would have to be begotten in a manner similar to that in which in the *Monk's Tale* Adam had been created by God: "With Goddes owne fynger wroght was he,/And nat bigeten of mannes sperme unclene." I have discussed how the Monk's lines are informed by the cosmic-union picture in Chaucer's opening lines. If we read the *Canterbury Tales* palimpsestically as tales whose full meaning lies in their interactions with each other as well as with the General Prologue, we discover that the sophisticated literary artist is playing a boldly heretical *game* in which he plays the Christian doctrine of Immaculate Conception against the notion of the chief god in Roman theology impregnating Earth. Chaucer is insinuating that the Prioress wishes to be impregnated by *God's clean sperm*:

> O mooder Mayde, O mayde Mooder free!
> O bussh unbrent, brennynge in Moyses sighte,
> That *ravyshedest doun fro the Deitee*,
> Thurgh thyn humblesse, the Goost that in th'alighte,
> Of whos vertu, whan he thyn herte lighte,
> Conceyved was the Fadres sapience,
> Help me to telle it in thy reverence! (VII 467-74, italics added)

The Prioress is projecting herself into Mary in the latter's function of Virgin Mother. The Prioress would like to have her heart cheered in the same way in which Mary's was: through impregnation by the Holy Ghost. Especially when the passage is read in light of the *descensus* picture in the opening lines of the General Prologue and in light of that picture's allusively functional analogue in Virgil, the Prioress' reference to the "Goost that in *th'alighte/* . . . whan he thyn herte *lighte*" becomes rather physical: in an instance of dissociating irony, Chaucer is insinuating that impregnation by the Holy Ghost would make the Prioress a "*laeta* coniux." This places the *th'alighte/lighte* rhyme in the startling stark-collocation category that Robert Jordan says is "possible" in Chaucer's art.

Chaucer in a dazzling linguistic game[29] has the present notion interact not only with the *descensus* pictures in the General Prologue and in Virgil but also—especially in the "ravyshedest doun fro the deitee"—with the *doun descende* in the *Merchant's Tale*.[30] This interconnection is fortified by the use of the word *vertu*, i.e., by the employment of a derivative of the Latin *virtus* ("courage," literally "man-ness," "that which befits a man") to describe that which impregnates Mary: *vertu* comes to mean the same as *corage* in the latter's sexual connotation,[31] and "Fadres *sapience*" (italics added) comes to mean *knowledge* in the sense in which *queynte Nicholas* "gets to know" Alison's "pryvetee." In fact, I would argue that Chaucer has the Prioress' hymn to the Virgin interact with the knowledge-and-*descensus* context and related notions in the fabliau of the *Miller's Tale*. An organic reading of the *Canterbury Tales* reveals that there is—to use Salzberg's term—an "unpleasantness" already about the Prioress' hymn, which some readers consider the very jewel of the *Prioress' Tale*.[32] And, as Condren has noted, "as a development of the *Prologue*, the *Tale* bears a closer relation to the five stanzas that precede it than has been supposed."[33]

My above reading of the Prioress' prologue does not assume that Chaucer intends her to be conscious of the double entendres in her hymn: the idea is that her words betray her secret wishes. Since in real life she is not sup-

posed to be a mother, she becomes a mother *poetically speaking*—by representing the recital of her tale as an act of giving birth:

> [O Lord,] in laude, as I best kan or may,
> Of thee and of the white lylye flour
> Which that the bar, and is mayde alway,
> To telle a storie I wol do my *labour*.   (VII 460-63,italics added)

The Prioress continues with the pregnancy imagery when she addresses Mary:

> My konnyng is so wayk, O blisful Queene . . .
> That I ne may the weighte nat susteene . . .   (VII 481-83)

Since the Prioress represents herself as giving birth to the story of the little
boy—an intolerably weighty, in modern jargon perhaps "heavy," story— she
poetically speaking gives birth to him,[34] and, consequently, by describing his
murder also kills him.

Up to this point in the Prioress' wish-fulfillment tale, i.e., in her prologue, Chaucer's characterization of the nun had not been totally unsympathetic; in her tale proper, however, Chaucer's satire on the bush that burns but
cannot marry becomes fierce.   The fierceness begins when Chaucer has the
Prioress unknowingly allude to the Apostle's advice on how to avoid burning
while she is actually mentioning the burning bush through which God spoke to
Moses.   She earns this fierceness in part because in her story she fails to make
the "connection between Moses and his people and the villains of the
story."[35] The Prioress not only makes the child into a Christ figure—a notion
which she is endowing with a special twist when she compares the Jews in the
story to the "cursed folk of Herodes al newe" (VII 574) who tried to kill the
Christ child[36]—but also apostrophizes the boy as a martyr confirmed to virginity:

> O martir, sowded to virginitee,
> Now maystow syngen, folwynge evere in oon
> The white Lamb celestial—quod she—
> Of which the grete evaungelist, Seint John,
> In Pathmos wroot, which seith that they that goon
> Biforn this Lamb, and synge a song al newe,

That nevere, flesshly, wommen they ne knewe. (VII 579-85)

Unlike Jesus who lived to be over thirty years old and thus had a choice in remaining a virgin, and unlike those men who, according to Jerome's *Adversus Jovinianum*, "have not polluted themselves with women [and] have remained virgins [and therefore] follow the lamb wherever he goes,"[37] the boy is only seven years old, so that there would be no need for the Prioress to state that he never knew women carnally but instead died as a "gemme of chastitee, this emeraude" (VII 609). In other words, when poetically speaking she kills the child at the age of seven, thus denying him a choice, the Prioress also poetically castrates the boy.[38]

There are several possible reasons why the Prioress does this. The simplest reason would seem to be that, being denied the pleasures of sex, she deprives someone else of those pleasures. Perhaps her father had sent her to a convent without her having a choice in that matter: especially since she applies the "sowded to virginitee" to a martyr, that term evokes associations with an iron chastity belt soldered shut—but, while a notion of the Prioress poetically putting in chains the genitalia of a seven-year-old boy would be sufficiently repulsive, the notion of what iron being soldered might do to the boy's genitals, not totally unreminiscent of what Absalom tries to do to a young wife with the "hoote kultour," is even more horrific. At any rate, the castration-reading would tie in with the obscenely heretical notion that, wedded to Christ by her vows of celibacy, the Prioress may be reminding her Bridegroom of His capacity as Holy Ghost: the Prioress could be angry at her Bridegroom for not living up to His job of impregnating the bride and, therefore, could be poetically castrating the Christ figure whom she has created in order to punish the Bridegroom who had been delinquent in paying His marital *dette*. Several possible motives may be simultaneously intended by the poet. The Prioress could be vicariously acting out on the boy her hostilities toward her father for having sent her to a convent. Or she could be castrating the boy to avenge herself on the opposite sex, with which she may have had unfortunate experiences: her overemphasis on Mary as "mayde *alway*" may suggest that, unlike Mary, the Prioress is *not* a "bussh unbrent"[39] and *not* a "white lylye flour," and despite the Apostle's remedy for burning was never married either.

I mentioned a moment ago the interaction between the Prioress' impregnation imagery and the *doun descende* in the *Merchant's Tale*, as well as the possibility that the Prioress is angry at Christ for being delinquent in his marital *dette* and not living up to His job of impregnating the bride. I now wish to argue that through the palimpsestic interaction between the *Prioress'* and the *Merchant's Tales* Chaucer is infiltrating the following notion into his presentation of the Prioress' bitterness: the marital relationship between Christ and the Prioress is of the same kind as that between January and May. As I will elaborate in Chapter V, the selfish January defines his marriage as "in this world . . . a paradys" (IV 1265). Brought to bear on the *Prioress' Tale*, January's definition transmogrifies Christ into a husband who selfishly has a paradise in this world with a woman whom he has been able to buy, or more precisely, whom thanks to its economic power the Church has been able to buy for him. To the Prioress, Christ's lovemaking is precisely what May considers January's: "nat . . . worth a bene" (IV 1854). Yet there is this allusively functional contrast: especially if Chaucer is using the word *bene* in its literal botanical sense to imply that, despite all his *labour* at plowing and sowing, January fails to impregnate his wife,[40] Christ does not even make such an attempt with His bride, the Prioress. Not only does Christ not *doun descende* in the secondary connatation in which Chaucer uses that term, i.e., ejaculate, but Christ does not even do so in the sense in which January himself uses that term: since Christ never mounts the Prioress' body, he does not have to dismount it.

Christ is so deliquent in His marital *dette* that He does not even deflower the Prioress. Chaucer is introducing the idea of defloration when he has the

Prioress' hymn interact with the impregnation picture in the General Prologue. Paul Ruggiers notes that the "Of whose vertu, whan he thyn herte lighte,/ Conceyved was the Fadres sapience" is a "conceit which we have seen in the opening lines of the General Prologue ('Of which vertu engendered is the flour.'), now more securely oriented to the great mystery of Christ's origin."[41] Needless to say that the *vertu* in the General Prologue has the same sexual connotation of "man-ness" as it does in the Prioress' lines, but what I would like to point out here is that Chaucer is establishing the following associations. April's "vertu" *engenders* flowers whereas the first sexual union traditionally *destroys* the flower, i.e., deflowers the virgin. In contrast to the sex act, but like April in the General Prologue, the Holy Ghost does not deflower Mary, who remains a "white lylye flour." There is nothing comical about these associations—until we begin to suspect that the Prioress may *not* be a "bussh unbrent."

The last point concerning the Prioress' past experiences with the opposite sex is, at least at this point in my discussion, mere speculation. What remains valid in any case, however, is the reading of the *Prioress' Tale* as a confession, a confession either of her secret wishes or of her fears—or both. Maybe the Prioress poetically speaking castrates the boy in order to come to terms with her fears of the opposite sex. A possible threat to her chastity would be the males in the clergy, for it should be noted that she calls the abbot who finally puts the boy to sleep by removing the grain from his tongue a holy man "As monkes been—*or elles oghte be*" (VII 643, italics added). The Prioress is aware of the fact that monks are not always as holy as they ought to be.

Through her acknowledgment that *monks* are not always as holy as they are supposed to be, Chaucer is ironically using the Prioress to reinforce the notion that *nuns* are not always as holy as they ought to be. It might not be an unfair illustration of Ridley's apparent naiveté in her reading of the *Prioress'*

Tale as a saint's tale that in her *Prioress* monograph she observed concerning the teller's remark about monks: "since [the Prioress] says that monks should be holy men, we must assume she knows that prioresses should be holy women:"[42] unless Ridley meant it ironically, which I doubt was the case, what was her point in telling us what we must assume the Prioress knows? Ridley later must have taken a more critical look at the Prioress' curious afterthought, "or elles oghte be," for she would note in the *Riverside Chaucer*: "Apparently a reference to the monk in The Shipman's Tale."[43] Yet Ridley would not modify her assessment of the *Prioress' Tale*, although her note seems to raise the following question: if the Prioress is referring to the lecherous monk in the *Shipman's Tale*, i.e., if she is making an aside which in a sense engages in a dialogue with the Shipman, is she still telling a saint's tale, simpleminded or not?

In fact, the Shipman's fabliau would have been a vivid reminder to the Prioress of any involvement with a monk. Such a reference, in turn, would lend support to my thesis concerning a sexual involvement, especially since there is a parallel on the one hand between the sexually unfulfilled wife in the *Shipman's Tale* who lets the monk make up for the marital "dette," and on the other hand the nun who is sexually neglected by her Bridegroom—and the interaction between the Shipman's fabliau and the Prioress' purported saint's tale might even suggest that the Prioress had used a monk for the debt which Jesus never paid. Such a sexual occurrence would explain why the Prioress so dramatically apostrophizes the little clergeon as a personified "emeraude," as a gem which, as Ridley points out, was considered a guard against lechery:[44] we would have the ironic implication that the Prioress now wishes that on that occasion she had had an emerald on hand—a medieval version of our modern cold-shower remedy for the Paulinian burning.

The biggest ironic implication of the idea of the Prioress having used a monk for the marital debt which Jesus never paid would be that she used a member of the Church founded by Christ to cheat her Bridegroom in an act of adultery. Such an idea will not seem too farfetched once we realize that in his presentation of the Prioress in the General Prologue Chaucer had associated her with a Biblical pronouncement on adulteresses. Douglas Loney made the following observations in his 1992 essay on "Chaucer's Prioress and Agur's 'Adulterous Woman'":

> There is, I believe, [an] oblique reference to scripture . . . in the . . . passage on the Prioress' manners at table—the three lines beginning "Hir over-lippe wyped so clene" (A 133-35). Compare the details here with Agur's observation in Proverbs 30:20: "Such is also the way of an adulterous woman, who eateth, and wipeth her mouth, and saith: I have done no evil." . . . of the many hundreds of such scriptural allusions identified already in Chaucer's poetry, Proverbs is the source more often than any other book of the Bible . . . And Alysoun of Bath (who would seem the more obvious choice as the butt of an esoteric joke about the ways of adulterous women), in the Prologue to her own tale (D 362-71), quotes verses 16, 21, and 23 from Proverbs chapter 30, thus bracketing the crucial twentieth verse and reserving it for the other important woman among the Canterbury pilgrims . . . *Of course I do not contend that by such an allusion Chaucer is inviting us to cast the first stone at Eglentyne; that would be entirely out of keeping with the mildness of his irony in the rest of her portrait* . . . It is much more likely that this muted allusion to the manner of an "adulterous woman" is meant to remind us again of the seductive power of the secular world, and its temptations to spiritual unfaithfulness.[45] (italics added)

The seeming mildness of Chaucer's irony in his portrait of the Prioress in the General Prologue is an integral part of the irony in his overall portrayal of that nun, an overall portrayal which includes what we learn about her from her tale and prologue. Once we have brought the *Prioress Tale* to bear on her portrayal in the General Prologue, we palimpsestically also reassess her description of her table manners in the light of the crucial twentieth verse of Proverbs which Chaucer will have the Wife of Bath bracket in her prologue and reserve for the Prioress.

Furthermore, the interaction between the description of the Prioress as fastidiously wiping her mouth and the passage in the Wife of Bath's Prologue is not limited to lines 362-71 and their Biblical implications as Loney has suggested; the intertextuality includes lines 372-75. Here is the passage from the Wife of Bath:

> Thou seydest eek that ther been thynges thre,
> The whiche thynges troublen al this erthe,
> And that no wight may endure the ferthe.
> O leeve sir shrewe, Jhesu shorte thy lyf!
> Yet prechestow and seyst an hateful wyf
> Yrekened is for oon of thise meschaunces.
> Been ther none othere maner resemblances
> That ye may likne your parables to,
> But if a sely wyf be oon of tho?
> Thou liknest eek wommanes love to helle,
> *To bareyne lond, ther water may nat dwelle.*
> *Thou liknest it also to wilde fyr;*
> *The moore it brenneth, the moore it hath desir*
> *To consume every thyng that brent wole be.* (III 362-75, italics added)

The lines I italicized as well as line 371 allude to Proverbs 30:16, to a verse which is heavily laden with sexual connotations, and it is against the background of verse 16 that we have to read verse 20 about the way of an adulterous woman and thus Chaucer's description of the Prioress' table manners. Whereas Loney cites from the Rheims-Douay translation of the Vulgate, let me quote Proverbs 30:16, 20, 21, and 23 from the Latin original:

> 16 *Infernus, et os vulvae,*
> Et terra quae non satiatur aqua;
> Ignis vero nunquam dicit: Sufficit.
>   . . . .
> 20 Talis est et via mulieris adulterae,
> Quae comedit, et *tergens os suum,*
> Dicit: Non sum operata malum.
> 21 Per tria movetur terra,
> Et quartum, non potest sustinere:
>   . . . .
> 23 Per odiosam mulierem, cum in matrimonio fuerit assumpta . . .
> (italics added)

Chaucer uses verse 21 about things which make the earth tremble to introduce things which trouble all this earth. His first example, ''an hateful wyf,'' which is Agur's *mulier odiosa*, is innocuous enough. And the comparisons of a woman's love to hell, to land which cannot be satisfied no matter how much water it receives, and to consuming fire likewise are relatively innocuous, even though these comparisons carry sexual connotations. The parables seem innocuous—until we consult the Latin text of the Vulgate. A closer look at the Latin of Proverbs 30:16 will show us that in the comparison of "wommanes love to helle" Chaucer is comparing to hell, to *Infernus*, not so much a woman's love as her *os vulvae*, literally the "mouth" of her vulva.[46]

The present chapter is not concerned with explicating the Wife of Bath's Prologue. What I am concerned with here is how Chaucer's portrayal of the Prioress is informed both by Chaucer's more extensively allusive use of Agur's pronouncements in the Wife of Bath's Prologue and by Chaucer's direct allusive association of the Prioress with Agur's specific pronouncement concerning the way of an adulterous woman. When Chaucer first allusively associates the Prioress with one specific pronouncement which Agur had made about women and then has the Wife of Bath bracket that specific pronouncement in her citation of several misogynistic dicta by Agur, the poet is calling on the reader to examine for possible allusively functional relevances the entire context from verse 16 to verse 23 in Proverbs 30.

The readers who heed Chaucer's call will not only remember that, shortly before citing Agur, the Wife of Bath had admonished her husband not to try to prevent her from giving her *queynte* to other men during her daytime outings,

> —Ye shul have queynte right ynogh at eve.
> He is to greet a nygard that wolde werne
> A man to lighte a candle at his lanterne— (III 332-34)

but they will also come to suspect that when Chaucer speaks about the Prioress wiping her "*over*-lippe" (italics added) he is slyly insinuating the following idea. While Chaucer probably did not know that the Hebrew word for "to eat" also had the slang connotation of "to have sexual intercourse"[47] and

Agur had probably created a pun in juxtaposing within four verses what would be translated into Latin as "Infernus, et os vulvae" and as *mulier adultera tergens os suum*, it would have been impossible for someone with Chaucer's imaginative power not to associate the *os vulvae* with the *os/mouth* which the supper-eating adulteress wipes clean (*tergens*) while saying she has done no wrong. Through his two-pronged allusion to Proverbs 30:16-23 in his portrayal of the Prioress, Chaucer is introducing the idea of a nun wiping clean her *lower* lips a.k.a labia and saying she has done no wrong—after an act of intercourse in which she committed adultery against her Bridegroom Jesus Christ.

Contrary to Loney's claim that Chaucer could not possibly be inviting us to throw stones at Eglentyne, I would argue that this is precisely what Chaucer is inviting us to do, regardless of whether he wants us to associate the sexually frustrated Madame Eglentyne with the woman's sexual insatiability that is attacked in the parables which the Wife of Bath cites from Proverbs 30. However, I believe there is no such thing as a "*first* stone" being thrown by the reader: it is part of the masterful operation of Chaucer's irony that some readers may be tempted to cast a stone when they catch the allusion to Proverbs 30:20 in the description of the Prioress' appearance, others perhaps after they discover that Chaucer has the lusty Wife of Bath bracket the twentieth verse, and others on the basis of the information offered by a palimpsestic interaction among the General Prologue, the Wife's prologue, and the Prioress' own tale. Or could it be argued that the Wife of Bath, who presumably had noticed the Prioress' table manners no less than Chaucer-the-pilgrim had, is throwing the first stone by actually *not* throwing it and, instead, bracketing the twentieth verse? At any rate, an organic reading of the *Canterbury Tales* suggests that the Prioress may be subject to a barrage of stones. Especially in light of the confessional nature of her prologue-and-tale, perhaps the Prioress is throwing a stone at herself, namely in the form of the "gemme of chastitee, this emeraude"—in the form of the "emeraude" which she creates in her

story because she didn't have such a precious stone on hand when she needed
it.

The implication of such an earlier occurrence would lend special irony
to the Prioress wearing a brooch with an "Amor vincit omnia" inscription. In
his discussion of the Prioress's "bedes" Condren observes that "It is useful to
keep in mind [the] irony . . . that *Amor vincit omnia* comes from Virgil's
Tenth's Eclogue, line 69, a monologue about frenzied love."[48] Condren fails
to catch in full the irony in Chaucer's use of what "comes from" Virgil, but
so had many scholars before Condren, including John Livingston Lowes who
back in 1919 made this often-quoted observation, an observation which
Condren cites at the beginning of his study: "Which of the two loves does
'amor' mean to the Prioress? I do not know, but I think she thought she
meant celestial love."[49]

Chauncey Wood seems to have come closest to appreciating Chaucer's
Amor vincit omnia, in a 1981 essay entitled "Chaucer's Use of Signs in His
Portrait of the Prioress," but he too didn't quite catch it. After quoting
Lowes, Wood observes:

> Now one would not want to state that *amor vincit omnia* could not have
> have a significance *in bono* in the Middle Ages; it could and did, and
> John Gower, for example, uses it in a good sense in the Prologue to his
> *Tripartite Chronicle* and in *Vox clamantis*, book 6, chapter 14. Howev-
> er, its original, Virgilian sense was almost certainly stronger, since it
> was undoubtedly a school text. Gower uses it that way in *Vox claman-
> tis*, book 5, chp. 3; it is used with an overt reference to Virgil in the
> climactic passages closing the *Romance of the Rose* . . . While it is not
> possible to resolve the matter definitively, it seems likely that the
> Virgilian sense would be so strong that the real joke is in the Prioress'
> inability to fathom the commonplace erotic sense of the text. Instead of
> stressing her innocence or puremindedness, as Lowes does, we might
> better stress her ignorance of Virgil, or perhaps her inability to distin-
> guish between *amor* and *caritas* . . . The joke about not knowing or
> understanding Virgil is precisely the same joke Chaucer used earlier in
> his portrait when he ascribed to her table manners that arose from a
> misreading or misunderstanding of the *Romance of the Rose*, and it is a
> piece of her knowing French, but only provincial French. Indeed, a

certain ineptitude with classical or foreign languages is a common
satiric touch in medieval English literature.[50]

Let me make a few suggestions which may help us "resolve the matter
definitively." Chaucer's "joke about not knowing or understanding Virgil"
and his satiric treatment of "ineptitude with classical . . . languages" goes far
beyond the rather general points which Wood has noted. There simply is no
way around looking at *Virgil's text*. What has been overlooked is the fact that
Chaucer built in a dissociating device by changing the word order in poor
Gallus' exclamation, "*omnia vincit Amor*; et nos cedamus Amori*": by changing the word order he changed the meaning. When Chaucer destroys the
dactyllic hexameter in one of the most famous of classical verses, he is indicating that he is inverting the meaning of the conclusion to Gallus' lover's com-
plaint: "Love conquers *all*; let us [i.e., me, Gallus] too yield to Love."
Peaceful, or at least resigningly acquiescent, Gallus unselfishly channels his
amor into wishing the best for the lover who has left him. The allusively
functional contrast is that, unlike the Gallus who wishes he could live in a
pastoral, ideal world but eventually accepts reality—*omnia* at the beginning of
Virgil's hexameter is the key word here—the Prioress is a poor loser: she
will, quite literally as we shall see, "raise hell" for, or at least on account of,
whoever she thinks has wronged her in her love life, and in the process she
will provide hell for herself. And she will provide the reader with what Salzberg calls "unpleasantness," beginning with her hymn to the Virgin Mother—in addition to the unpalatable aspects which Chaucer had already provided
in the General Prologue through allusions radiating from his description of her
table manners.

Chaucer is employing the Prioress' use of impregnation-and-birthing
imagery to endow her story with an "unpleasantness" which goes beyond,
but, as I will show, thematically ties in with, her display of anti-Semitism.[51]
Chaucer is doing so through the manner in which he has her combine the

description of the slaying of the boy by the hired murderer and that of the disposing of his body:

> This cursed Jew hym hente, and heeld hym faste,
> And kitte his throte, and in a pit hym caste.
> *I seye that in a wardrobe they hym threwe*
> *Where as thise Jewes purgen hire entraille.*
> O cursed folk of Herodes al newe,
> What may youre yvel entente yow availle?
> Mordre wol out, certeyn, it wol not faille,
> And namely ther th'onour of God shal sprede;
> The blood out crieth on youre cursed dede. (VII, 570-78, italics added)

Tying the Jewish matzo blood sacrifice to King Herod is a clever stratagem on the Prioress' part in her attempt to present the murder of the boy who sings the "Alma redemptoris" as a Jewish attack on the Christian religion, as clever as is her association of the murderer with the most famous hireling in history, Judas Iscariot. Equally clever is her association of the Jewish matzo blood-sacrifice with the notion of the blood spilled by the murder as actually increasing God's honor.

This is an intellectual-theological exercise performed in the honor of God substituting for the regular ways in which a nun is supposed to honor the Lord, the regular ways in which the Prioress has failed in her worship. And this may very well be the point where Chaucer's irony in the *Prioress' Tale* is at its most ingenious. Just as "Mordre wol out," it is in this context that the poet gives the impression that he may be letting out the main one of the Prioress' failures at honoring God. For what does it mean that her fairly brief description of the murder committed by the hireling and the intellectual-theological legerdemain frame the detailed graphic description of the Jews throwing the child's body into the privy where they purge their entrails? Which associations does the murder of a child—a child whose *very* young age is being emphasized if we bring to bear the Prioress' reference to Herod's infanticide—and its disposal into a privy evoke? There are several possible answers, and I now wish to argue that the sophisticated literary artist wants the reader to toy with several associations, associations which, instead of being mutually exclusive, all contribute to the poet's complex portrayal of a prioress who insinuates to her fellow pilgrims that not all monks are as holy as they ought to be.

Chaucer is inviting the reader to contemplate the possibility that the Prioress may once have been pregnant—which should shed new light on our reading of her hymn to Mary, supposedly the jewel of her entire tale, with its copious imagery of impregnation, conception, and breast-feeding—and gone through an abortion: "mordre wol out." Condren has made the tantalizing observation that a "body stuffed in a privy hole suggests a reversal of birth,"[52] but he does not inquire into what a suggestion of a child being stuffed back into the *pryvetee* might tell us about the expressly stated subject of his article, namely Chaucer's portrayal of the teller of a saint's tale: "The Prioress: A Legend of Spirit, a Life of Flesh." Let us therefore take a look at Chaucer's description of the birth reversal:

> For thennes forth the Jues han conspired
> This innocent out of this world to chace.
> An homycide therto han they hyred,
> That in an aleye hadde *a privee place*;
> And as the child gan forby for to pace,
> This cursed Jew hym hente, and heeld him faste,
> And kitte his throte, and in a pit him caste.
> I seye that in a wardrobe they him threwe
> Where as thise Jewes purgen hir entraille. (VII 565-73, italics added)

In 1987 Boyd had observed concerning *privee*: "Pun hunters have not re-marked on the possibility here of (proleptic) wordplay. At line [VII 571] the body of the slain boy is thrown into a *pit*, specified in line [VII 572] as *wardrobe*, i.e., a privy."[53] In his 1989 article (which obviously was written before the *Prioress Variorum* became available), Condren, knowingly or unknowing-ly, was one of the pun hunters close to catching what—to use Ross' metaphor which I employed in Chapter I—may have been Madame Eglentyne's *pryvetee*: "mordre wol out."[54]

As has been argued in a 1990 essay, Chaucer may have named his Prioress after "Belle Aiglentine," an aristocratic young woman in a fragmentedly surviving French romance whom her mother, suspecting her daughter to be pregnant—"Why are you so pale and swollen?", she asks her—forces into a "shotgun marriage" with the count whom Aiglentine admits she has had sexual intercourse with.[55]   If, in giving his Prioress the name Eglentyne Chaucer alludes to Belle Aiglentine's fate, then he is indeed insinuating that the Prioress once had been pregnant.   But in that case Chaucer is also insinuating that, regardless of whether an abortion had taken place, the Prioress had been forced by her parents into a marriage with the Church.   Yet let us further inquire into the birth reversal.

Roger Ellis has observed concerning the disposal of the boy's body: "The pit into which the body is cast . . . reminds us of the fate of the Old Testament patriarch Joseph, the youngest . . . child of Jacob and preternaturally wise; his jealous brothers threw him into a pit and then sold him into slavery."[56]   Ellis does not elaborate on the significance of this similarity: Ellis merely states that "an archetype [is] at work here."[57]   I would argue that a *literary allusion* is at work here.   The Jews and the Christian boy are in one sense brothers, or at least half-brothers, and the Jews are jealous of their much younger brother because he is, like Joseph, preternaturally wise, namely in the sense that he is a little Christian "clergeon" (VII 502).   There is the ironic twist that his wisdom in religious matters makes the young boy a *step*-brother to the Jews.

Even more heavily fraught with irony is the allusive contrast between the boy who is "sowded to virginitee" and the Joseph who lived to be a patriarch, and himself was a genealogical extension of Jacob, the patriarch who sired the tribes of Israel.   For what does it mean that in his description of the disposing of the young boy's body Chaucer is presenting us with a Joseph figure who is cast into a privy?   In terms of the tale's treatment of Jews, that presentation means that the Prioress is putting in a demeaning place Jacob's youngest but most famous son. She is not doing this deliberately, but when Chaucer has her use the word "pit," he has her unknowingly establish a connection with Jacob's youngest son. Furthermore, since she poetically kills and disposes of into a privy the young boy whom she unknowingly connects with Joseph, she unknowingly is doing away with a *very* young son of the man who fathered the tribes of Israel. Which associations does Chaucer's "game" with the prolifically procreative patriarch and his son evoke? Regardless of whether Chaucer intends to insinuate the fiercely ironic notion that in a story in which a Christian nun vituperates the Jews she unknowingly is aborting one of the sons of the father of the tribes of Israel, he is lending weight to the suggestion that the Prioress may have had an abortion.

The place where the fetus was disposed of would not necessarily have to be a privy, but the Prioress would be associating the abortion with the evacuation of bodily waste. Regardless of whether the Prioress knows from personal experience that monks are not always as holy as they ought to be, she would also be establishing an association with the evacuation of bodily waste[58] in the case of a miscarriage, in the case of the murder of a newborn, and even in the case of a separation from a newborn after a pregnancy as a result of which her parents sent her to a convent. The possibilities which the ironist Chaucer leaves us with are legion, but a close reading of his text suggests that the entire *Prioress' Tale* is a confession. Chaucer, then, is presenting the Prioress as a severely disturbed person, and he employs the character portrayal of the Prioress to dissociate himself from her anti-Semitic tirade—an interpretation for which I will provide more evidence later in the chapter.

This is where I disagree with Kendrick's approach to the *Prioress's Tale*—and with her approach to some of the other tales which she calls "abreactive fictions." Kendrick observes:

> The purpose of pathetic, abreactive fictions . . . is to work through
> anxieties by repeatedly replaying fearful situations . . . , thus gradually
> leading *the reader* to accommodate him to a difficult reality, . . . to
> lead *the reader* to accept his own inability to control his life. This
> eventual acceptance, however, is based on illusion. *The interpreter's
> accommodation to reality* takes place within a safe, fictional world
> where his private reality is represented indirectly, figuratively, by the
> experiences of the fictional characters.[59] (italics mine)

I could perhaps agree with Kendrick's approach if her abreactive-fiction
theory were a reader-response theory along the lines of Norman N. Holland,
where the artist mollifies unconscious fears or forbidden fantasies by trans-
forming them into conscious, literary content, in an adaptive strategy with
which the reader can identify if it also transforms fantasy content of his own.[60]
But Kendrick is not talking about Chaucer *unconsciously* doing something that
might accommodate the reader's unconscious by mollifying the reader's own
fantasy content. Instead, Kendrick is talking about what she perceives Chau-
cer-the-conscious-interpreter-and-artist to be doing for the reader strictly within
the confines of Church-sanctioned festive play. It is because of this monolo-
gizing of Chaucer in Bakhtinian festive-play terms that Stevens, after his initially enthusiastic review of Kendrick's "often scintillating study," expresses
some disappointment: "There are no radiant discoveries, no daring new theoretical positions . . . At base Chaucer may have been conservative in his view
toward the institutions of his time, but he also voiced some fundamental discontents that did not simply assert themselves at moments of carnival only to
reconstruct themselves."[61]

I see some of Chaucer's fundamental discontents manifest themselves in
his portrayal of the Prioress as a severely disturbed person. While a case of
festive, carnivalesque play could be made for some of the tales told by the
churls, Chaucer definitely is granting no such carnivalesque License of Fools
to the Prioress although, as I have attempted to show, her contribution is no
less heretical—and for Chaucer the artist no less dangerous—than the contribu-

tions made by the churls. I wish to suggest an abreactive-fiction thesis different from Kendrick's, although I don't offer it as a daring new theoretical position. In fact, the position could be called an old one in the sense that the teller of the tale is revealing to us something about himself or herself, as in the case of the Wife of Bath whose story about an old woman turning young again has customarily been interpreted as a wish-fulfillment story. Where my position is perhaps new is that I read the *Prioress' Tale* as abreactive fiction not on Chaucer's but, instead, on the Prioress' part. It is the Prioress, not the poet, who is working through anxieties in order to adapt to a difficult reality: while I earlier spoke of her tale as a confession, I will now more specifically call it an anxiety-release story.

In the present discussion I prefer to use the term anxiety-release over confession. For once we have discerned in the Prioress certain elements of unhappiness about her sexual status, I can use the notion of anxiety release to interpret her prologue and tale as an expression—if I may apply Stevens' remarks about Chaucer to the Prioress herself—of some fundamental discontents which the Prioress has toward the institutions of her time, in particular toward the Church. While she may be angry at her father for selling her to a convent, perhaps angry at a social system which did not allow her to get married because her father was unable—or unwilling—to offer the dowry, maybe even angry at a less-than-holy monk who had seduced her into committing adultery against the Bridegroom who neglected to pay His marital debt, the focus of her discontents is the institution which she is married to. Since the Church is a husband who exists only in her mind, like the boy's mother in her story the Prioress is, if not exactly a widow, at least an unmarried woman who is looking for the child, real or imagined, that she has lost. In fact, it is worth noting that the Prioress concludes her tale with a prayer in which she asks God to reunite her with the child. "This holy monk, this abbot," has removed the grain from the child's tongue,

> And in a tombe of marbul stones cleere
> Enclosen they his litel body sweete.
> There he is now, *God leve us for to mete*!
> O yonge *Hugh of Lyncoln*, slayn also
> With cursed Jewes, as is notable,
> For it is but a litel while ago,
> *Preye eek for us, we synful folk unstable,*
> That, of his mercy, God so merciable
> On us his grete mercy *multiplie,*
> For reverence of his *moder Marie.* Amen. (VII 681-90, italics added)

I deliberately spoke of the Prioress's wish for *re*union with the boy in her story, because poetically she had given birth to a child and also killed him—and done some other not so nice things to him. She indeed had been so "synful" and "unstable" that she needs all the prayer she can get from the murdered Hugh of Lincoln, as well as mercy from God.

The confessional nature of the *Prioress' Tale* finally also explains her excessively negative portrayal of the Jews. It does so mainly in the phrases I italicized in the closing couplet, where the "Amen" is merely an adjunct to the "mercy multiplie"/"moder Marie" rhyme, a stark collocation rhyme. However, the adjunct is needed to rehabilitate a tale in which the teller has just been playing havoc with Christian ideas. The Prioress has been playing havoc especially with the Holy Trinity. There is nothing objectionable about her expressed desire to meet in heaven the boy whom her story had been about, except that she has presented the boy as a Christ figure and, mostly unconsciously, presented herself as a Mary figure, thus arrogating a place for herself in the operation of the Holy Trinity. Even her final plea to Hugh of Lincoln, to one of the real-life models of the young martyr in her own story, to pray that God may *multiply* His great mercy on "us," i.e., first and foremost on the Prioress herself,[62] for reverence of *His mother Mary*, is a bizarre inversion of the "hooly Trinitee," which she had earlier mentioned explicitly in connection with the little clergeon (VII 646).

The Prioress' plea to Hugh of Lincoln inverts the Trinity in the sense that it pits the *Hebrew* God of Genesis who had told mankind to increase and multiply ("Crescite et multiplicamini") against the *Christian* God who is called upon to have mercy on the Prioress because of the manner in which she has just celebrated the mother who according to the Trinity has procreated Him.   Or more precisely, the Prioress is pitting Christianity, which has condemned her to celibacy and to what Milton will call "wilful barrenness,"[63] against the Hebrew religion which preached and practiced procreation. And since, at least on an unconscious level, the Prioress vituperates the Christian much more fiercely than the Jewish religion, she has to compensate by presenting the procreation-preaching religion as a destroyer of life: not merely as killing a child but as actually treating the disposal of the child's body as the evacuation of waste matter, regardless of whether she has an association with abortion in mind.

It might seem attractive to argue that if my reading of the *Prioress' Tale* as abreactive fiction as outlined above is correct, Chaucer could be using the Prioress as a spokesperson for his own discontents toward Church practices, especially in light of the fierce satire to which he subjects members of the clergy throughout the *Canterbury Tales*. I will address such a possibility in a moment; for now I would like to connect the confessional part of the *Prioress' Tale* to the historical part with which she opens her tale proper:

> Ther was in Asye, in a greet citee,
> Amonges Cristene folk, a Jewerye,
> *Sustened by a lord of that contree*
> *For foule usure and lucre of vileynye,*
> Hateful to Crist and to his compaignye;
> And thurgh the strete men myghte ride or wende,
> For it was free, and open at eyther ende. (VII 488-94, italics added)

It is important to determine carefully who in this opening statement is being satirized and/or castigated, and who is *doing* the satirizing and/or castigating, since the two need not be the same. It is possible to castigate someone without satirizing him since satirizing normally involves the use of irony whereas merely castigating need not do so. Presumably the Jews are being castigated, both by the Prioress and by Chaucer himself, for their practice of usury. But the irony in the Prioress' statement about a community of Jews which is actually maintained by the lord of the country for the purposes of foul usury and villanous lucre—actions hateful to Christ and His followers—identifies the Prioress as an object of Chaucer's satire if she is castigating the Jews but not the people running the country the Jews live in.

While the Prioress does not specifically identify the "lord of that contree" or the "greet citee" in Asia as Christian, two facts emerge: the country's lord is at least on friendly terms with the Christians and the number of Christian residents in that city is so sizeable that there is within their community (*"Amonges* Cristene folk,'' italics added) a Jewish community—so that we are at least dealing with a case of a Jewish ghetto within a Christian community. I said *at least* because, as F. N. Robinson pointed out long ago, "It is unknown what suggested to Chaucer the localization in Asia, which has not been noted in any other [of the twenty-odd versions] of the legend. The conditions described remind one of the situation in Norwich, England, where the Jewish colony was under the protection of the King.''[64] Let me offer a possible answer to the question of why Chaucer localized that event in Asia. It is the teller herself who relocalizes the story to Asia. Since the lord of that mysterious Asian country actually maintains the Jewish colony for the purposes of foul usury and villanous lucre, the localization of such a colony in a Christian country would be *too* embarrassing. That the lord of that country, whose provost not only duly punishes the Jews but expressly does so in his capacity as a Christian—we remember that

> He cam anon withouten tariyng,
> And herieth Crist, that is of hevene kyng,
> And eek his moder, honour of mankynde—

is at least allied with the Christians residing there is already embarrassing enough, as is the fact that the usury-practicing enclave is "Sustened . . . Amonges Cristene folk." Whether or not the Prioress realizes it, she is implicating the Christians as accessories to the sinful practice for which they say they hate the Jews: Chaucer's own version of the old legend where a Christian boy is murdered by Jews is anything but simplistic—and Chaucer may well be satirizing the hypocrisy involved in the conditions which had existed under William of Norwich. At any rate, since the Jewish enclave is maintained *within* a Christian community, we know who Chaucer implies were willing participants in the money-loaning transactions and, thereby, proved themselves to be hypocrites.[65]

I would argue that the Prioress is implicating the Christians *deliberately*—and that she is doing this in an act of rebellion against the Church. *She* is pointing to the hypocrisy in her religion which, due to whatever the specific circumstances had been, has forced upon her a life which she considers unnatural. My reason for offering such a reading of the opening stanzas of the actual tale, stanzas whose possible implications for Chaucer's attitude toward Christian institutions have never been evaluated in terms of an overall understanding of the *Prioress' Tale*, is that at the conclusion of her tale the Prioress is returning to the notion of "foule usure and lucre of vileynye,/Hateful to Crist and to his compaignye," i.e., to the notion of Jews *multiplying* their money by charging interest on loans, when in her final stanza she associates God's "multiplication" of His mercy with the "cursed Jewes" mentioned four lines earlier.

I now wish to argue that Chaucer is very subtly, and very cautiously, using the Prioress as a spokesperson for some fundamental discontents which he himself had toward certain practices of the Church. We may assume that Chaucer shared with his Prioress the criticism she voices in her tale of the Jews for their practice of lending money for interest. What immediately comes to mind is the scene of an adult Jesus chasing the merchants and money changers out of the temple. In the *Prioress' Tale* it takes the murder of a child to at least temporarily put an end to that practice—a practice which the Christians in the tale hypocritically are part of. While the Prioress voices disagreement with that monetary kind of "multiplication," she is deeply troubled by the prohibition of a kind of multiplication which the first chapter of the Bible had promised her, a kind of multiplication which the "cursed Jewes" believe in, but which the Church has declared off limits for her. She is displaying her being troubled over this confusing prohibition in the final stanza of her tale—a stanza which is just as filled with dazzling linguistic games as the hymn to the Virgin had been.

I have discussed how the Prioress' situation crystalizes in the final stanza, a stanza in which, admitting that she is one of the "synful folk unstable," she asks God to "multiply" His mercy. Yet I have also shown that the Prioress associates God's multiplication of His mercy with the "cursed Jewes," not only with the Jews' money-making practices but, mostly unconsciously, also with their Biblical preoccupation with propagation. I will now take the next step and argue that Chaucer is using the Prioress as a vehicle to criticize the Church both for its sexual and for its economic politics—and that Chaucer is actually combining both criticisms into one. I mentioned earlier the Prioress' possible resentment toward a system which denies her the fulfillment of what she considers natural—and, it should now be added, God-given—desires because her father does not offer the dowry. In my fourth chapter I will deal with the case of a woman whose lack of a dowry enables a man to buy her as wife and, consequently, abuse her. While I will not exactly be lenient in my treatment of the Marquis Walter, in the final analysis the Prioress deserves just as much pity as does Patient Griselda: in light of the emphasis which the Prioress places on the Jews' practice of making money, apparently needlessly because this hate-generating practice seems irrelevant to the tale's main action involving the little clergeon, I will now argue that the Prioress' primary resentment is over having been sold to a convent. Or let me rephrase this: the Prioress resents the Church for having been able to *buy* her and keep her "sowded to virginitee," or at least keep her "sowded" inside what is tantamount to a chastity belt.

In a sense, then, Chaucer is attacking the Church for using its economic power to force its sexual doctrine on women who might have wanted to lead a different life, but whose fathers grasped the economic opportunity of turning over their daughters to the Church like chattel: if a man wants to join the clergy and lead a celibate life, then that is his own choice. The satiric result is that the Prioress avenges herself on the Church, to which she is "sowded" as a bride, by poetically castrating the man in whose model she has created the boy in her story, a story the account of which she had started in an attempt to sublimate her maternal instinct. She is also castrating her own father for turning her over to the Church,[66] but in so doing she could be viewed as likewise trying to castrate a "father" with a capital "F."

Ellis has pointed out an interesting connection between the Prioress' speech about the "martir . . . sowded to virginitee" and the Christians' attitude toward the Jewish money lenders:

> [Chaucer] carefully distances himself from the speaker in the very moment when she is so volubly commending the martyr's chastity, by means of the little phrase 'quod she' . . . That little phrase warns us against identifying ourselves too easily with the teller and her story. The reason is not far to seek, and it has everything to do with the presentation of the Jews . . . The saints may condemn their way of life . . . , but the Jews are not necessarily worse than those they live amongst.[67]

Ellis makes this comment in a book chapter entitled "Saints' Tales: *The Prioress' Tale.*" My discussion so far has already raised the question: *is* the tale really a saint's tale? I would now like to suggest that Chaucer is in a sophisticated literary *game* parodically playing against each other the popular

genres of the saint's tale and of the story about Jews as Christ-killers.[68]   The
intent of this parodic game is to satirize simultaneously the Church's economi-
cally enforced sexual repressiveness and hypocrisy among the clergy.   Yes,
Chaucer "carefully distances himself from the speaker" during her commendation of the martyr's chastity in the sense that her commendation is a panegy-
ric that is rather strident; but Chaucer *makes* those lines strident because the
Prioress, whom he uses as a spokesperson, does not truly believe in all those
wonderful things she says about chastity: the poet, who had in dissociating
irony thrown in a "quod she" two lines into her hymn to the Virgin Mother,
expects the more perceptive reader to recognize that the Prioress protests too
much, and protests too much because with the help of the Church's economic
power life has short-changed her.

I purposely used the term "short-changed" because the Prioress associates the Jews she is inveighing against with the money which her father either
did not possess or did not want to spend on her dowry.   Giving the Jews-as-
Christ-killers motif an ingeniously ironic twist, and thus further dissociating
himself from the apparently obsessive nature of the Prioress' anti-Semitism—
if as a product of his time Chaucer himself was anti-Semitic, as an artist he
was too sensitive to ignore its hypocritical and its most excessive aspects—
Chaucer has the Prioress provide for the little clergeon's murder by the Jews a
sexual basis.   Chaucer has the Prioress describe what triggers the Jews' violent
reaction to the young boy who has been walking through their ghetto singing
the *Alma redemptoris*:

> Oure firste foo, the *serpent* Sathanas,
> That hath in Jues herte his own waspes nest,
> *Up swal*, and seide, "O Hebrayk peple, allas!
> Is this to yow a thyng that is honest,
> That swich a boy shal walken as hym lest
> In youre despyt, and synge of swich sentence,
> Which is agayn your lawes reverence?"   (VII 558-64, italics added)

Quoting from this stanza the portion from "Our" to "swal" and italicizing *serpent* and *swal*, Maurice Cohen observes that the Jews in the tale "function as imagos of the phallic father, at once provocative and dangerous, and, in obviously genital imagery, are associated with Satan, the negative father imago par excellence." And Cohen interprets the murder of the boy as an "incestuous rape fantasy" on the part of the Prioress.[69]

While I don't agree with the point about incestuousness, Cohen does deserve credit for having pointed out the phallic imagery in the passage, and it is surprising that nobody seems to have pursued this idea further: after all, Chaucer uses the serpent *both* as a phallic symbol *and* of course as a Satanic symbol in his presentation of the "adder" and "foe" Damian in the *Merchant's Tale*.   In the Middle Ages, the Jewish religion was frequently associated with Satan by those who believed and preached that Judaism was bent upon the destruction of Christianity.   According to that belief, "Oure firste foo . . . Sathanas" could indeed be considered a father of sorts to the Jews,[70] in a somewhat oblique analogy to the Adam in Genesis who was the physical father of all mankind and was victimized by the Serpent which, in contrast to the Hebrew religion, Christianity came to equate with Satan.

It is somewhere along the lines of this belief that the Prioress is thinking when she describes the "serpent Sathanas" as instigating the murder of the clergeon.   But it is not the Prioress herself who wishes to present the Satanic Serpent as phallic—it is only the poet.   Chaucer is using her nonsexually intended statements about what Satan does in the story to satirically play off against each other the anti-Semitic Satan-association and his own Church's sexual repressiveness. He does so by presenting the "serpent Sathanas" as an advocate of the Hebrew practice of prolific "multiplication," i.e., as an advocate of the Hebrew "lawes" which according to the "serpent Satanas" have been violated by a Christian singing the *Alma redemptoris* and thus preaching Christianity on Jewish turf.[71]

It depends on the individual reader whether or not Chaucer is actually turning the tables on those Christians who condemned the Jews as a threat to the Christian religion; I personally think he is. At any rate, I hope that in the course of this chapter, in which I have exposed the apologetic fallacy, I have also succeeded in laying to rest what could be called the anti-Semitism fallacy, i.e., the notion that in writing the *Prioress' Tale* the artist unfortunately was expressing agreement with, perhaps even trying to propagate, the anti-Semitism of his time. In dissociating irony Chaucer is satirizing the religious conflict of Christians-versus-Jews by reducing it to sexual terms, or more precisely, by reducing it to a conflict between the Hebrew preoccupation with multiplication and the Church's shift of emphasis to celibacy. The Church's emphasis manifests itself in the Prioress who resents being a prioress because that vocation, which had been imposed on her against her will, denies her the turgid ("Up swal") "serpent."

Alan T. Gaylord remarked in an article entitled "The Unconquered Tale of the Prioress" in 1962: "I say we would like to think that Chaucer was fully aware of the quality of anti-Semitism displayed here, but I do not see that completely satisfactory proof can be adduced . . . Chaucer not only reproduces these elements [from models for the *Prioress' Tale*] but elaborates on them."[72] I don't know whether I have been able to to adduce completely satisfactory proof, let alone conquer the *Prioress' Tale*, but I do hope I have provided fairly strong evidence. When in his elaboration on the model of the Satan-Jews association Chaucer transforms the "serpent Sathanas" into a phallic agent, not only is he satirizing anti-Semitism but he is also showing awareness of the "quality of anti-Semitism displayed here": a cultural anti-Semitism that has been personalized by an unhappy individual. As I have been arguing throughout this chapter, attacking anti-Semitism is not Chaucer's main intent: what complicates Chaucer's satire on anti-Semitism is that such satire is imbedded in satire against certain practices of the Church; within this double-satire it is not always immediately clear whether Chaucer is satirizing anti-Semitism or the unhappy individual who has personalized the cultural anti-Semitism.

Whether or not we consider the "Up swal the serpent Sathanas" context a *dazzling* linguistic game on the part of Chaucer, the poet is successfully using the supposedly pro-Jewish but most assuredly phallic-aggressive "Sathanas" to poetically cut down to size the sexually repressive self-righteousness of the Church. Chaucer's making "ernest of game" here is of course dangerous.[73] Yet what had been announced as a celebration of the *Alma redemptoris mater* (literally "nourishing mother of the redeemer") would be even more dangerous if we could assume that Chaucer is in a linguistic "game" playing the notion of the *plena gratia Dei* against the swelling "serpent," implying that the Prioress had wanted to swell up *plena*—never mind the *gratia Dei*.[74] But then Chaucer would only be expressing the Prioress' personal feelings and therefore really would not be to blame. In fact, could we even blame the Prioress? Or if we do wish to blame the Prioress for entertaining such wicked thoughts, would we wish to deny her the multiplication of the mercy she is asking from a God who in the first chapter of the Bible had commanded us, males and females, to swell up and multiply? Wouldn't such a denial violate the Christian spirit in the same manner in which that spirit is being violated when the Christian provost not only shows absolutely no mercy toward the Jews but actually "multiplies" their punishment, and does so "by the lawe"—which looks more like the Old (Jewish) than the New (Christian) Law?[75]

What does my foregoing interpretation of the Prioress and her tale add to our understanding of Chaucer's dispensation of *solaas* and *sentence*? The answer will depend on our attitude toward satire. If we believe in the archetypal killing-power of satire as Robert C. Elliott has described it in *The Power of Satire: Magic, Ritual, Art*,[76] then Chaucer has poetically killed the Prioress—which is the fate that, in my reading, the Prioress deserves. The Prioress "deserves" that fate in two ways. I have discussed how Chaucer's satire poetically punishes her; if we like truculent humor, we will appreciate how Chaucer turns the tables on her for her special use of the contemporary custom of associating the Jews with Satan—for her special use of the Jews who, as David has pointed out, "in the tale are primarily religious symbols."[77] To me, it is an instance of earnest exuberance when the sexually and procreatively frustrated Madame Eglentyne uses Satan to instigate the Jews' murder of the boy, only to have Satan turn into a phallic agent who retroactively aborts the most famous son of the father of the tribes of Israel: as I will elaborate in the final chapter, in which I discuss the origins of satire from phallic ritual, Chaucer's narrative move of having the Prioress tell a story in which the "serpent Sathanas" plants the seed of a wicked deed in the "waspes nest" that he has in the "Jues herte" could be seen as satire in its original ritual form.

Perhaps, as my study so far may have been suggesting all along, I possess a sense of humor that is slightly perverse, but to me Chaucer's poetic punishment of the Prioress is a special kind of *solaas*—and perhaps it is this special type of *solaas* that has made it dangerous to teach the dangerous art of the *Prioress' Tale* in the classroom. Or put differently, it is the oversight of the *solaas* that has made the teaching of the tale such a controversial subject. But then, my discovery that Chaucer uses the Prioress as a vehicle for satirizing the Church's sexual repressiveness, a repressiveness which is *oppressiveness* insofar as it is econonomically based, might give rise to a new kind of concern.

On the other hand, such a concern might not be *entirely* new. Peggy Knapp has recently observed that the Prioress "is a frustrated mother displacing her maternal feelings into her story, a woman with a case of arrested development, . . . but the social likelihood of the Prioress' particular characteristics raises it from a personal neurosis to a cultural pathology."[78] It is this intertwinement of individual personality and cultural context that actually provides the *sentence*: the cultural context, a context created by a long tradition of males who felt Divinely called upon not only to choose celibacy for themselves, but also to impose that lifestyle on some women, thus denying them, in Milton's words, "what God declares/Pure, and commands to some, leaves free to all" (*Paradise Lost*, IV, 746-47), can easily lead to personal neuroses. Chaucer is presenting the Prioress as such a victim of the cultural pathology.

I said a moment ago that the Prioress "deserves" death in two ways. One kind of death is by means of satire, and I have discussed how Chaucer executes that type of punishment. The Prioress also deserves physical death, namely as a way out of her misery. Regardless of whether she indeed has had a sexual involvement, she has done enough for her Church, has suffered enough for her religion. When she pathetically apostrophizes the young boy, "O martir, sowded to virginitee," she is giving expression to the wish that *she*, a "martir" of sorts herself, with or without the "virginitee," could be "in a tombe of marbul stones cleere." When she says about the boy, "Ther he is now, Gode lete for us to mete," she may well be uttering a death wish; in any case, consciously or unconsciously, she is telling us that the cool marble stone would relieve her from the kind of burning which the Apostle Paul, with more than just a modicum of self-righteousness, had condemned. And since in her tale it was Satan who had helped the boy to his martyrdom, it is one of the great ironies of literary history that the Prioress would have answered in the affirmative Milton's question:

> Our Maker bids increase, who bids abstain
> But our Destroyer, foe to God and Man? (IV, 748-49)

And I don't think I am making game of earnest if I suggest that Chaucer would have agreed with the Protestant Milton. That is the *sentence* which I see in the linguistically and otherwise dazzling *solaas* of what purports to be a saint's tale but, upon closer examination, turns out to be a fierce satire on what under the cloak of the cloth men can do to women—while it is at the same time also a satire on religious prejudice.[79]

CHAPTER III

Revealing the Church's *Pryvetee*: The Pardoner and Various Otherworldly Loins

In the preceding chapter, I interpreted the *Prioress' Tale* as a fierce satire on what under what under the cloak of the cloth and thanks to the Church's economic power men can do to women. One of the sources for the Church's economic power during the Middle Ages was the practice of selling indulgences, and if, as I have argued, Chaucer is criticizing the Church for using its financial resources to impose celibacy on women, it is natural to suspect that Chaucer's attitude toward the practice of selling absolution may not have been much more favorable than it was toward the Jewish practice of usury: both practices take advantage of people who are in need or, more precisely when money is being charged for forgiveness of sins, may have been swindled into *believing* they are in need of the kind of help that is readily being offered. In fact, as I will attempt to show, Chaucer establishes a thematically important connection between the Pardoner on the one hand, and on the other the religious symbolism which the Jews held for medieval Christianity, a symbolism I elaborated on in my discussion of the Prioress in the preceding chapter.

People who ask for financial help usually *know* they need the help and have some concrete idea of how the money intended for investment may help them; they have a certain amount of control over that money, which, however, is not the case with buying indulgences. When Chaucer has his Pardoner admit that he is interested solely in the money and not in saving souls, Chaucer is expressing his knowledge that some pardoners hold that attitude, but he could also be voicing his suspicion that such an attitude is a reflection of the Church's attitude in selling indulgences in the first place. On the other hand, the Pardoner whom Chaucer presents to us is such a monstrosity, such a caricature, that the poet could not possibly be *ernest* in portraying the Pardoner as representative of the Church's economic policies—or could he?

Answering that question will require a close reading of the text. Such a textual analysis will reveal the following characteristics which the *Pardoner's Tale*, including the prologue and the concluding episode, shares with the *Prioress' Tale*: both tales are reflections of what the tellers consider anomalous states of sexuality. For example, in the General Prologue Chaucer tells us about the Pardoner:

> A voys he hadde as smal as hath a goot;
> No berd hadde he, ne never sholde have;
> As smothe it was as it were late shave;
> I trowe he were a geldyng or a mare.   (I 688-92)

The poet's casual comment that he believes this fellow pilgrim to have been "a geldyng or a mare" has directed a great deal of critical attention to the question of the Pardoner's sexual nature. In her chapter on "Eunuch Hermeneutics," Dinshaw observes concerning the possible implications of the poet-pilgrim's "notorious speculation" *I trowe*:[1]

> We can't read "trowe" here too easily and ironically: [C. David] Benson stresses the uncertainty of any knowledge of the Pardoner's sexual makeup. Moreover, he suggests that recent critical emphasis on the Pardoner's sexuality is a modern distortion: "The real perversion of this pilgrim is not sexual but moral" . . . *While I agree with Benson that the Pardoner's portrait confounds any sure knowledge of his sexu-*

ality, I would argue that the issue of sexuality was in fact central to medieval audiences of this text: as . . . has recently [been] stated, sexual practices, from the late twelfth century on, were "taken as indicators of doctrinal orthodoxy," so that sexual deviance implied spiritual deviance . . . Indeed, the moral cannot be opposed to the sexual, but it is deeply implicated in it.[2] (italics mine)

Then, however, Dinshaw contends: "But the Pardoner, that sexually peculiar figure, . . . does not allow himself to be stripped and revealed, as it were: he won't allow himself to be known, won't reveal his intentions, his meaning, his truth. He expends much energy on keeping a veil on, on keeping himself screened from the gaze of others."[3] I will attempt to strip the Pardoner's veil, to reveal his *pryvetee*, as it were, and I will do so with help from the poet, of course, but also with the help of one of the poet's and the Pardoner's fellow pilgrims.

Until fairly recently the prevalent critical opinion had been that with his high-pitched voice and his lack of facial hair the Pardoner is a eunuch. One problem with this interpretation always has been that it could easily miss one half of Chaucer's portrayal of the Pardoner, since it does not address the fact that in the preceding lines Chaucer had been hinting at a possible sexual relationship between the Summoner and the Pardoner. Chaucer was hinting at such a possibility when in response to the Pardoner singing, "Com hider, love, to me," the Summoner "bar to him a stif burdoun" (I 672-73): while the Summoner provides the "stif burdoun" in the meaning of bass, the technical term for which is *cantus firmus*,[4] in their singing together the Summoner could also provide their togetherness with something else, with a stiff and firm penis ready to unburden itself through seminal ejaculation.

It was mainly the insinuation of a possible sexual relationship between the Summoner and the Pardoner that led to the re-interpretation of the Pardoner as a homosexual, especially after Monica McAlpine, in her 1980 study on "The Pardoner's Homosexuality and How It Matters,"[5] not only pointed out that "mare" has the meaning of homosexual male but also demonstrated that

"while the establishment of this gloss does not eliminate the alternative interpretation as a 'geldyng' or eunuch, it does obligate us to explore the the implications of the Pardoner's possible homosexuality.'' The interpretation of the
Pardoner as homosexual now seems to have replaced the earlier interpretation
of him as a eunuch.

However, are these two readings really what McAlpine calls "alternative interpretation[s]," are they mutually exclusive? Even as a eunuch the
Pardoner would still be able to engage in anal intercourse in which he is the
recipient of the *stif burdoun*, and a portrayal of the Pardoner as a "geldyng"
and a "mare" would endow the equivocation in Chaucer's "a geldyng or a
mare" statement with special meaning: if the Pardoner cannot be a stallion in
sexual relations, he can still be quite literally, i.e., anatomically, the "mare."
And the Beryl Rowland who in her 1979 article on "Chaucer's Idea of the
Pardoner" had remarked, "The ambiguity of the statement 'I trowe he were a
geldyng or a mare' is obvious. *The man cannot be both*" (italics mine),[6] and
contended that "eunuchry preclude[s] homosexuality,"[7] may be in for a surprise. But so may be McAlpine who, citing the twelfth-century Latin poem on
which in 1973 Jill Mann had based her reading of the Pardoner as homosexual,[8] argued, in my opinion correctly, that "We need not wait for the discovery
of more supporting texts,"[9] correctly because all the information we will ever
be able to use will have to come from close-reading Chaucer's own text[10]—
that is, from close-reading palimpsestically in light of each other passages in
the General Prologue and at the conclusion of the *Pardoner's Tale*.

This is not to say that the intriguing readings offered by Rowland, who
interpreted the Pardoner to be a hermaphrodite, or by McAlpine, who saw the
Pardoner as a homosexual without eunuchry, have sent us in the wrong direction; the contrary is true. What probably did delay further insight into Chaucer's portrayal of the Pardoner once that character had been interpreted as a
homosexual was that in 1987 the *Riverside Chaucer* declared that the Pardoner

is not a eunuch because "a eunuch would have been ineligible for holy orders (Deut. 23.1)."[11] Deuteronomy 23:1 reads: "Non intravit eunuchus, attritis vel amputatis testiculis . . . , ecclesiam Domini" ("A eunuch, whose testicles have been crushed or cut off, shall not enter into the assembly of the Lord"). I contend that according to the teachings of the Bible a eunuch is *not* ineligible for holy orders, for the message in the pre-Christian book which Christians refer to as Deuteronomy is superseded by Acts 8:38, which describes Philip as baptizing a eunuch. As I will demonstrate, a goodly part of Chaucer's portrayal of the Pardoner is based on the interaction between the conflicting messages in the Deuteronomy and Acts passages.[12]

In light of the possibility that Chaucer could be presenting the Pardoner as a "geldyng" who is a "mare," let us examine the appropriateness of the teller's relation to his tale, a relation about which David has commented: "an excellent case could be made that the Pardoner's Tale [is the best of the tales of 'moralitee and hoolynesse']. If we look simply at the tale, forgetting about the Pardoner, it is certainly a powerful exemplum of sin and retribution, but of course it is impossible to forget about the Pardoner."[13] I wish to argue that what makes the *Pardoner's Tale* an excellent case of "moralitee and hoolynesse" is Chaucer's very portrayal of that member of the clergy, because the portrayal in itself is a powerful exemplum not of sin and retribution but, instead, of sin and redemptive forgiveness.

After the delivery of his tale, the Pardoner asks the Host to buy some of his sacred relics, relics which he has already admitted to be counterfeit. Harry Bailey replies:

> Thou woldest make me kisse thyn olde breech!
> And swere it were a relyk of a seint,
> Though it were with thy fundement depeint!
> But by the croys which that Seint Eleyne fond,
> I wolde I hadde thy coillons in my hond
> In stide of relikes or of seintuarie.
> Lat kutte hem of, I wol thee helpe hem carie;
> They shul be shryned in an hogges toord! (VI 948-55)

What is the significance of the Host's bawdy response to the Pardoner?

Lindahl, who views the Pardoner as a homosexual rather than a eunuch, interprets the Host's outburst in this scene as

> a quintessential festive inversion, momentarily substituting the Pardoner's sexual "relics" for St. Thomas's shrine, and invoking the comic priniciples present at the Feast of Fools when dung rather than incense was burned in Church censers to convert the sacred to the utterly profane. But the Host himself is not the appropriate person to mock the Pardoner. Unlike the Bishop of Fools, he is not a lowborn man assuming temporary control over his equals . . . It is necessary here that the Knight step in to reimpose order. This gentil, who has acted in a manner consistent with his class, merits the respect he demands in telling Host and Pardoner to kiss and make up. He displays the deference wise nobles extended to churls on holiday and reasserts the festive equality of the two men.[14] (Italics, except for gentil, are mine)

I submit that the Host is indeed the appropriate person to mock the Pardoner, because we are dealing here not with a situation where a participant in a festive performance breaks the order of the "game," but dealing instead with a genuinely psychological event whose nature is totally lost on most members of the audience alias pilgrims.

If the Host suspects, as some of us readers do, a homosexual relationship between the Pardoner and the Summoner, or more precisely, if the Host suspects that in addition to being a "geldyng" the Pardoner is a "mare," then we can interpret the Host's statement that he wishes he had the Pardoner's testicles rather than his relics in his hand as a homosexual gesture. Or rather, the Host's gesture is one of homosexual rejection, since the Host is sarcastically suggesting that the Pardoner have his nonexistent testicles cut off so that the Host can bury them in a hog's feces. But then an act of rejection would have to be preceded by an act of solicitation. In one sense, the Pardoner is indeed issuing a sexual solicitation when he asks the Host to buy some of his false relics:

> Com forth, sire Hoost, and offre first anon,
> And thou shalt kisse the relikes everychon,

Ye, for a grote! Unbokele anon thy purs. (VI 954-45)

McAlpine has observed concerning this passage: "The latent aggression in the Pardoner's statement that Harry [shall kiss the relics] and the latent sexual implication in his command to Harry to 'Unbokele anon thy purs' . . . turn the scene into one of implied seduction or even rape; the Pardoner uses his homosexuality as a weapon."[15]

Here I can only in part agree with McAlpine. The word *purs* is of course a slang term for scrotum.[16] I would argue that while the Pardoner is *not consciously using* that term in its sexual connotation, the Host *perceives* it in that meaning—i.e., Harry perceives the request that he open his "purs" to buy the false relics as a homosexual advance at himself, and he extends this perception of a homosexual gesture to include the request that he kiss the false relics. The Host perceives an equivalence which according to McAlpine is perceived only by the reader: "the symbolic equivalence between the relics and the Pardoner himself becomes almost explicit. For many readers, Harry's crudity must suddenly and explosively bring to consciousness a truth they have already apprehended subliminally."[17] What I would like to suggest is that it is not only the reader's consciousness that is explosively affected by the scene. And what explosively affects the Host, as well as some readers, is not merely a "symbolic equivalence" between the relics and the Pardoner. Instead, the Host reacts so vehemently because all of a sudden he recognizes that there exists a causal relation between the sexual nature of the Pardoner and his selling of false relics: the Pardoner sells fake relics since he is a fake as a man. The Pardoner is a fake as a man not simply because he is a homosexual, but because the lack of a "purs" restricts him to being a "mare" who receives the "stif burdoun."

This mental process is a perceptive psychoanalysis of the Pardoner not only by the poet, but also by one of Chaucer's own characters, the Host. At the same time it is a clever psychological study of the Host: the Host is responding in such a vehemently repulsive manner because he is horrified at the discovery of the causal connection between the sexuality of the Pardoner and his spiritual state, and the bawdy outburst is the only way in which he can cope with that horrible discovery. This discovery, which is a direct result of his perception of having been sexually solicited by the Pardoner, makes the Host precisely the appropriate person to "mock" the Pardoner, if I may employ Lindahl's term in a different meaning: *to mock* would be the wrong term if I were using it, as Lindahl presumably is, to connote a quintessential festive inversion in a staged "game" such as the Feast of Fools.

Chaucer continues his psychological study of the Pardoner and the Host by describing the former's reaction to the latter's remarks:

> This Pardoner answerde nat a word;
> So wrooth he was, no word ne wolde he seye. (VI 956-57)

Why is the Pardoner unable to answer? The reason is that he has been totally stripped of his defenses because he has been hit by the same recognition as the Host: the recognition of a causal relation between his sexual anomaly of gelding-and-mare and his selling of false relics. Up to this point the Pardoner had been able to crack jokes about his own physical handicap, e.g., when he said he had a wench in every town or when he announced in response to the Wife of Bath's Prologue that she had caused him to change his mind about his planned marriage, a response which will play an important part in my assessment of the Pardoner. Such remarks were a relatively easy defense mechanism vis-à-vis an audience most of whose members the Pardoner *expected* to be aware of his eunuchry. In making such joking remarks, the Pardoner was still in control, both of his audience and of himself. He loses that control as soon as Harry unearths—and depending on the quick-mindedness of the other members of the audience, *exposes*—the causality between the Pardoner's sexual anomaly and his selling of false relics.[18] The Pardoner knows that the Host has 'psyched him out.'

The Host, in turn, is aware of the Pardoner's act of self-recognition and therefore observes in a conciliatory tone:

Now . . . I wol no lenger *pleye*
With thee, ne with non oother angry man. (VI 958-59, italics added)

The Host realizes that his dialogue with the Pardoner is no longer a joke. In contrast, the other pilgrims are laughing because the full depth of the meaning of the confrontation is lost on them. An exception is the Knight who, when he sees everybody laughing, pleads for a reconciliation:

"Namoore of this, for it is right ynough!
Sire Pardoner, be glad and myrie of cheere;
And ye, sire Hoost, that been to me so deere,
I prey yow that ye kisse the Pardoner.
And Pardoner, I prey thee, drawe thee neer,
And, *as we diden, lat us laughe and pleye*".
Anon they kiste, and ryden for hir weye. (VI 962-68, italics added)

To the Knight the confrontation between the Pardoner and the Host is no laughing matter, as the Knight makes clear when he suggests that the pilgrims should laugh and *play as before*: it could even be argued that in the portion I italicized Chaucer is expressly pitting his written/literary playing-around against the folkloric *game*-tradition, especially since the meaning of the confrontation is lost on the audience, on the listening pilgrims. The Knight, however, likewise is hit by the sudden recognition of a causal relation between the Pardoner's sexual state and his spiritual state of selling false relics. Yet the Knight not only perceives the psychological situations which the Pardoner and the Host, respectively, are in, but he also attempts to help them overcome their dilemmas, much in the manner of a spiritual counselor. There is of course the irony that a layman, the Knight, would try to spiritually help the Pardoner, a member of the clergy; yet this ironic aspect has a counterpart in the irony of a situation in which the Host unintentionally aids the Pardoner in grasping the truth about himself: in his cathartic encounter with the Host, the Pardoner comes to realize not only that he is both physically and spiritually isolated from humanity, but also that there exists a causal relationship between the two types of isolation.

The Pardoner has to have this recognition scene first before he can be reintegrated into humanity. The act of reintegration is being initiated by the Knight when he asks the Host to kiss the Pardoner: the kiss, which the Host had earlier perceived as a homosexual gesture, is here transformed into a means of helping the Pardoner overcome a spiritual separation which has a physical equivalent in his sexual anomaly of gelding-and-mare. In one sense, then, Lindahl is correct when he says that "It is necessary here that the Knight step in to reimpose order"; but it is quite possible that Chaucer is dissociating himself here from the Feast of Fools tradition through the reimposition of an order which has been inverted by a physical anomaly whereas the listening audience thinks the Knight is merely restoring the order of what looks like a Feast of Fools to them: the equality which the Knight is reasserting between the two men is much more than just "festive"—it is existential.

The above interpretation of the conclusion of the *Pardoner's Tale* sees religiously redeeming values in what otherwise would seem to be an unnecessarily bawdy episode, and in fact would seem to be a totally unnecessary episode, and it also sees more depth in the confessional aspects of the *Pardoner's Tale*. In his prologue, the Pardoner confesses to his fellow pilgrims that he gives sermons and sells pardons not in order to help people spiritually, but in order to accumulate wealth. This is of course not intended as a confession in the Christian sense; instead, it is an instrument for manipulating his listeners: in order not to appear to be like the Pardoner himself, the personification of the very vice he preaches against, avarice, they will freely give him their money. This confession trick might have worked on a less perceptive listener, but it fails when the Pardoner uses it on the Host, who occupies a key function within the religious-didactic context of the *Canterbury Tales* in that he had declared that he who tells a tale which is the most entertaining but also the most filled with *sentence* shall have a free meal. Chaucer poetically punishes the Pardoner by forcing him into a confession that is genuine.

What we are dealing with is a case in which the pseudo-confession by a sinner displaying his sinfulness finally leads to a genuine confession that may actually achieve the salvation of the sinner. The sin which the Pardoner initially admits to is that of being a crook who cynically takes advantage both of people who have sinned and of people whom he may have persuaded into fearing that they have committed a particular sin. What turns out to be one of the Pardoner's greatest sins, however, is *the pose* of his confession: his sin here is not his crookedness but the hubristic manner in which he confesses, or rather, flaunts, his crookedness. In the bold flaunting of his crookedness the Pardoner is trying to compensate for his "mareness," for his lack of maleness—and in his cathartic confrontation with the Host the Pardoner comes to realize that there exists a causal relation between his flaunting and his sexual anomaly: he had been trying to show that he 'has balls.'

But then, wasn't Charles A. Owen, Jr. voicing a similar interpretation almost four decades ago when he stated: "The Pardoner's physical disability has isolated him from some of the normal satisfactions in life. In revenge he has rejected the professed morality of other people and uses it against them to attain the power and comfort that wealth brings. His income is thus a symbol of his victory over physical inadequacy and of his superiority over the normal and stupid louts who are his victims."[19] Owen was of course speaking about eunuchry, yet what he said about the rejection of professed morality remains applicable if in addition to being a eunuch the Pardoner is a "mare."

The point I have been trying to make contrary to Owen's reading is that Chaucer is not presenting the Pardoner's "revenge" as a conscious act: if it were a conscious act, the Pardoner would not be shocked to the point of being speechless—and he would not be deserving of the Host's conciliatory statement in lines 958-59 as well as the Knight's intercession. It would make much more sense if the revenge were *unconscious*—so that the sinner would indeed deserve forgiveness once he has gone through the recognition scene. If Owen observed that "we see the Pardoner but he cannot see himself,"[20] I would now like to add that Chaucer is presenting what is probably the bawdiest dialogue among the pilgrims in the entire *Canterbury Tales* as precisely the point where the Pardoner gets an opportunity to see himself. After the Pardoner has finally seen himself, he receives not, as McAlpine would have it, merely "a kiss of ambivalent social tolerance"[21] but instead that which, according to McAlpine's study, he seems to be denied forever: "the redemptive kiss," "the kiss confirming his part in the Father's creation and in the Son's redemption."[22]

There are yet many more aspects to the angry encounter between the Host and the Pardoner, some of which have never received critical attention. For example, if we assume that the Host believes the Pardoner to be a eunuch who is homosexual, then we interpret the Host's statement as to what he would like to do with the Pardoner's testicles as a comment on what Harry thinks of anal intercourse: according to the Host, the Pardoner's seed if he had any to sow would deserve to be enshrined in a hog's feces. Yet what is important for the *sentence* in Chaucer's portrayal of the Pardoner is that at the same time the Host is drawing what Melvin Storm, interpreting the Pardoner to be a homosexual but not a eunuch, has called an "analogy between the seed lost in carnal sodomy and the seed of the word of God wasted by the simoniac,"[23] i.e., an analogy between the Pardoner's physical sodomy and what Wycliffe had called "spiritual sodomy":[24] namely, simony. And the *toord/word* rhyme in "They shul be shryned in an hogges toord."/This Pardoner answered not a word" is a reference to the word of God wasted by the Pardoner, and a formal device by Chaucer to insinuate that the Pardoner too recognizes the analogy between the two things whose waste he has been causing, especially since the next line states that the Pardoner "ne *word* ne wolde . . . seye": Chaucer is insinuating that after his encounter with the Host the Pardoner will try his best to discontinue his practice of casting the word of God onto a dunghill.

The Pardoner's discontinuation of that practice may very well be a device on Chaucer's part for converting into earnest the game in which, in Lindahl's words, "dung rather than incense was burned in church censers to convert the sacred to the utterly profane." At any rate, the irony is of course that the seed the Pardoner has been causing to be wasted is not his own. It is the Summoner with his "stif burdoun" who had been casting his seed onto a dunghill of sorts—an activity which the Host thinks the Pardoner is inviting him to join when he asks him to kiss the relics and open his "purs": instead of kissing that which symbolizes the Pardoner's spiritual separation from mankind and opening his "purs," the Host kisses the sinner in an attempt to help him overcome that spiritual separation.

Since the Host is aware of the Pardoner's eunuchry, he considers the "Unbokel anon thy purs" not only a homosexual advance, but a sexual advance by what the Host would consider the "feminine partner" in homosexual anal intercourse between males. Such a reading might raise the following question: is the Host guilty of homophobia? Perhaps he is, but what is more important about the Host's treatment of the Pardoner, more important because it is an integral part of Chaucer's scintillatingly broad-ranging presentation of male-female relationships throughout the *Canterbury Tales*, is that the Host is frightened by the "female" threat he perceives in the homosexual eunuch's command. For in the Host's perception the Pardoner poses something that is comparable to a psychological-castration threat in that it threatens the Host's sense of control over his own life, a control which for him is symbolized by possessing a *purs*, in both meanings of that word.

This does not mean that I am now retracting what I said earlier about the Host, and as a result also about the Pardoner, experiencing a recognition scene with respect to the Pardoner selling fake relics. On the contrary, the moment the Host is hit by the recognition that the Pardoner is selling nonexistent relics because owing to his eunuchry he is nonexistent as a man, the Host relates the manner in which the Pardoner has sexual intercourse to the selling of allegedly sacred relics. For even before the Host mentions the "relikes of a seint" he talks about kissing the Pardoner's old underpants,[25] and even before he mentions the testicles, he refers to stains which the Pardoner's anus ("fundement") has caused on these underpants.

While the Host is suggesting that, like the Pardoner's nonexistent testicles which he designates to "be shryned in a hogges toord" and like his relics, his preaching words are manure, he is more importantly referring to anal intercourse, namely to stains caused in part by the sex partner's ejaculate. The Host resents being called upon to contribute his share to such "wet-spots." The Host is gladly conceding that function to the Summoner, in a relationship where the Summoner provides a loaded phallus and the Pardoner is the feminine recipient.[26] In fact, Harry had perceived the Pardoner's request to kiss his false relics and unbuckle his "purs" specifically as an invitation to join the Pardoner *in sin*, for the Pardoner had called on him first because as an innkeeper the Host was most involved with sin:

> I rede that oure Hoost heere shal bigynne,
> For he is moost envoluped in synne.
> Com forth, sire Hoost, and offre first anon . . . (VI 941-43)

And Harry may even have understood that the Pardoner was linking the Host's alleged sinfulness to sexual behavior when, by playing on false etymology, he called Harry "moost en*volup*ed in synne": the Pardoner was suggesting that Harry was enveloped in sinful *voluptas*. Regardless of whether Harry caught the clever accusation, it is important in terms of this scene's moral significance that the Host, whom in a wildcat etymology the poet had in the General Prologue introduced as "A *semely* man" (I 751, italics added), refused to spend his semen on the Pardoner.[27]

In terms of the sexual theme programmatically symbolized by the cosmic-union picture in the opening lines, the Pardoner is incapable of "raining
upon" anybody and only capable of "being rained upon" himself: when
Chaucer has the Host make reference to anal intercourse, our poet is relating
the Pardoner's sexuality to the *descensus* notion.   While if it were not for his
eunuchry the Pardoner would be able to give seed, he is only capable of receiving it.   However, although the Pardoner can receive seed, he cannot produce a crop.   Or more precisely, the Pardoner would not be able to to produce
a *physical* crop.   For there is the ultimate irony that the intercourse between
the Pardoner and the Host, a *verbal* intercourse, does produce a harvest,
namely the Pardoner's recognition scene and resulting forgiveness and reintegration: in contrast both to the wasting of seed in carnal sodomy and to the
wasting of the seed of God's word by the simoniac, the Host's sexual response, sexual insofar as he grabs the Pardoner by his nonexistent testicles,
has a religiously healing effect on the Pardoner. Through his crude response
bringing the Pardoner to self-recognition, the Host sows the seed of the word
of God in the Pardoner.[28]

David has commented that the Pardoner's "Prologue and Tale and the
brief episode that follows it constitute a morality play in which the stake is not
the soul of some ordinary representative sinner but the worst that may be.
The Pardoner represents the ultimate challenge to the healing power of St.
Thomas."[29]   I trust that I have been able to show that what makes the healing
power of St. Thomas work for the Pardoner is the power of Confession.
Since the Pardoner makes his confession before the pilgrims reach the shrine
of St. Thomas, the Pardoner ironically is well ahead of other pilgrims seeking
spiritual healing, pilgrims most of whom do not even realize that they *have
been overhearing* a confession and perhaps even think that what they have just
heard was a "game" which was first staged by the Host when he called upon
the Pardoner to tell a tale, then bone-chillingly delivered by the monstrous

Pardoner, crudely upstaged by the master of ceremonies himself, and brought to a proper conclusion by the Knight, the highest-ranking person on the pilgrimage.[30]   Little do the pilgrims know about the "earnest" psychomachia which went on not only in the Pardoner, but also in the master of ceremonies[31] and, albeit to a lesser extent, even in the gentle Knight.   Most of the pilgrims do not know that they have been watching a morality play.

Since the Pardoner has been living with his irreversible sexual nature at least since prepubescence and therefore should have been able to accept it by now, or more precisely, should have never had a problem to begin with, why has he, in Owen's words, "[i]n revenge . . . rejected the professed morality of other people"?   Actually, the Pardoner has done much worse than what Owen accuses him of and the question should be: why has the Pardoner rejected Christianity by making a mockery of a profession that is an important part of that religion, important because the pursuit of that profession is directly authorized by the earthly representative of that religion's God?   The answer is that the Pardoner has rejected Christianity because he prefers the message conveyed by Deuteronomy 23:1, conveyed in that part of the Bible which Christians call the "*Old* Testament"—conveyed by the *Old* Covenant.   It would be more convenient for the Pardoner to belong to a religion which because of his physical handicap automatically makes him an outcast—and thus would provide him with a legitimate reason for treating that religion in a spiteful fashion.[32]

As I discussed in Chapter II, in the *Prioress' Tale* Chaucer presents the Jews as religious symbols, as representatives of a force which medieval Christians tended to consider a threat to their own religion; associating the Jews with Satan, Christians could also use them as scapegoats whom they could blame for any major misfortunes that might befall society, such as droughts and, of course, the Black Plague.   I now wish to argue that the Pardoner uses the Jews as scapegoats in a manner whose perverseness precisely reflects the perverseness of his sexuality: not of course his eunuchry alone or his homosexuality alone but, instead, his practicing of the sodomy of gelding-and-mare. The Pardoner is playing off against each other the Christian and the Jewish religions in the same deviously self-serving fashion in which he plays off against each other eunuchry and homosexuality, not only using eunuchry to justify homosexuality but actually blaming his own homosexuality on his eunuchry.

The Pardoner knows that according to the teachings of the Bible his practice of sodomy is sinful, but he is able to rationalize his sexual behavior on the grounds that Deuteronomy 23:1 would deny him legitimate entry into the assembly of the Lord anyway. He of course also knows that the New Testament account of the baptism of a eunuch supersedes Deuteronomy, but he could always claim that he is a representative Christian whose religion-and-religiosity has been severely hurt by the Satanic Jewish religion as represented by Deuteronomy 23:1. The Pardoner can claim that he is a personal victim of the very existence of that Satanic religion—by the very existence of Deuteronomy 23:1 within the holy text of the Christian religion. I trust, then, that it now has become clear why I dealt with the portrayal of the Prioress before dealing with that of the Pardoner although I will return to the Prioress later in this chapter: I am trying to examine the Pardoner palimpsestically in the light of the Prioress' use of the Jews as religious symbols.

I base my argument that the Pardoner is playing the Old Law of the Jews as represented by Deuteronomy 23:1 against the New Law of Christian mercy and grace as represented by the baptism of a eunuch in Acts on a passage in the *Canterbury Tales* which has received a great deal of critical attention, because it is one of the highlights in the Wife of Bath's Prologue, a passage, however, which seems to have been neglected with respect to what it may be telling us about the Pardoner. After comically outlining *her* idea of the marital ''dette''—''An housbonde I wol have . . . /Which shal be bothe my

dettour and my thral" (III 153-54)—the Wife of Bath treats us to the following
sermon on sexuality:

> " . . . I have the power durynge al my lyf
> Upon his propre body, and noght he.
> Right thus the Apostel tolde it unto me,
> And bad oure housbondes for to love us weel.
> Al this sentence me lyketh every deel"—
> *Up stirte the Pardoner, and that anon,*
> "Now dame," quod he, "by God and by Seint John!
> Ye been a *noble prechour* in this cas.
> I was aboute to wedde a wyf; allas!
> *What sholde I bye it on my own flessh so deere?*
> *Yet hadde I levere wedde no wyf to-yeere!"* (III 158-68, italics added)

The Wife of Bath has proven herself a "noble prechour" by distorting to her
advantage what the Apostle had said about marital relations in 1 Corinthians
7:3-4: she has left out that the wife in turn is a debtor to her husband who has
power over her body just as she does over his. The Wife's hilarious distortion
of a Biblical text causes the Pardoner to announce that he will postpone his
wedding plans because he now sees no reason for getting into the marital-debt
relationship if he has to pay so dearly with his own "flessh." Since the Pardoner expects most of his fellow pilgrims to know that he is a eunuch, he is
making his announcement as a deliberately self-ironic response to the Wife's
"sermon" which of course everybody knows is a distortion: *what* "flessh"
would he be able to draw upon to buy into such a relationship?

Yet in the Pardoner's sprightly response—and in the poet's own
sprightly *presentation of* that response as a phallicism: "Up stirte the Pardoner, and that anon"—Chaucer is making earnest of game: Chaucer is already
setting the stage for his portrayal of the Pardoner as a consummate cynic in the
pursuit of his profession within the Church. In particular Chaucer is establishing a parallelism between the Wife of Bath playfully omitting the second half
of a Biblical passage about sexuality on the one hand, and on the other the
Pardoner resentfully omitting, perhaps I should say *excising*, from his Chris-

tian belief the New Testament passage that supersedes the Old Testament passage, the "Jewish" passage as it were, which because of his state of sexual omission if not excision would have excluded the Pardoner from the assembly of the Lord (in fact, I cannot help seeing a palimpsestic interaction between "Up stirte the Pardoner" and the ironic, ironic because unintended, phallicism in the Prioress' statement that the Jews' ally, "the serpent Sathanas, . . . Up swal"). The Pardoner *wants* to be a religious outcast—in order to have a legitimate reason for treating his religion in a spiteful fashion. As I suggested earlier, the object of his spiteful treatment would have to be the *Jewish* religion; but since the Pardoner is after all Christian, and as a clergyman familiar with the passage in Acts, his response to Deuteronomy 23:1 is nothing but a desperate attempt to use Judaism for the purpose of mocking Christianity.

As a eunuch, the Pardoner is in particular targeting for mockery a statement which Jesus made about eunuchry in Matthew 19:12: "Sunt . . . eunuchi, qui de matris utero sic nati sunt: et sunt eunuchi, qui facti sunt ab hominibus: et sunt eunuchi *qui seipsos castraverunt propter regnum caelorum*" ("There are eunuchs who come that way from the mother's womb, there are eunuchs who have been made so by men, and there are eunuchs *who have castrated themselves for the kingdom of heaven*" [italics added]). Jesus is talking about men who make themselves *eunuchi* for the kingdom of heaven, i.e., he is talking about men who voluntarily adopt the lifestyle of celibacy in order to serve God: Jesus does not literally mean the self-mutilation of testicular amputation when he speaks both about eunuchs and about dedication to a religion that would have to be considered a radically new one. The Pardoner, however, whom I interpret to have been born a eunuch, tries to cheat God by playing Jesus' notion of *eunuchus Dei* against that of the *eunuchus de navitate*. Since the Pardoner was born without testicles and therefore is incapable of erection and penetration, he has no problem with being a male who voluntarily chooses eunuchry as Jesus had meant that term—for

Jesus had said nothing about what a "geldyng" for the kingdom of heaven should *not* do, i.e. not be a "mare."

Chaucer's Pardoner had chosen the profession of a pardoner in order to seek vengeance against what he considered God's cruelty of having preordained him as a eunuch. The Pardoner chose that profession to 'show' God by entering into His service as an *eunuchus* in the customary sense of that word, i.e, as a male without *coillons*, but instead of being what Jesus had called an *eunuchus propter regnum caelorum*, the Pardoner made a habit of the sin of what in the context of our present discussion could be called passive sodomy. Or put differently, while rejecting celibacy and adopting sodomy, the Pardoner can literally, in the sense never intended by Jesus, be an *eunuchus propter regnum caelorum*—and in his pursuit of serving God accumulate wealth by selling fake relics: the irony here is the parallel between the selling of fake relics and the Pardoner being a fake *eunuchus* in the sense of fake celibate.

The Pardoner is cheating God because he feels that God has cheated him by making him a eunuch like those who "facti sunt ab hominibus." The Pardoner avenges himself on God by making a mockery of the Church's practice of male celibacy, by selling pardons without being in the least interested in the purchasers' spritual well-being, and by actually flaunting the cynicism with which he conducts his profession. The ability to dispense absolution gave him a sense of power, even if the money for pardons did not necessarily become his own but the Church's. And having acquired a taste for power, the Pardoner later in one sense arrogated the Church's power by extending the selling of pardons to, if not replacing it with, the selling of false relics. It was a case of power corrupting a man who was susceptible to corruption because physically he was not a man. Or to use a term which I applied to Chaucer's description of the fate of the Prioress: since the Pardoner had been "short-changed" by life, he decided to short-change both God and man and line his purse in the process.

In fact, Chaucer may well be using the Host's outburst as a vehicle for satirizing the Church's practice of selling pardons. The Host probably is not attacking that practice but, instead, only this particular pardoner's attempt on his own *purs*, in both meanings of that word. If the Host were to comply with the Pardoner's request as he perceives it, namely as a homosexual advance, the Host would be allowing the Pardoner to castrate him. For the kind of *purs* which the Pardoner has consciously appealed to, but which Harry consciously confuses but unconsciously equates with the other kind, is the *purs* alias money bag which gives the Host a sense of control over his life, and which the Pardoner has just called upon him to unbuckle so that the "feminine" Pardoner's own *purs* might fill up. The Host knows that he would be wasting his money—in an oblique analogy which Chaucer establishes both to the simoniac wasting the seed of the word of God and to a man wasting his seed and providing more stains on another man's underpants. In this most Freudian scene in all of the *Canterbury Tales* the castration threat which the Pardoner poses to the Host, then, pertains also to Harry's financial state.

Chaucer is pointing to this double castration threat when the poet has the Host's verbal defense of his *purs* palimpsestically interact with the description the General Prologue had given us of the physical locale where the Pardoner carries the indulgences, significantly just before Chaucer mentioned his high-pitched voice and lack of facial hair:

> His walet, biforn hym in his lappe,
> Bretful of pardoun comen from Rome *al hoot*.
> A voys he hadde as smal as hath a goot.
> No berd he hadde, ne ever sholde have;
> As smothe it was as it were late shave.
> I trowe he were a geldyng or a mare. (I 686-91, italics added)

Dinshaw comments on the Pardoner carrying his pardons in his lap: "As rolled-up parchments with seals dangling from them, the Pardoner's documents and bulls, placed conspicuously in his bulging 'male' (6:920), present an icon-

ographic substitute for his own lacking masculinity.''[33] I don't know why
Dinshaw chose not to put it more precisely and speak of lacking testicles sub-
stituted for by the *male* (i.e., bag or sack): whether or not we wish to read
the *hoot/goot* rhyme as a stark collocation which contrasts the Pardoner to the
proverbially lascivious goat,[34] Chaucer is already insinuating that the Pardoner, who in his tale will treat us as well as his pilgrim audience to a sermon on
the *radix malorum*, the root of all evil, speaks with a high-pitched voice because the only thing he has in his lap that is hot is a bagful of pardons. Or let
me rephrase this: Chaucer is insinuating that all the Pardoner ''has got *left*''
in his lap that is hot is a sack of pardons.

This ''got *left*'' idea is exactly what Chaucer will be elaborating when
he has the Host correlate the Pardoner's *coillons* to his *relikes*: ''relics''
derives from the Latin past participle *relictus* meaning ''left behind,'' ''remaining.'' While Chaucer probably is not attributing this pun to the Host as
an intended witticism, when he has Harry establish a correlation between
testicles and relics our ironist comes closest to letting us know what it is that
the Pardoner either hasn't got left—which in all likelihood is what the Host in
his anger is thinking of—or never had to begin with, yet what we expect a
man to have in his ''lappe'' but wouldn't be able to find there. Chaucer's
relikes pun is close enough for me to warrant an interpretation of the Pardoner
as eunuch,[35] but that isn't even the point I've been trying to make in my argument in the last few paragraphs, an argument which I started by suggesting
that Chaucer could be trying to satirize the Church's practice of dispensing
absolution in return for money. I therefore will now relate the Host's attempt
to protect from the Pardoner his own *purs*, consciously in the meaning of
money but, more or less unconsciously, also in the meaning of testicles, to this
eunuch's chosen profession of a pardoner.

I said a few paragraphs ago that Chaucer has the encounter between the
Pardoner and the Host palimpsestically interact with his description, in the

General Prologue, of the physical location of the pardons. I quoted earlier
Dinshaw's observation that the description presents an iconographic substitute
for the Pardoner's "lacking masculinity." Dinshaw continues her argument in
the following fashion: "[The Pardoner] emphatically declares that these bulls
validate his body, make it legitimate and unquestionable. Exhibitionistically he
brags: 'my bulles shewe I, alle, and some./Oure lige lordes seel on my
patente,/That shewe I first my body to warente' (336-38)."[36] Let me add to
Dinshaw's line of argument that the moment Chaucer correlates the Pardoner's
nonexistent *coillons* to the fake relics with which the Pardoner tries to cheat
people out of their money, the poet is retroactively implying that there is
something phony also about the the bulls which the Pardoner uses to declare
the validity of his body.

By this I don't mean that Chaucer is implying that the pardons are *not*
"comen from Rome al hoot." On the contrary, there is no reason to doubt
the veracity of the Pardoner's statement about "Oure lige lordes seel," because what makes Chaucer's portrayal of the Pardoner so fascinating is that
the Pardoner has absolutely no reason to lie: he is used to having his way by
telling his audience the truth about himself, for example that his relics are fake
and that he doesn't care whether his pardons will save anybody's soul. Therefore Chaucer must be attacking a *radix malorum* that is more deeply rooted
than the greed of an individual pardoner who became a pardoner because his
lack of a sexually functional root drove him to the depths of avarice. That
Chaucer may be attacking the avarice of the Church will strongly suggest itself
when we compare the fates of the Pardoner and the Prioress, the former being
a financially opulent representative and the latter a sex-starved victim of the
economic power of the Church.

I have discussed how, in a morality play of sorts, the Pardoner over-
comes the spiritual handicap which resulted from physically not being a man; I
will now contrast the Pardoner's physical dilemma to that of the Prioress.

Unlike the Prioress' celibacy, the Pardoner's physical state is irreversible. And this contrast ironically highlights the Prioress' problem. After his recognition-and-reintegration the Pardoner can truly dedicate, or, perhaps more precisely, can *re*-dedicate, himself to being an *eunuchus propter regnum caelorum* by simply no longer trying to compensate for the lack of urges which he never possessed to begin with, but which he thought a man must have to be a worthy human being. After all, the Pardoner has *always and forever* been "sowded to virginitee" in the heterosexual sense in which the little clergeon is a virgin.

Although the Pardoner presumably had experienced being *plenus* from the Summoner's "stif burdoun," he had only been able to compensate for the impossibility of one kind of "multiplication" with another kind—with the kind of multiplication for which the Prioress knowingly chastises the Jews while at least unconsciously she is groping for the other kind. I mentioned earlier why I dealt with the portrayal of the Prioress first: I have been trying to read-and-explicate the portrait of the Pardoner palimpsestically in the light of the Prioress' portrait. While the Prioress may or may not have been, but certainly at one point or another had felt the desire to be, *plena*, after his recognition-and-reintegration the Pardoner can become *plenus gratia Dei*, become "full by the grace of God"—because the Host, who had refused to do what the replenishing Summoner had done, has planted in the Pardoner the seed of the word of God by bringing him to self-recognition.

And like Mary, the Pardoner will be a virgin "always and forever." If I am reading Chaucer's palimpsest correctly, then he is using his characterization of the Prioress to present a gender-reversal of sorts between her and the Pardoner, a gender-reversal which involves a perverse kind of irony. I argued in Chapter II that there is something suspicious about the Prioress apostrophizing Mary as "mayde alway," one possible implication being that the Prioress is *not* a virgin. I will now add that as a self-appointed *eunuchus propter regnum caelorum* the Pardoner is trying to arrogate Mary's sexual status. If Christian religion claims that Mary always remained a virgin, the Pardoner can become a living parody of Christianity by in one sense equalling Mary.

It could be argued that, when the Pardoner decided to avenge himself on God for his having been born as a male "sowded to virginitee," he also decided to become an anal-erotic version of Mary. While heterosexually the Pardoner had no choice with regard to virginity, he could still cheat by choosing a type of sexual activity in which he would remain a virgin: after all, who would ever think of accusing someone of a loss of anal-erotic virginity? At any rate, Chaucer allows the Pardoner to equal Mary in her perpetual virginity by having him retain his own kind of virginity and, through the Host's kiss in the final lines, receive redemption. No such redemption, I wish to argue, is granted to the Prioress, not because Chaucer was a male-chauvinist and/or misogynist but, on the contrary, because Chaucer wanted to depict the injustices of what Peggy Knapp, whose comments on the Prioress I quoted in Chapter II, calls a cultural pathology.

In her point about a cultural pathology in the Middle Ages, Knapp approaches Chaucer from a sociological stance which, while it is critical of the Establishment, resists the temptation to reduce the cultural pathology to gender-issues. I wish to argue, however, that Chaucer was not being far behind us moderns when in an organically functioning work of literature he presented a scenario in which a male born without testicles is granted the redemptive kiss, but a female born sexually-and-procreatively intact is not. In this scenario a male-dominated Church has made the female into an *eunucha propter regnum caelorum*, so that she is quite literally, although not anatomically, one of the "eunuchi, qui sunt facti ab hominibus."

One aspect of organic unity between the *Pardoner's* and the *Prioress' Tales* lies in Chaucer's establishing of a pointed contrast between the conclusions to the Pardoner's and the Prioress' respective performances. Whereas the Pardoner's performance ends, not with the laughter of those pilgrims who didn't see the underlying reason for Harry's supposedly comical outburst of obscenities but, instead, with the Host and the Pardoner kissing each other and all of them riding off together, the Prioress' performance leads to this scene at the beginning of the Prologue to *Sir Thopas*:

> Whan seyd was al *this miracle*, every man
> As sobre was *that wonder was to se*,
> Til that oure Hooste japen to bigan . . . (VII 691-93, italics added)

The absence of applause for the preceding tale and the strange silence have been adduced by some of the Prioress' "hard critics" as evidence that the pilgrims, and thus by implication Chaucer himself, do not approve of her treatment of the Jews.

In that regard, I would add that the pilgrims are feeling uncomfortable because in her final stanza the Prioress had tried to make them part of her "miracle" tale, not only by asking Hugh of Lincoln that he pray for

> *us*, we synful folk unstable,
> That in his mercy God so merciable
> On *us* his grete mercy multiplie, (italics added)

i.e., by means of a plea which, as I demonstrated in Chapter II, is intended mainly to gain mercy for the Prioress herself, but also by trying to make the pilgrims accomplices in her treatment of the Jews. For when she says,

> O yonge Hugh of Lyncoln, slayn also
> With cursed Jewes, *as it is notable*,
> For it is but a litel while ago, (italics added)

she is trying to insinuate herself with her fellow pilgrims: "You know what happened to Hugh as well as I do—after all, it happened only a short while ago."

Of course the pilgrims know what happened to Hugh, but at least some of them resent her devious attempt to include them among those Christians that had the Jews who had been suspected of involvement in Hugh's murder executed: the Prioress is trying to make the pilgrims participants in something that had occurred in 1255, more than four generations earlier. Regardless of whether we can assume that some of the pilgrims or even Chaucer himself suspected that the Hugh of Lincoln story might have been a fabrication,[37] they resent her for distorting history—"it is but a litel while ago"—in her attempt to manipulate them into complicity with her treatment of the Jews, a treatment which began when immediately after her hymn to the Blessed Virgin she introduced the usury-practicing Jews as antagonists, "Hateful to Crist and to his compaignye." The pilgrims feel that this was an unhealthy way to begin a tale whose stated intent was to glorify Mary. No "wonder" they are "sobre" when at the end she asks them to identify with what she had done in her tale.

But the pilgrims' negative reaction to the Prioress' plea to identify with her goes beyond her needlessly malicious treatment of the Jews, needlessly malicious because it does not add anything at all to a celebration of Mary. The pilgrims are even more perturbed by her attempt to get them involved in matters of a more personal nature, for at least some of them are aware that the Prioress' miracle tale about a "gemme of chastitee" had been an expression of her unhappiness with her state of celibacy. They feel uncomfortable that this nun has let them in on a *pryvetee* which is much more perturbing than what, with the help of the Host, the Pardoner had unveiled to them. Most of them already knew that the Pardoner was a eunuch, although some of them may not have known that he was also homosexual. Very few of them perceived the recognition scene, the scene in which the Host, the Pardoner, and eventually the Knight were hit by the recognition of a causality, but all of the pilgrims were relieved to see the Pardoner and the Host kiss each other. The difference is that, in contrast to the Pardoner's case where Harry was personally angered by the ecclesiastic's request that he unbuckle his *purs* and therefore responded with a personal attack, there is nothing the Host can do to censure the Prioress for her unsavory "miracle"—or is there?

The Prioress' tale has left the company in a gloomy atmosphere, which Chaucer-the-poet has the Host try to dispel by calling on Chaucer-the-pilgrim to tell the group a cheerful tale:

> Whan seyd was al this miracle, every man
> As sobre was that wonder was to se.
> Til that oure Hooste japen tho bigan,
> And thanne at erst he looked upon me,
> And seyde thus: *"What man artow?"* quod he;
> "Thou lookest as thou wouldest fynde an hare,
> For evere upon the ground I se thee stare.
> Approche neer, and looke up murily.
> Now war you, sires, and lat this man have place!
> He in the waast is shape as wel as I;
> *This were a popet in an arm t'embrace*
> *For any womman, smal and fair of face.*
> *He semeth elvyssh by his contenaunce,*
> *For unto no wight dooth he daliaunce.*
> Sey now somewhat, syn oother fol han sayd;
> Telle us a tale of myrthe, and that anon." (VII 691-706, italics added)

If the Host wants Chaucer-the-pilgrim to tell a cheerful tale so that they all can put the Prioress' perturbing tale behind them, why does he approach this fellow pilgrim in a less than friendly manner? The *Riverside Chaucer* offers the following observation:

> Because the Host's description of Chaucer as abstracted [*elvyssh*] and unsociable appears to conflict with the gregariousness of [the General Prologue] I.30-34, [a 1910 reading] took the description to refer, not to permanent characteristics, but to a temporary mood of seriousness induced by The Prioress's Tale. But Chaucer portrays himself as generally unsociable in [*The House of Fame*] 644-60; and 694-95 here suggest that the Host is noticing him for the first time. Harry's condescension to Chaucer, as an obscure and unpromising participant in the tale-telling, provides an apt introduction to the ensuing tale.[38]

Whatever portrait the speaker in *The House of Fame* is or is not giving of the poet himself, I believe that the poet-and-pilgrim in the Prologue to Sir Thopas is none other than the gregarious person in the General Prologue who, "Redy to wenden on [his] pilgrymage,/To Caunterbury with ful devout corage," had spoken with each of his fellow pilgrims: "So hadde I spoken with hem everichon/That I was of hir felaweshipe anon'' (I 31-32). As a matter of fact, I wish to argue that when Chaucer has the Host refer to the pilgrim-poet as unsociable, the poet is sending us a strong signal in the following direction: the pilgrim Chaucer is being unsociable because he is deeply troubled by what he has just heard the Prioress say. While we need to distinguish between what Chaucer-the-poet and the creator of a character named Eglentyne knows about the Prioress and what Chaucer-the-pilgrim has been able to pick up, Chaucer-the-pilgrim knows enough. So does the Host, who, I would suggest, is not necessarily noticing Chaucer here for the first time: how would Chaucer-the-pilgrim be able to know that? Likewise, are we really expected to believe that the Host means literally his statement, ''For evere upon the ground I se thee stare''? It seems to me that both of them are protesting too much.

I would suggest that the Host is vicariously using his fellow pilgrim to vent his feelings toward the Prioress. Harry is trying desperately to break the uncomfortable silence. When he notices that Chaucer-the-pilgrim looks what the Host calls ''elvyssh,'' Harry seizes the opportunity to turn to him—perhaps turn *on* him would be a more appropriate phrase—and overdramatizes his request by complaining that Chaucer speaks to nobody. The pilgrim Chaucer is indeed ''abstracted'' as the *Riverside Chaucer* translates the term *elvyssh*, but Harry is saying much more when he uses that word. Harry is saying that Chaucer's facial expression looks *otherworldly*,[39] and he is doing so in order to place Chaucer in the same category as the Prioress, who has just delivered an otherwordly tale and is otherwordly herself in the sense that as a nun she is married to Christ and therefore lives in celibacy. When Harry first asks Chaucer, ''What man artow?'', and then says that he looks elfish-inhuman-other-worldly, he is impugning Chaucer's sexuality.[40]

Moreover, when Harry, presumably the manliest of all the men among the pilgrims, a ''semely man,'' points out that ''this man'' alias this human being possesses a midsection as lovably huggable as his own, he is referring to

the female-male sexual embrace. This in turn endows with a special meaning
Harry's rebuke that Chaucer does not have social intercourse with human
beings ("unto no *wight* dooth he daliaunce"):   the *daliaunce*, which here
initially means no more than sociability or sociable conversation and probably
is best rendered by the modern-usage term "mingle," receives a sexual twist.
That is, when the Host justifies his assessment of Chaucer-the-pilgrim as
"elvyssh" with the "For unto no wight dooth he daliaunce" declaration, he is
attributing to Chaucer a state of sexuality which facilitates celibacy but is
unnatural in the same way as the sexual state of the Prioress—and as unnatural
as her mention of the sexual state of the young boy in her story.

The Host either does not know that his supposedly taciturn fellow
pilgrim feels the same way about the Prioress' "miracle" as Harry does, or he
is challenging Chaucer to "quyte" the Prioress by contributing a cheerful tale
that will exorcise the Prioress' unwholesome presentation. In any case, Chaucer-the-pilgrim complies gladly and with a vengeance. I purposely used the
term "vengeance" because there exists an interaction between the *Sir Thopas*
and the Host's long-winded request on the one hand, and the immediately
preceding *Prioress' Tale* on the other. Chaucer-the-pilgrim's "vengeance" is
directed both at the Prioress and, in one sense, at the Host, but both acts of
revenge in the final analysis serve the same purpose: to "quyte" the Prioress.
As requested by the Host, Chaucer does tell a "tale of myrthe," but in that
tale he pays the Host back for calling him *elvyssh* and thus sneaking in sly
innuendoes concerning the teller's sexuality. When Chaucer tells a burlesque
about a knight who dreams not only that an "elf-queene" shall be his lover
but actually that the fairy queen shall sleep under his knightly cloak, he is
adroitly responding both to the Host's question "What man artow?" and to his
remark that Chaucer has a body which a woman simply couldn't resist wanting
"t'embrace." The idea of a knight aspiring after a fairy queen was of course
a stock motif in medieval literature, but Chaucer-the-pilgrim having his knight

explicitly describe how and where he would "embrace" his lover is engaging-ly grotesque: it "quytes" the Host for having referred to him as an other-wordly sort of man.

More importantly, Chaucer-the-pilgrim is fiercely parodying the Prior-ess when he has Sir Thopas call upon the Blessed Virgin and tell her his dream:

> "*O Seinte Marie, benedicite!*
> What eyleth this love at me
>   To bynde me so soore?
> Me dremed al this nyght, *pardee,*
> An elf-queene shal my lemman be
>   And slepe under my goore.
> "An elf-queene wol I love, ywis,
> For in this world no womman is
>   Worthy to be my make
>   In towne;
> Alle othere wommen I forsake,
> And to an elf-queene I me take
>   By dale and eek by downe." (VII 784-95, italics added)

Actually, as the juxtaposition of the *O Seinte Marie, benedicite* and the ever-so-innocuous-seeming *pardee* suggests, Sir Thopas is calling both on Mary and on God—just as the Prioress had done in her Prologue, where she expressed her desire to be ravished.

Here it is even doubtful whether Sir Thopas has in mind any ravishing at all. If "in this world" no woman is worthy to be his mate, what is it he intends to do "under [his] goore" with his "lemman," the "elf-queene"? Sir Thopas has no earthly idea, and Mary isn't going to tell him. Maybe someone like the Prioress could tell him, since she had decided, or rather had been forced to decide, that "in this world" no man would be worthy to be her mate and she therefore chose an "elf-king" of sorts: we would have a female case of arrested development dispensing advice to a developmentally retarded male whose dreams have encouraged him to ascend to elfish aspirations.

On the other hand, we shouldn't waste our time worrying about the fate of a young man who *is* what the Prioress wishes she *had in her possession*. After all the learned statements which seriously inquiring scholars have made about the "emeraude" and other gems of chastity in the *Prioress' Tale* and about the topaz as a guardian against lust,[41] why has very little been made of Chaucer having his pilgrim alter-ego match the Prioress' story about otherworldly love with a tale about a character who is pointedly introduced as "chast and no lechour" (VII 745) and who is named "sire Thopas"?[42] In a tale which, while it burlesques simpleminded romances, also parodies the simplemindedness of miracle tales, Chaucer is presenting Sir Thopas as a little clergeon who has survived the assault by the Jews but remained at the stage of sexual development which the Prioress had poetically assigned to him for eternity—except that, instead of "folwynge evere in oon/The white Lamb celestial" and singing "a song al newe," this "gemme of chastitee, this emeraude" spends his time hunting. In other words, Sir Thopas is a spiritually benign and sexually innocent version of the Pardoner.[43]

In fact, Chaucer is establishing a connection between the Pardoner and the tale with which he parodies the performance by the *eunucha propter regnum caelorum* when he has the Host stop Chaucer-the-pilgrim's doggerel by echoing a passage from the poet's description of Harry's encounter with the Pardoner:

> "Namoore of this, for Goddes dignitee . . .
> . . . .
> Myne eres aken of thy drasty speeche.
> Now swych a rym the devel I biteche!
> This may wel be rym dogerel," quod he.
>   "Why so?" quod I, "why wiltow lette me
> Moore of my tale than another man,
> Syn that it is the beste rym I kan?"
>   "By God," quod he, for pleynly, *at a word,
> Thy drasty ryming is nat worth a toord!* . . . ."
>   (VII 919-30, italics added)

We remember in what context the Host had used the term *toord* and the poet had employed a *toord/word* rhyme. Here Chaucer is presenting the Host's assessment of something as being worth even less than a *toord*: in his earlier outburst the Host assigned the same value as that of a *toord* both to the Pardoner's word as a preacher and to his nonexistent testicles. But is it really the teller's "drasty [i.e., crude, excrement-like, crappy] ryming"[44] that the Host is condemning as "nat worth a toord"? Put differently, is it really the verse form of Chaucer-the-pilgrim's story that drives the Host to repeating the obscenities he had hurled at the sexually anomalous Pardoner?

I suggest that the Host is reacting to the *Sir Thopas* vicariously to vent his resentment of another story that had been otherwordly, sexually and otherwise, and his resentment of another teller who is otherworldly, sexually and otherwise. The Host finally gets to vent his anger at a person whom a sexually anomalous life had caused to tell a tale that was indeed *elvyssh* and, at least in one sense, *drasty*—and when the Host refers to feces three time in eight lines the poet is in fact having him allude to a "crappy" passage in that tale. When the Host condemns Chaucer's tale about Sir Thopas as "drasty," then, he is really saying that the *Prioress' Tale* was "nat worth a toord."

I would even argue that in his "drasty" encounter with Chaucer-the-pilgrim the Host is experiencing a recognition scene obliquely analogous to the one he had experienced with the Pardoner, except that the present recognition scene involves not only the person he is talking to but also a third person—who happens to be the unnamed subject of their dialogue. When the Host called Chaucer *elvyssh* and asked him to tell a "tale of myrthe," he was challenging the supposedly taciturn fellow pilgrim to "quyte" the Prioress. When the Host criticizes Chaucer's doggerel as "drasty speche," he is acknowledging that this unassuming fellow has lived up to the challenge by parodying the Prioress' in formal terms exquisite but contentwise gratuitous tale about otherwordliness. But the Host's use of the terms *drasty* in line 923 and *toord* a few lines later lets us as well as Chaucer-the-pilgrim know that the Host is bothered by something in the *Prioress' Tale* which *Sir Thopas* failed to address: the Prioress' acount of the boy being thrown into the "wardrobe . . . /Whereas these Jewes purgen hir entraille."

The Host may not even have consciously been making that connection, but when Chaucer-the-pilgrim seemingly innocuously asks him why he interrupted his own tale rather than someone else's, it occurs to the master of ceremonies that it would have been his duty to interrupt the Prioress at that point in her tale—just as he had shut up the Pardoner when he perceived the latter's request that Harry unbuckle his purse as obscene. Such an interruption would have spared the pilgrims the description of the punishment of the Jews—and, more importantly, would have spared them the Prioress' embarrassing attempt to make them privy to her personal business with God concerning her deprivation of "multiplication." It certainly would have spared the pilgrims the in this context embarrassing apostrophe to "this gemme of chastitee, this emeraude."

Once we recognize the interaction among the *Tale of Sir Thopas*,[45] the Prioress' performance, and Chaucer's portrayal of the Pardoner, there is the ironic implication that the Pardoner had come into this world as an "emeraude," as a "gemme of chastitee," i.e., with a suitability for an ecclesiastic profession which the Prioress never had. This fact and the fact that the Pardoner himself debased the "emeraude"—turned it into a "toord," as it were—should eventually put the Prioress in a less negative light than the Pardoner, but these two facts don't bestow such a favor on the nun: whereas with the help of the Host and the Knight the Pardoner gains the kiss of redemption, the Prioress' "miracle" alienates her from the pilgrims. As I said earlier, the reason is not that Chaucer was a male-chauvinist or misogynist but, on the contrary, that he wished to depict the injustices inflicted on women by a male-supremacist Church run by self-righteous males.

Chaucer-the-poet of course sympathized with a woman whom the Church's economic power forced into a situation where pent-up feelings of deprivation eventually drove her to an exhibitionistic behavior, a behavior which is comparable to the exhibitionism with which, as Dinshaw's scrutiny has exposed, the Pardoner uses the sack of pardons in his "lappe" to validate his male body. Chaucer-the-poet sympathized with a woman to whose "lappe" the Church denied plenitude while it filled the Pardoner's with bulls which could bear fruit—bear fruit, that is, for the Church. God's representative on earth, then, himself committed to celibacy, has impregnated with parchments "comen from Rome al hoot" a eunuch who had put his physical determinism to use and played *eunuchus propter regnum caelorum*. Madame Eglentyne could not possibly match that source of Church income unless she was willing to sell her *pryvetee*—which of course would be "synful" whereas the Pardoner's sodomitic way of life as gelding-and-mare is venial as long as his physical status, which symbolizes an inability to give that resulted in an eagerness to receive, keeps him "sowded" to the coffers of the Church. After all, no matter how often the Pardoner is *plenus*, there is no danger that a "swelling up" might expose this ecclesiastic's double-life—and his stained underpants are much better hidden than his sack bulging with pardons.

I do not wish to make Chaucer into a pre-Reformation Martin Luther, but I would argue that the Chaucer who presented a redemption scene for the Pardoner denied a similar denouement for the Prioress because he wanted to satirize the sexo-economic politics of the Church. I spoke a moment ago about the celibate pope having impregnated with documents the "lappe" of a pardoner incapable of multiplication other than financial. I discussed in my first chapter how in the *Monk's Tale* Chaucer parodically uses Pope Innocent III's pronouncement on the quality of human sperm to insinuate the comic notion that God used clean sperm in His creation of Adam. In the earlier discussion I tried to defend Innocent III on the grounds that he was speaking as a theologian who attempted to distinguish between postlapsarian propagation on the one hand, and on the other the Holy Ghost impregnating a Mary who was free of Original Sin, a sin which made human propagation dirty. Yet it is difficult not to react to Innocent's remark about human sperm with anger or at least with cynicism. Maybe something like this was in Ross' mind when he noted: ''Not a bawdy but a rather unhealthy reference occurs in the 'Monk's Tale' . . . where Adam is described as being made with God's own finger, not of 'mannes sperme unclene'.''[46] As I showed earlier, the reference *is* bawdy; but as a theological pronouncement on human propagation, some of us will consider the reference also unhealthy. Or did Ross see, as I did, a reference to a masturbating God and considered *that* unhealthy? Why did he keep his interpretive *pryvetee* to himself?

Some of us will consider as applicable to Innocent III the assessment which Milton gives of those theologians who argued that if it had not been for Original Sin human propagation would occur without sexual intercourse:

> Hypocrites . . .
>
> . . . .
> Defaming as impure what God declares
> Pure, and commands to some, leaves free to all.
> (*Paradise Lost*, IV, 444-47)

In my second chapter I quoted Milton's lines to discuss the Prioress' resentment over the state of celibacy which the Church had imposed upon her, and I said that Chaucer would have agreed with the Protestant Milton. While Milton does attack the Catholic Church's command of celibacy for ecclesiastics, Milton's attack actually goes all the way back to the origin of the Catholic command, namely to the alleged origin of sexual intercourse. It is one thing to argue, as St. Augustine does, that as a result of Original Sin human sexuality underwent a drastic change, but it is another to claim that sexual intercourse is a result of Original Sin. Chaucer would therefore reply to Innocent's theory

by having the Wife of Bath in her marital-debt sermon make the following
assertion about the function of the penis:

> Now wherwith sholde he make his paiement,
> If he ne used his sely instrument?
> Thanne were they *maad upon a creature*
> To purge uryne, and eek *for engendrure*. (III 131-34, italics added)

In a low-blow parody of Pope Innocent III, Chaucer has the Wife of Bath first
acknowledge that the male possesses a penis for the purpose of urination but
then point out that God *created* the penis also for the purpose of propagation.
Actually, this is a *double* low-blow parody of Pope Innocent III: if this theologian thought that had it not been for Original Sin human propagation would
occur without the penis emitting that dirty sperm, did Pope Innocent III think
either that urine was cleaner than sperm or that prelapsarian Adam didn't have
to urinate?

If we read the *Canterbury Tales* as possessing an organic unity, we
realize that Chaucer is playing a dangerous *game* throughout that work, a
game that probably reaches its climax in the poet playing havoc with the declaration by Pope Innocent III—but also with some papal policies in general. The
Chaucer who in the opening lines of the General Prologue displays a positive—nowadays we might say healthy—attitude toward sexuality must have
considered Innocent's view of sexuality degrading to humanity even if, or
perhaps *because*, the idea of human sperm being something dirty was commonplace in the Middle Ages.[47]   Therefore Chaucer poetically puts Pope
Innocent III in his place. According to the *Parson's Tale*, even God's representative on earth would be subject to nocturnal "polucioun"; so how does the
pope get a handle on that problem? The solution is quite simple: if he doesn't
handle it in the manner in which, apparently, the Monk does, he can unload
his "stif burdoun" by filling pardoners' laps with papal bulls.

Chaucer, then, presents the pope who had been enthroned with the
trade name "Innocens Tertius" as a practitioner of the sin whereof according

to the Parson one dare not speak. There simply is no way around this interpretation once we read palimpsestically the Monk's story about the creation of
Adam and Chaucer's portrayal of the Pardoner. It's a wonderfully innocent
way to get rid of one's sperm and transform into a holy element something
that had been innately dirty—and lining one's papal purse in the process.
What in Chaucer's view was dirty was not the human act of multiplication but,
instead, the Church's practice of selling pardons to multiply its economic
power, power which it could then use to force vulnerable women into a life of
celibacy. In satirizing this practice, Chaucer did not hesitate to expose not
only one particular pardoner's but also the pope's "pryvetee," and the exposure showed an unwholesome relationship between the two *elvyssh lappes*—a
relationship which had been forged between two otherwordly loins for the
purpose of a *multiplicatio spurcissima*, a multiplication that is much dirtier
than the human act of reproduction.

CHAPTER IV

Feminist Jokes and the Story of
Patient Griselda

Whereas the *Prioress' Tale* is about a woman whose lack of economic power has "sowded" her into celibacy, the *Clerk's Tale* is about a woman whose lack of economic power solders her into marriage. What Griselda has in common with the Prioress is that, just as the Prioress is married to Christ to whom she owes absolute obedience, the *Clerk's Tale* has traditionally been read as an allegory in which the wife's absolute obedience to her husband is an integral part of an exemplum that preaches man's obedience to God.[1] Interpretations along those lines usually try to solve the problem of accounting for Walter's and Griselda's strange behaviors by classifying, as Elizabeth Salter did in 1962, the exemplum as a "secular saint's tale."[2] More recently critics have been examining the *Clerk's Tale* for satiric elements. Lindahl, for example, has made the following observations:

> When [the Marquis Walter] decrees that Griselde shall be sent naked back to her father's house, the Marquis abuses simultaneously his wife and his lower-class subjects. The clerk, then, questions the morality of the *gentils*: rulers, like parents and husbands, *should* be benevolent monarchs, but is it not possible that they be evil? Nearly all of Chaucer's subtle additions to Petrarch's narrative exploit the failure of the *gentil's* [i.e.,Petrarch's] tale to provide solutions to the problems of social injustice . . . [The] few additions undercut any positive value that

may be ascribed to the behavior of the powerful. The oppressed Griselde remains a heroine, but the world in which she suffers holds no hint of virtue.[3] (The italics in *When* to *naked* are mine)

I wish to argue that underneath the disguise of what Lindahl considers an anti-elitist message the *Clerk's Tale* there is a satire directed against a different type of arrogation of supremacy.[4] In fact, as I will attempt to show, Lindahl's statement as to what the Marquis "decrees" for Griselda is a reflection of the Clerk's irony. While the text tells us that Griselda returns home wearing a smock, Chaucer's reader is easily misled into assuming, as Lindahl does, that, in an attempt to humiliate the peasant girl who had brought Walter no dowry, the Marquis had initially issued such a decree but then was persuaded by Griselda's plea to let her keep her smock.[5]

Here is the scene of Griselda's departure from Walter's palace:

Biforn the folk hirselven strepeth she,
And *in her smok, with heed and foot al bare,*
Toward her fadre hous forth is she fare. (IV 894-96, italics added)

It is Griselda herself who, after Walter reminds her that she had brought him no dowry from her father's poor house, introduces the idea of nakedness, including the notion of her returning home naked, into their dialogue—and she does so rather massively:

"My lord, ye woot that in my fadres place
Ye dide me strepe of my povre weede,
And richly me cladden, of youre grace.
To yow broghte I noght elles, out of drede,
But feith, and *nakednesse, and maydenhede;*
And here agayn your clothyng I restoore.
And eek your weddyng ryng, for everemore . . .
 . . . .
" . . . Naked out of my fadres hous," quod she,
"I cam, and *naked moot I turne agayn.*
Al youre plesance wol I folwen fayn;
But yet I hope it be nat your entente
That I smoklees out of youre paleys wente . . . "
                    (IV 862-75, italics added)

It is important for our understanding of the *Clerk's Tale* that Chaucer's text does not report Walter as having said anything about a possibility of Griselda going home naked. In fact, Griselda's request, "But yet *I hope it be not your entente*/That I smokless out of your paleys wente" (italics added), indicates that Walter has not ordered her to leave the palace naked. After urging her to immediately vacate the palace for his new wife who he said was already on her way, Walter had advised her:

> " . . . thilke dowere that ye broghten me
> Taak it agayn, I graunte it of my grace;
> Retourneth to your fadres house," quod he;
> "No man may alwey han prosperitee;
> With even herte I rede yow t'endure
> The strook of Fortune or of aventure." (IV 807-812)

While there is nothing in his words indicating that Walter means anything more than that she will have to return from riches to poverty, Griselda either feels the need to make sure that he does not mean literally his offer to let her take her dowry with her: since in her father's house he had stripped her of her "povre wede" which he replaced right there with fine clothes, if he meant his order, "thilke dowere that ye broghten me/Taak it agayn," in a literal sense, then he would be ordering her to go home naked. Or, as I would argue is the case, she is trying to force his hand by *creating the impression*, in the "open audience" (790) which he had convened, that he has just told her she will have to go home naked.[6]

That we are dealing with the presentation of a male-female relationship rather than a social criticism of the elite's treatment of the lower classes is suggested by the sexuality-laden argument with which Chaucer has Griselda react to Walter's banishment of her. By bringing in all kinds of sexual aspects, Griselda beats Walter to the punch no matter what his *entente* may have been. She does so first by pointing out to him what his order would mean if it was intended literally, namely "nakednesse," and second by tying the idea of "nakednesse" to what *she* contributed to their marriage, her "maydenhede"—which, unlike the fine clothes and the wedding ring which she is returning to him, cannot be "restored": even if he at one point did consider sending her home naked, since he cannot restore the dowry of her virginity[7] he now has no choice but to grant her request that she be allowed to wear a smock on her way home. After all, the entire dialogue takes place in the "open audience" which Walter had convened for the purpose of announcing the divorce.

Dinshaw has observed in her "Griselda Translated" chapter that when Walter "orders [Griselda] to return to her father's house, she *demands* a smock in return for her lost virginity" (italics mine).[8] Griselda is dramatically reinforcing her demand when she says, "Naked out of my fadres hous . . . /I cam, and naked moot I turne agayn," for she is pointedly punning on Job's "Naked came I out of my mother's womb, and naked shall I return thither": whether or not she is actually trying to present herself in a Job-like role, she is now using all her cards. In what Judith Ferster calls a "bargaining scene,"[9] Griselda is playing her trump card when, after first reminding Walter and the "open audience" indirectly that he had taken something from her which he would never be able to restore, she makes an appeal to his sense of *personal* honor, an appeal in which she makes his honor contingent on giving her something in recompense for the virginity she had given to him:

> "Ye koude nat doon *so dishonest a thyng*.
> The thilke wombe in which your children leye
> Sholde biforn the peple, in my walkyng,
> Be seyn al bare, wherfor I yow preye,
> Lat me nat lyk a worm go by the weye . . .
> Wherfor, *in guerdon of my maydenhede,*
> *Which that I broghte, and nat agayn I bere,*
> As voucheth sauf to yeve me, to my mede,
> But swich a smok as I was wont to were,
> That I therwith may wrye the wombe of here
> That was youre wyf." (IV 877-88, italics added)

What makes Griselda's request for a smock-in-return-for-virginity barter an offer which the Marquis cannot refuse is that she ties this request to the suggestion that he would not want to dishonor *himself* by exposing to the public the womb in which his children had lain: what through the combination of these two ideas Griselda is really suggesting is that by exposing her womb to the common folk he would be allowing the common folk to repeat symboli- cally what he had done physically, i.e., to take her virginity. Griselda, then, is using his divorce decree not only to save her own honor alias chastity but also to punish him by publicly exposing him as a woman-abuser,[10] for he is scarcely able to speak:

> "The smok," quod he, "that thou hast on thy bak,
> Lat it be stille, and bere it forth with thee."
> But wel unnethes thilke word he speak,
> *But wente his weye*, for routhe and for pitee.
> Biforn the folk hirselven strepeth she,
> And in her smok, with heed and foot al bare,
> Toward her fadre hous forth she is fare. (IV 890-96, italics added)

Note the parallel which Chaucer establishes between Griselda's plea with Walter, "Lat me nat lyk a worm go by the weye," an addition to Pet- rarch but also a "stock expression meaning naked,"[11] and the narrator's state- ment that the almost-speechless Marquis "wente his weye." The parallelism suggests that the Marquis himself walks away "lyk a worm," i.e., naked: the Marquis knows that he has just been exposed not only to Griselda, but also to the "open audience" which he had convened for a public spectacle. He had planned to display the male's ultimate power over the female, but he is ex- posed by the woman whom he divorces on grounds of what her naked poverty socially symbolizes. In the light of Griselda's frequent mention both of her womb and of the never-to-be-restored *maydenhede*—as Dinshaw notes, vis-à- vis its source Griselda's mention of "feith, and nakednesse, and maydenhede" has been "augmented by Chaucer to include her virginity"[12]—the following interpretive move will not be overly Freudian. I will carry the notion of the

Marquis having been made into a naked "worm" further and interpret the implied picture of a worm crawling on the ground as symbolic castration, as a reduction to "im-potence" in the literal sense of that word: the Marquis is "power-less" in the sense that he almost has lost his speech and bows out, or rather *crawls* out, of the dialogue which he had publicly staged to humiliate Griselda.   At any rate, regardless of whether he himself actually feels that because of his male-supremacist bevavior he has deservedly been taken down a peg, Griselda is icing her "open audience" victory over Walter when she seemingly finalizes the divorce on what now she has managed to make her own terms by undressing herself of the rich garment in which he had clad her but keeping a smock.[13]

Not even Griselda's father realizes the victory she has gained over the Marquis:

> this olde poure man
> Was evere in suspect of hir mariage;
> For evere he demed, sith that it began,
> That *whan the lord fulfild hadde his corage,*
> Hym wolde thynke it were a disparage
> To his estaat so lowe for t'alighte,
> And voiden hire as soone as ever he myghte. (IV 904-910,italics added)

The irony here is that Walter's discarding of Griselda has absolutely nothing to do with the "lord" having had "fulfild . . . his corage," with *corage* in in its sexual meaning.[14] The Marquis is discarding his wife for reasons which have nothing to do with first lusting after a lower-class girl—if we can trust the Clerk, "Walter noght with wantoun lookyng of folye/His eyen on hire, but in sad wyse/Upon hir chiere he wolde hym ofte avyse" (236-38)—and then getting tired of her sexually: if anybody can be said to be stripping the Marquis of his *corage*, it is Griselda psychologically castrating him by the manner in which she responds to his own divorce decree.

The *Clerk's Tale*, then, is about a battle not so much between the common folk and the aristocracy as it is between the female and the automatically supremacy-arrogating male.[15] This idea is reinforced by Chaucer's following addition to Petrarch[16] when he has the Clerk, who in his prologue had informed his audience that he would tell them a story which he had learned from Petrarch (IV 40), compare Griselda to Job:

> Men speke of Job, and most for his humblesse,
> As clerkes, whan hem list, konne wel endite,
> Namely of men, but as in soothfastnesse,
> Though clerkes preise wommen but a lite,
> *Ther kan no man in humblesse hym acquite*
> *As womman kan, ne kan been half so trewe*
> *As wommen been* . . . (IV 932-38, italics added)

Since according to the Clerk's summary toward the end—"for oure beste is al [Goddes] governaunce;/Lat us thanne lyve in vertuous suffraunce" (1161-62)— the *sentence* of the tale is the advocacy of Job-like humility and Job-like unquestioning acceptance of what life has in store for us, i.e., an advocacy of equanimity in the face of adversity, the Clerk's comparison of Griselda with Job is first of all a tremendous compliment to Griselda, but also a tremendous compliment to all women. However, it is also a declaration of defeat for the Marquis who had just advised Griselda "With even herte . . . t'endure/The strook of Fortune or of aventure"—a piece of advice which Chaucer added[17]— but almost lost his speech and went away "lyk a worm" when she used his own divorce decree to put *him* on the spot: the psychological castration of the self-righteous male-supremacist provides a measure of *solaas* in this tale.

Especially in light of the Clerk's clever employment of sexual or sex-related terminology, I agree with Lindahl's final assessment of the *Clerk's Tale*: "the Clerk has turned the morality of the romance against itself . . . we might label the Clerk's romance a *Schwank* [i.e., a humorous, fabliau-like story] in disguise."[18] Lindahl's departure from the traditional interpretation of the *Clerk's Tale* as strictly an exemplum is both refreshing and convincing. I do, however, wish Lindahl had adhered to what the text says, for what really makes the tale "a *Schwank* in disguise" is not the anti-elitist message that

Lindahl wishes to see in Walter's abuse of Griselda, but instead a feminist message. In praising Griselda the Clerk does say early in the story that in addition to her wifely qualities she also "The commune profit . . . koude redresse" (431), and "*The commune profit* . . . has been called a 'favorite phrase of fourteenth-century socialism'."[19] Yet when in the Envoy—the scribe designated it "Lenvoi de Chaucer," but the Clerk refers to it as his own "song" (1176)—the teller calls upon women to assume the "governaille" (1192) for the sake of the "commune profit" (1194), the Clerk's use of the phrase *commune profit* in the Envoy ironically informs the context in which he had used that phrase earlier:

> Nat only this Griselde thurgh hir wit
> *Koude al the feet of wyfly hoomlinesse,*
> *But eek, whan that the cas required it,*
> *The commune profit koude she redresse.*
> Ther nas discord, rancour, ne hevynesse
> In al that land, that she no koude appese,
> And wisely brynge hem alle *in reste and ese.*
> Though that hire housbonde absent were anon,
> If gentil men or othere of hire contree
> Were wrothe, she wolde bryngen hem aton;
> So wise and rype wordes hadde she,
> And juggementz of so greet equitee,
> *That she from hevene sent was, as men wende,*
> *Peple to save and every wrong t'amende.* (IV 428-41, italics added)

The comic interaction between the Envoy's call upon women to assume leadership for the common good and the passage just quoted operates as follows. Not only does Griselda manage "al the feet of hoomlinesse," but during the Marquis' absences she also adminstrates the country so efficiently that his subjects think heaven had sent her to save people and right every wrong: the Clerk is playing off her wifely qualities against her capabilities as governor, in both of which she excels. The Clerk continues the playing off when in the subsequent lines he has the wife give birth to a daughter and thereby prove that "she nys nat bareyne" (448), i.e., prove that she may be able to give birth to the son who will continue the Marquis' lineage—which is the reason his people had entreated the reluctant Walter to get married in the first place. In what I suggest we read as a feminist *Schwank*, Griselda has now employed her *wifely* qualities to serve the "commune profit."[20]

Yet what does the husband-and-governor do in response to his wife's assisting him in his public affairs not only in one but actually in two ways? In the immediately following lines the Clerk presents the Marquis as jeopardizing the marital "reste and ese," just as the child is being suckled:

> Whan that this child had souked but a throwe,
> This markys in his herte longeth so
> To tempte his wyf, her sadnesse for to knowe,
> That he ne myghte out of his herte throwe
> This merveillous desir his wyf t'assaye;
> Nedelees, God woot, he thoght hire for t'affraye.
> He hadde assayed hire ynogh bifore,
> And foond hire evere good; what neded it
> Hire for to tempte, and alwey moore and moore,
> *Though some men preise it for a subtil wit?*
> *But as for me, I seye that yvele it sit*
> *To assaye a wyf whan that ther is no nede,*
> *And putten hire in angwyssh and in drede.*
> (IV 450-62, italics added)

This is the most important instance where the Clerk expresses disapproval of Walter's oppressive treatment of his wife, because in the lines I italicized Chaucer is adding to Petrarch[21] and thereby pointedly dissociating himself from the allegorical intentions which the vastly popular Patient Griselda legend originally had, i.e., the idealizing exemplum of wifely obedience.[22] In the passage I quoted, the Clerk uses the words *tempte* and *assaye* two and three times, respectively. The fact that he uses a verb meaning "to test" five times within ten lines and later toward the end compares Griselda's being tested to Job being tested by God has the following implications: Walter is trying to play God with Griselda—which the banished wife will (sarcastically?) acknowledge by associating her situation with Job's.

It could be argued that in playing God with Griselda the Marquis is only doing what malevolent monarchs do with their subjects anyway. But what speaks against such a generalizing interpretation is first that the Marquis never deliberately wrongs his subjects; on the contrary, he is complying with their wishes when he gives up his freedom for what he calls the "servage" of marriage (446). He even invites them to the "open audience" in which he discards his first wife for a new one whom he says his people will find better suited to their monarch and thus eventually also better for their country. What also would seem to invalidate such a simplifying socialist-message reading is the fact that in his narration of the disposal of both children the Clerk mentions their breastfeeding: the daughter is disposed of while she is still being suckled, the son after he has been weaned from his nurse's breast (617-18). The Clerk mentions the breastfeeding in the contexts of the children's disposal because nursing is a matrimonial event that is as important as the acts of procreation and birthing: the Clerk pointedly mentions the breastfeeding to suggest that, when Walter disposes of the children, in a symbolic sense he is retroactively trying to undo the acts of procreation and birthing—a point which I will elaborate later in this chapter by relating it to the "servage" of an entirely different type of marriage, namely to the Prioress' service under Christ.

Walter's perverseness as husband-and-father is illustrated the most strongly in the Clerk's description of the first case of child disposal: "*Whan that this child has souked but a throwe* [i.e., only for a short while],/This markys *in his herte longeth* so to tempte his wyf, her sadnesse [i.e., steadiness] for to knowe,/That he ne myghte out of his herte throwe/This merveillous desir his wyf t'assaye" (italics added). Regardless of whether we are to assume that Walter is actually witnessing the nursing of his daughter when he is overcome by "This merveillous desir," the Clerk's juxtaposition of these two occurrences, a juxtaposition whose verbal order may suggest to some readers a cause-effect sequence between the suckling and the disposing of the child, has the following implications for our understanding of Chaucer's portrayal of the Marquis. At a time when one would expect the father to be, perhaps if not filled with loving "long[ing]" for his child and his wife, then at least concerned about the welfare of the *very*-newborn, Walter's heart is filled with a strong "longing" to test the steadiness of his wife who has just undergone the "tests" of carrying a child, of going through labor, and of giving birth. When the Clerk mentions Walter's strong longing but not any emotion which would be *natural* in this situation, he is subtly disqualifying the Marquis as a tester of a woman's character. Walter would be much better off testing the qualities of hawks and hunting dogs, a passion which Walter gave up when he acceded to his subjects' plea to get married.

It could even be argued that when the baby, a female to boot, is making *her* "desir" known, she is seen as making the Marquis' own desires secondary. While Walter at least had part in the procreation, he cannot participate in the breastfeeding. His "merveillous desir" could therefore have as an underlying motive jealousy—which might explain why he takes the infant away after "but a throwe" whereas in the case of the second child Walter will tolerate the child (who, perhaps fortunately for the child, happens to be male) for two years. For it is interesting to note that while in the case of the second child Chaucer will expressly mention a nursemaid, in the first case he does not say who does the breastfeeding. Could this be an ambiguity intended to make the reader wonder whether Griselda herself nurses the baby girl, in which case Griselda would be seen by the Marquis as shutting him out? Such a scenario would cause Walter to use a nursemaid for the second child (he certainly wouldn't want his wife to devote any of her intimate time to another *male*, would he?), which in turn would help explain why he allows Griselda to keep the second child for two years.

All this is of course speculation, but the point is that in the *Clerk's Tale* Chaucer is not simply putting down in writing a piece of folklore where no motivation for the characters' actions is needed. Nor is the Clerk, who in his prologue had informed his audience that he would treat them to a tale he had learned from what Petrarch *had written* (40) and who displays his literary talents through his additions to and transformations of Petrarchan materials, simply telling a folktale. Once Chaucer has had the Clerk insinuate that morally-mentally Walter is not qualified to test Griselda, one could argue that both the Clerk and Chaucer are also implying that, after the loss of her daughter, Griselda is no longer bound by her oath of obedience to the Marquis. I will address that point in a moment. Let me now mention that for Walter even Griselda giving birth to a girl is a test of sorts. Since the first child is not the "knave child" he had initially hoped for (444) but whom she will duly deliver four years later, the procreation of the "mayde child [that] coome al bifore" (446) had merely been a biological test for Griselda—a trial run, as it were.

The Clerk is offering the following explanation for Walter's "merveillous desir" when the Marquis 'tests' Griselda by disposing of the son. This time he mentions the breastfeeding in a different context:

> Whan it was two yeer old, and fro the brest
> Departed of his norice, on a day
> *This markys caughte yet another lest*
> To tempte his wyf yet ofter, if he may.
> O nedelees was she tempted in assay!
> *But wedded men ne knowe no mesure,*
> *Whan that they fynde a pacient creature.* (617-23, italics added)

Here the Clerk comes forward and attributes Walter's strange behavior toward Griselda to the kind of marriage they have. While he is not letting Walter off the hook, he is saying that wives should be careful not to be overly "pacient" because such behavior is likely to cause the husband to lose all restraint: it is important for our assessment of the Clerk's warning to wives that Chaucer added the warning to the original source.[23] More specifically, the Clerk is implying the following criticism of Griselda. The Griselda who had between her wedding and her first child displayed the wisdom and judgment required to restore peace and order in the country during the Marquis' absences should have communicated with him concerning their sex life. She would have been able to do so, the Clerk is suggesting, even if she felt she could not renege on her rash nuptial promise and stand up to him when he claimed that for socio-political reasons he needed to dispose of the daughter as best he could: "Nat as I wolde, but as my peple *leste*" (490, italics added).

That the Marquis had the been lying to the woman whom his people had just come to regard as a heaven-sent savior is made explicit by the inter-action with the Clerk's mention of "yet another lest" in line 619, but the interaction between the two contexts also suggests that Walter threw overboard all *mesure* when she gave in to him with respect to the first child—and when she continued to have sexual intercourse with him presumably without discuss-ing the possible consequences: what did she expect he would do if she had another child? Why didn't this "flour of wyfly pacience," as the Clerk will—sarcastically?—call her shortly after the divorce spectacle (919), point out to her husband that he would be confronted with the same socio-political problem if they had another child? Each time she had sexual intercourse with him at a time when conception was a possiblity she was consenting to potential infanticide. And that is exactly what Walter had been planning on when he stipulated that, whatever he did, she would not "grucche it, *nyght* ne day" (354, italics added).[24]

There is no need to consider medieval laws concerning what a husband could and could not do sexually to his wife, first of all because the Marquis' own (Italian) subjects come to hate him as a "mordrere" (732). More impor-tantly, it is not so much a legal question of the validity of the oath of obedi-ence which Griselda had sworn to her husband-and-monarch; instead, it is a moral question which the Clerk's audience is in a unique position to appreci-ate: they are on a pilgrimage to the shrine of a man who had refused to fol-low his king's orders because they violated his understanding of what was right, in Saint Thomas à Becket's case the law of the Church. For the most part, the Clerk's audience therefore would have consented to Griselda reneging on her nuptial promise, especially since, a few lines after mentioning that his people had come to hate the Marquis because they thought he was a murderer, the Clerk reports the Marquis as misinforming "the court of Rome" with false documents and even having papal bulls forged which gave him dispensation to cast off his first wife and marry someone else—bulls which he published in their entirety (737-59). Some of the pilgrims certainly knew that the pope himself became outraged by King Henry's machinations when the king avenged himself on the archbishop of Canterbury, whose prerogatives included coronations, by having the archbishop of York conduct the coronation of Prince Henry as the successor to the throne; the pope even went so far as to suspend the archbishop of York.

It is also in the light of this historical background that we have to assess Walter's actions and also Griselda's own situation: the Clerk knows that Griselda morally would have been in the right had she opposed Walter. As I will show, she would have been in the right even before Walter played his dirty game with the Church, which the Clerk describes as follows:

> He to the court of Rome, in subtil wyse
> Enformed of *his wyl*, sent by message,
> Commaundynge hem swiche bulles to devyse
> As to his crueel purpos may suffyse,
> How that the pope, as for his peples reste,
> Bad hym to wedde another, *if hym leste*. (IV 737-43, italics added)

The key phrases here are *his wyl* and *if hym leste*. I have discussed the thematic significance of Chaucer's use of the words *lest* and *leste*: Walter does with his wife just as he pleases. However, in a context which presents Walter as dealing with the pope's court, the Marquis' self-indulgence takes on a new dimension. In a context in which the Marquis pretends to have communicated his desire to God's representative on earth, which associations is the Clerk's use of the phrase "his wyl" intended to evoke? The answer is: "Thy will be done" ("Fiat voluntas tua," Matthew 6:10). The crucial point of the tale here, then, is that Walter is not only inflicting his will on his wife but also imposing his will concerning his treatment of his wife on the pope—ironically, the pope does not even know what Walter's will is—and by implication trying to impose his will on God Himself. God of course does know what Walter's will is, but there is an insinuation that, as in the case of the pope, the Marquis thinks he can impose his will on God behind His back.

We therefore need to take a look at Walter's relationship with God. The Clerk first introduces the Marquis as a worthy person, but we soon learn that he has one fault, initially uncommented upon by the teller, i.e., in his apparently perpetual hunting and hawking Walter has neglected one of his obligations towards his subjects: to get married and guarantee the continuation of their leadership by his well-proven dynasty. When Walter finally accepts his responsibility toward his citizens and agrees to the "servage" of marriage, he outlines to them how he will go about his newly accepted duty:

> I truste in Goddes bountee, and therfore
> My mariage and myn estaat and reste
> I hym betake; *he may doon as hym leste.*
> (IV 159-61, italics added)

Walter is reassuring his subjects that he is placing his marriage, his political affairs, and his peace of mind in God's hands. But does Walter really mean what he says? The reader probably does not worry overly much about what Walter is doing to his own peace of mind when he decides to play extremely stressful mind-games with his wife, but when in the context of the disposal of the son the Clerk almost nonchalantly says, "This markys caughte yet another lest/To tempte his wyf yet ofter," Chaucer has that statement interact with Walter's earlier public announcement that he will let *God* "doon as he leste." In other words, Chaucer has the Clerk himself endow the Marquis' announcement with an ironic twist: even if Walter did mean what he was saying to his people back then, he must have "caughte . . . another lest" shortly thereafter when he spelt out to Griselda the condition on which he would marry her:

> *be ye redy with good herte*

To all my lust, and that I frely may,
As me best thynketh, do yow laughe or smerte,
And never ye to grucche it nyght ne day? (IV 351-54, italics added)

The reader who examines the text closely will detect that Chaucer is playing the notion of Walter's own lust/wish/pleasing against what Walter had proclaimed he would leave to God's "lust." Thus when in his speedily performed negotation with Griselda Walter stipulates that she agree with "al his lust," he is hastening to reclaim to his own dominion that which he said he had turned over to God. This verbal maneuver reinforces the suggestion that Walter is trying to play God with Griselda, and that he had planned on doing so even before he fed his people the line about placing his marriage-plus-politics in God's hands. He had planned from the very beginning to subject to Job-like tests the potential wife he had picked already before his citizens pressed him on that subject. In this, Walter is playing God not so much with his subjects as he is with his wife.[25] Therefore, after discussing Walter's relationship with God, let us take another look at his relationship with his wife.

The Clerk does not grant us a look into Walter's and Griselda's bedroom, but Griselda's later references to the Marquis having stripped her suggest that at some of the times they were having sexual intercourse the woman whom he had forced to sacrifice the child they had procreated together must have felt as though she was being sexually abused. Such a notion would tie in with the psychological castration with which she punishes the Marquis during the "open audience" spectacle. Or did Walter perhaps tell Griselda that the next child would be a different case if it turned out to be a son who would be able to carry on Walter's noble lineage? The Clerk of course doesn't say, but it is worth noting that, whereas at the time of the birth of Griselda's daughter the mother would have preferred a "knave child" (444), after the eventual birth of a boy the Clerk reports everybody to be completely happy—"all [the] contree"(615) presumably includes Griselda—even to the point of crediting

God for the event. After pointedly observing that, following the disposal of
the girl, Griselda never said a word about her but was "As glad, as humble,
as big in servyse,/And *eek in love*, as she was wont to be" (603-604, italics
added), the Clerk tells his audience:

> *as God wolde,*
> A knave child she bar by this Walter,
> Ful gracious and fair to beholde.
> And whan that folk it to his father tolde,
> *Nat oonly he, but al his contree merye*
> *Was for his child, and God they thanke and herye.*
> Whan it was two yeer old . . . . (IV 611-17, italics added)

This passage may well be the culmination in what I have called the
Clerk's feminist *Schwank*. Through his seemingly innocuous brief statement,
"as God wolde," the Clerk instills the following ironic note into his tale. The
Clerk had made no mention of God's will with respect to the "mayde child,"
although, as the Clerk of all people would be one of the first to know, her
birth too fell under the Church's doctrine that the main purpose of sexual
intercourse was to increase the flock of God's children. Therefore, when the
tale's narrator omits any mention of God's will in the case of the first child,
whom everybody would have preferred to be a boy, but then mentions God's
will in the case of the second child, the Clerk is sarcastically joining the Marquis and his subjects in their merriment and expression of gratitude toward
God—*sarcastically* because the Clerk knows, and immediately proceeds to
report, what will happen to the boy. But the Clerk's "as God wolde" has yet
further ironic implications. That three-word remark interacts with the notion
of the Marquis trying to impose his will concerning his marital matters on
God. Through this interaction the Clerk may be suggesting that Walter
equates "his wyl" to have a son who can carry on his lineage with God's will.
More seriously, the Clerk may be suggesting that it is Walter's belief that,
when he engaged in the sex act which finally turned out to produce the son he
had wished for, he had willed God into making sure that his union resulted in

the procreation of a male: after all, having God participate in the procreation of his son more than makes up for being excluded from breastfeeding his baby!

I earlier discussed how the Marquis' pride-governed behavior toward his wife, which I also have established includes the sin of pride toward God, is punished by Walter's psychological castration during his "open audience" divorce spectacle. But wouldn't all this suggest that in the final analysis the *Clerk's Tale* carries a socialist, or at least populist, message? After all, couldn't I take what would seem to be the path of least resistance and argue that the tale is a *Schwank* simultaneously with both a feminist *and* a socialist message? I cannot do so for several reasons. First there is the Clerk's strongly worded condemnation of the fickleness of the populace which had come to hate its Marquis as a murderer but then expresses its delight when Walter brings in the person who everybody thinks is his new wife:

> "*O stormy peple! unsad and untrewe!*
> Ay undiscreet and chaungynge as a fane!
> Delitynge evere in rumbul that is newe,
> For lyk the moon ay wexe ye and wane!
> Ay ful of clappyng, deere ynogh a jane!
> Youre doom is fals, *youre constance yvele preeveth*,
> A ful greet fool is he that on yow leeveth." (IV 994-1001, italics added)

There is the ironic refraction that the Clerk tries to give the impression that his condemnation of the "stormy peple" is only second-hand, since he assigns lines 994-1001 to some of the more stable members of the city: "Thus seyden sadde folk in that citee" (1002). This is a clever rhetorical device on the Clerk's part: he first voices what appears to be his own, and sound, judgment, but then qualifies his statement by saying he has only been reporting the opinion voiced by stable citizens. This playing down of the "stormy peple" condemnation in turn enhances the Clerk's credibility, and he is now able to almost unnoticeably join those citizens who are critical of the populace for cheering the Marquis—just as in dissociating irony the Clerk had earlier joined the people cheering the Marquis after the birth of the first child:

> Thus seyden sadde folk in that citee,
> Whan that the peple gazed up and doun;
> For they were glad, right for the noveltee,
> To han a newe lady of hir toun.
> Namoore of this make I now mencioun,
> But to Griselde agayn wol I me dresse,
> *And telle hir constance and hir bisynesse.* (IV 1002-1008, italics added)

In the narrative in lines 1003-1005 the Clerk is tersely expressing agreement with the opinion which the "sadde folk" have of the *peple*, and then he proceeds to contrast the *peple*'s lack of *constance* to Griselda's own character.[26]

Why does the Clerk, who has just condemned the *peple* for their lack of *constance*, mention in one breath Griselda's *constance* and her *bisynesse*? Is the Clerk perhaps implying that the populace also lacks Griselda's industriousness or at least her reliability in fulfilling a task? For it should be noted that the lines from "O stormy peple" to "hir bisynesse," i.e., lines in which the Clerk cites the stable citizens' opinion to lay a firm foundation for his own opinion, are additions, *the Clerks's* own additions, to Petrarach.[27] At any rate, the Clerk goes on to illustrate how Griselda's *bisynesse* is part of her *constance*: she busies herself with the wedding preparations which the Marquis has asked her to help him with. One of Griselda's functions is to receive the aristocratic guests. Griselda does a splendid job as we might have expected, but what we may not have expected is that the upper-class guests, instead of expressing contempt for Griselda being meanly dressed, give her due praise:

> ay they wondren what she myghte bee
> That in so povre array was for to see,
> And koude swich honour and reverence,
> And *worthily they preisen hire prudence.* (IV 1019-22, italics added)

While throughout their marriage the Marquis had kept reminding Griselda of the rags he had liberated her from, then, not *all* members of the aristocracy are portrayed as abominable monsters. Or to express it in Lindahl's words which I quoted at the beginning of my discussion of the *Clerk's Tale*: "the world in which [the] oppressed Griselde remains a heroine, . . . the world in which she suffers," does indeed "hold hint[s] of virtue." These hints come from the aristocracy of whose undeniably existing evils Walter is a representative, a representative, however, whose caricaturing portrayal addresses the question of male-female relationships rather than that of class struggles: as Ferster puts it, "[the noblemen] are worthy for seeing her worth and prudent in seeing her prudence."[28]

In fact, I would argue that it is precisely because Griselda has received deserved praise from the aristocracy that she finally dares to criticize the Marquis for his treatment of her, even if she does so in a roundabout way.   After Griselda has wished Walter and his new wife happiness, she cautions him:

> O thyng biseke I yow, and warne also,
> That ye ne prikke with no tormentynge
> This tendre mayden, as ye han doon mo;
> *For she is fostred in hire norissynge*
> *Moore tendrely, and to my supposynge,*
> *She koude nat adversity endure*
> *As koude a povre fostred creature.*   (IV 1037-43, italics added)

Griselda is vicariously doing for the Marquis's new wife what because of her promise of absolute obedience she had been unable to do for herself: she is standing up to him.   Yet as if to make her plea appear less personal, she is expressing her criticism of the Marquis in terms of a class-struggle argument when she tells him that she is afraid the new wife could not endure the adversity as could somoeone who had been brought up in poverty.

If Griselda really means what she says about the significance of her social background, she is making a fool of herself through a display of monomania not totally different from that of the Marquis.   Part of Chaucer's irony in the present context is that Griselda is unwittingly standing up for herself since, in accordance with the Marquis' plan, she will continue to be his wife. And the other part of Chaucer's irony here is that Griselda is trying to impress upon the Marquis an anti-elitist message of sorts when she says that only someone with her own social background is capable of enduring the adversity he has been heaping on her. This, I wish to argue, is a case of snobbishness-in-reverse, even pride: we need to remember that the humble Job to whom the Clerk compares Griselda, and to whom Griselda had even compared herself, had *not* been a "povre fostred creature" when adversity hit him.

Yet Chaucer's ironic treatment of Griselda in this context extends even further. Chaucer is poetically punishing Griselda for her class-related pride, for laying sole claim to a certain capability simply because she was "fostred" (literally "nourished" or "fed") *in poverty*. Chaucer—or perhaps more precisely the Clerk, whose poor-scholar role had been emphasized in the General Prologue where his coat is described as "thredbare" (I 290)—is bringing here to bear on his characterization of Griselda the first breastfeeding context. When Griselda claims, or perhaps in an attempt to feign modesty in the lecture which she delivers to the Marquis on class differences says she *supposes*, that Walter's new wife does not possess the capacity which she herself possesses for enduring adversity—"For she is fostred in hire *norissynge*/Moore tenderly, and to my *supposynge* . . . " (italics added)— Griselda is embarrassingly far off the mark: note the rhyme between the two words I italicized. Griselda does not know that, while the other woman's upbringing eventually had been more genteel-and-gentle than her own, that woman's *norissynge*/"souk[ynge]" (450) had been traumatically disrupted, literally by the abduction at the hands of the cruel sergeant, but more importantly when after "but a throwe" of her *soukynge* her father was overcome by "This merveillous desir." In her monomaniacal class-selfconsciousness Griselda even is unwittingly belittling the character of her own daughter.

In Griselda's class-difference speech Chaucer is endowing the tale's theme of *gentilesse* with an ironic twist. Bernard S. Levy has observed concerning that theme:

> Walter, the marquis, is the highborn aristocrat who decides to marry a
> woman of true, not inherited, *gentilesse* . . . [Walter] decides to follow
> the theory, already presented by the Hag in the *Wife of Bath's Tale*,
> that *gentilesse* is not a matter of birth, but rather of goodness derived
> from divine grace, and thus can be found in a person of the humblest
> origin (155-61) . . . [When he tests Griselda] Walter is thus trying to
> justify his decision to marry a woman of low birth, because he himself
> is not yet sure that his decision was in fact the right one.[29]

Levy's perspicacious observations raise the following question: who or what
gives Walter the right to examine whether Griselda possesses the true *gentilesse* which is derived from Divine grace? I provided the answer earlier: when
Walter decides to subject Griselda to Job-like tests, he is arrogating a right
which is God's and God's only—Walter is playing God with his wife.

The ironic twist here is that what Levy calls "Walter's lack of true
gentilesse in his scandalous treatment of his wife"[30] frees the lowborn woman
of her illusions as to where *gentilesse* is to be found. In Levy's words again,

> It is, ironically, the "povre Griselda" . . . who humbly accepts the
> theory that high birth is a requisite of *gentilesse*, while it is the noble
> marquis who promotes the view that *gentilesse* is a matter of virtue,
> goodness given through God's grace, rather than aristocratic birth.[31]

Both are wrong: Griselda is wrong in her humble acceptance of the socially
based definition of *gentilesse*, and Walter in trying to test the validity of the
view he himself promotes. I will later discuss how Walter undergoes a conversion; Griselda undergoes a conversion of sorts at the latest when the putative personification of *gentilesse* breaks his marriage vow—as result of which
the *gentil* becomes a "worm." Griselda is further expressing her disillusionment from her original notion of *gentilesse* in her "povre fostred creature"
lecture to the Marquis. In fact, her disillusionment is so strong that she goes
overboard and becomes guilty of what I have called class-based pride, unwittingly belittling the charcater of her own daughter.

Any class-oriented message which readers might want to attribute to the
Clerk's Tale because of the speech Griselda delivers to the Marquis on how

not to treat his new wife and *why not* to treat her in such a fashion is being negated moments later when she learns that she has all along been the victim of male-supremacist pranks. At this point at the latest Griselda realizes that, if she had had her wits about her when the Marquis surprised her with the marriage proposal *and the conditions attached*, she would have declined. After all, he did not force her to marry him—but perhaps the opportunity to move from rags to riches was too tempting: when she was offered such a gigantic opportunity she knew "no mesure" just as the Marquis knew none when he found a "pacient creature." It might therefore not be impertinent to quote John M. Gamin's comment concerning the monstrosities taking place in the tale: "There was a time when the critics agreed that the problem of the *Clerk's Tale* was the monstrous Walter, but there is now some disagreement as to who the real monster of the tale might be. After all there are ways in which Griselda herself seems monstrously passive, or to be more accurate, passive/aggressive."[32]

I would argue that Griselda *is* passive/aggressive in several instances, most prominently in the "open audience" where she brings up the idea of nakedness in order to be able to reduce Walter to a "worm." It could also be argued that she was, consciously or unconsciously, challenging the scouting Walter when she presented him with her "chiere"—that she was in fact *teasing* him in a nonerotic sense. It could then be argued that this challenge led to a long battle of wills which she won because she was so "pacient"—in the literal Latin sense of "allowing oneself to and being able to suffer"—that she could will herself into identifying her own will with Walter's: she engaged in what Ferster calls "meta-willing, the willing to will."[33] Let us therefore return to the Marquis' will.

The Clerk tries to explain Walter's obsession by using the following comparison:

But ther been folk of swich condicion

That whan they have a certeyn purpos take,
They kan nat stynte of hire entencion,
But, *right as they were bounden to a stake*,
They wol nat of that firste purpose slake. (IV 701-705, italics added)

In an article partially entitled "Walter at the Stake," Thomas A. Van quotes the Clerk's comparison and observes: "We might expect to see the image of a person at the stake used to describe the saint in a legend such as this, but not the saint's oppressor."[34] And Van goes on to elaborate on Walter's unsaintly machinations, for example his "outrageous lies about the nobility, the commons, and even the Pope." I would argue that the Clerk's application to Walter of the image of a person at the stake is precisely suited to the point the Clerk is trying to make. The function of the image is to convey the ironic notion that, when the Marquis pretends to be committing acts which cause *him* agony for the sake of his country, he is playing saint.

Walter is playing saint when he tells his people that for their sake he will subject himself to the "servage" of marriage. This is *playing* saint because, unlike the martyr and future-saint who must make a choice between life or his beliefs, Walter really has no choice but to do what a man in his social position is supposed to do: since apparently he has no brothers whom his subjects could turn to for the continuation of the dynasty, it is his duty to get married and sire a successor. And this is where I see the reason for Walter's "merveillous desir": since fate has left him no choice but to get married, he decides that he will take control of every event from now on, especially of events having to do with his wife, whom he perceives as the personification of the fate which had "bound" him to the "servage" that forced him to give up his passion for hunting. As Van points out,

> [Walter's] hunting has been an outlet for romantic energy and an escape from the servitude or loss of control he fears in marriage, for as a hunter he initiates and disposes of things as he pleases. When he continually chances to see Griselda while out on his hunts, the hitherto opposite activities of hunting and love-making elide, for she is the new game, which he will stalk after with customary intensity.[35]

Chaucer is establishing an equivalence between Walter's passion for hunting and his stalking after Gridelda as he has the Clerk make the following comment on the manner in which Walter would look at Griselda when, as happened quite frequently during his hunting expeditions, he caught sight of her:

> upon Griselde, this povre creature,
> Ful ofte sithe this markys sette his ye
> As he on huntyng rood paraventure;
> And when it fil that he myghte hire espye,
> Walter noght with wanton lookyng of folye
> His eyen on hire, but in sad wyse
> Upon her chiere he wolde hym ofte avyse . . . (IV 232-38)

I earlier observed concerning the Clerk's comment, "if we can trust the Clerk," an observation by which I meant to imply that the Clerk's voiced assessment of Walter looking at Griselda might be open to interpretation. While I still maintain that the Clerk is absolving Walter from sexual motives, I will now add that the Clerk is attributing to Walter a motive which indeed is less than innocent. While Walter is not guilty of "wantoun lookyng of folye," there is something about his looking at Griselda which is indeed *wantoun*: Walter will replace his unruly passion for stalking after game with an equally unruly obsession with stalking after a woman. However, whereas Walter's hunting had been, in Van's words, "an outlet for romantic energy," in its transferred form that energy is deromanticized: the Clerk's disclaimer of romantic motives in Walter's inspection of Griselda's *chiere* foreshadows a total absence of eroticism in Walter's marriage. As a matter of fact, in one sense Walter is already married to Griselda while he is inspecting her: already long before his subjects ask him to enter into the "servage" of marriage, he *knows* that he will marry this girl—in compliance with his duty as monarch. Or more precisely, he is performing the "servage" of being monarch when he takes time out from his hunting to inspect the peasant girl.

Chaucer is expressing this linkage between Walter's marriage and his duty as monarch when he has the spokesman of the people, trying to persuade Walter to marry, make his request in the following manner:

> Boweth youre nekke under that *blisful yok*
> *Of soveraynetee*, noght of servyse,
> Which that men clepe spousaille or wedlok . . .
>   (IV 113-15, italics added)

Ferster notes that lines 113-114 contain a *contre-rejet*, i.e., "the continuation of an enjembed unit [which] forces the reader to return to the first line to reassess its meaning":[36] the speaker

> seems to be referring to the commonplace image of the yoke of marriage . . . until "soveraynetee" makes us revise our expectations. Although he is actually referring to marriage, [the spokesman's] wording emphasizes that Walter would be in a superior position in marriage. He seems to think that his request can be made more appealing if it is couched as a request that Walter rule.

I would suggest that Walter is gladly taking the spokesman up on his request when he lords it over his wife. Walter knows that the spokesman is trying to manipulate him when he makes palatable the pill of the yoke of marriage by covering it with the sugar-coat of *soveraynetee*. Walter therefore will avenge himself by compensating for the *soveraynetee* of the hunter which he has to give up with the superior position in the marriage which has been forced upon him. Walter is quite literally a husband with a vengeance: he avenges himself on the institution of marriage for the loss of of control over his own life which the social position of monarch has inflicted upon him.

Unfortunately for Griselda, Walter has no choice but to direct his revenge at the yoke which has been laid on his shoulders: since the passionate hunter must perceive the spokesman's word-play involving sovereignty, servitude, and marriage as hypocritical, he will act out his own word-play, one in which he will have "soveraynetee" in marriage by subjecting to his "servyse" which he is being assured is *not* his fate her who personifies the yoke—an arrangemant which, he could justifiably argue, "men *clepe* spousaille or wedlok" (italics added). Walter will tyrannize his wife and "call it marriage." Taking the people who ask him to get married at their word, Walter will be able to "call marriage" anything he wishes to do with his wife. As a matter of fact, for his own arrangement of that which "men clepe spousaille or wedlok" Walter has been authorized by God, because the spokesman is expressly bringing in God's will when he appeals to Walter:

> Delivere us out of al this bisy drede,
> And taak a wyf for hye Goddes sake. (IV 134-35)

Ferster notes that "This is a command in the familiar singular (as opposed to the earlier, more polite 'Accepteth,' 1. 127)."[37] I would add that the spokesman's command is impatiently urgent, perhaps best rendered in Yiddish-influenced Modern English as "Take a wife for God's sake *already*." In his appeal the spokesman, then, is laying the foundation for Walter's equating of his own will with God's will, especially when he asks Walter to "deliver" the people of their political fears concerning the continuation of the dynasty, which places Walter in the role of a savior. The spokesman is in fact asking Walter to *play Christ*—which endows with an ironic twist the Clerk's later comparison of Walter to someone "bounden to a stake": Walter becomes a Christ whose martyrdom consists of sacrificing himself in marriage. The fact that Christ's bride is the Church, in turn, enables the self-appointed Christ-figure Walter to even supersede the pope.

In setting up this arrangement, the Marquis is not being a malevolent monarch. As Ferster observes, "The session ends, each side having won something. They do not begin as equals, but Walter does not misuse his power, and the poeple do not underestimate theirs. Each side compromises and both are partners in the decision."[38] I would argue that Griselda too is a partner in that decision. Chaucer is giving us a signal in that direction when in Walter's stipulation that, whatever he does, Griselda will not "grucche it, nyght ne daye" (354), he has the Marquis echo his earlier declaration that he is willing to enter the "servage" of marriage if his subjects agree not to "grucche ne stryve" (170) about his choice of bride and the manner of their wedding. There is, however, an important difference with respect to the situation Walter is in when he makes his stipulation. When his subjects ask him to get married, they are exercising the *soveraynetee* they have over him in the sense that his social position leaves Walter very little choice but to comply with their request—so that his stipulation that they not *grucchen* him is a defense mechanism on Walter's part. He is converting this defense mechanism into an *offense* stratagem when he confronts Griselda with the same stipulation: in exchange for going from rags to riches, Griselda has to promise him unwavering obedience. Or more precisely, Walter is able to exact such a price only from a lower-class girl. This explains Walter's choice of Griselda—perhaps even more so than Griselda's *chiere* does, although her *chiere* might suggest to Walter that she would be a perfect object for his experiments.

Walter's selection of a peasant girl in turn provides motives which make a happy ending possible. There is the ironic twist that Walter finally ceases his testing games with Griselda when she unwittingly reminds him of the reason he had chosen her for a wife: when she tells him that only someone brought up in poverty could stand the adversity he had heaped onto her, she is unknowingly rubbing in the fact that he had married a peasant girl because such a marriage would allow him to make a stipulation enabling him to avenge himself on the fate that forced him to give up his *soveraynetee* and fulfill his duty as a monarch. In fact, that Chaucer intends this as a recognition scene for Walter[39] is being suggested when Walter acknowledges to her not only that she possesses the constancy he supposedly had been looking for, but also that *with her own body* she had actually helped him fulfill his duty as the monarch of his subjects:

> This is thy daughter, which thou hast supposed

To be my wyf, *that oother feithfully*
shal be myn heir, as I have ay disposed;
Thou bar hym in thy body trewely.
At Boloigne have I kept them prively . . . (IV 1065-69, italics added)

The portions I italicized have the following implications. In his recognition scene Walter not only realizes why he had started his testing game, namely because he had felt mistreated by fate, but also that he should have stopped the game after Griselda had given birth to a boy. At that point, less than five years into his "servage," he had fulfilled his duty toward his subjects—and as far as they were concerned, he could have resumed his passionate hobby of hunting instead of continuing to stalk after his wife: isn't there a suggestion that if it had not been for his monomania—first his unruly passion for hunting, which was partly based on his desire to remain unmarried, and then for stalking after his wife—he would have been able to strike a happy medium between both?

Since Walter continued his stalking even after the birth of their son and, in fact, negated the birth of his heir by pretending to have had him killed, he still had not yet fulfilled his main duty towards his subjects, i.e., the continuation of his lineage. Thus, when he finally restores to their identity the children whom he had everybody believe were dead, he is not only restoring Griselda to her status as wife but also in a sense repeating with his wife the act of procreation. When Chaucer has Walter unveil the children whom Griselda "bare in [hire] body trewely" but whom Walter "At Boloigne . . . kept . . . pryvely," Chaucer may well be having a sexual innuendo in mind, especially in light of the massive sexual-and-birthing imagery which Griselda had treated Walter to during the divorce spectacle—in which case Walter would now be pointedly alluding to her use of such imagery during that spectacle. In any case, *Chaucer*, who had presented the Walter-Griselda relationship up to this point as conspicuously devoid of eroticism— during his 'courtship' Walter had not been guilty of "wantoun lookyng of folie"—is

presenting the reunion scene in terms of a procreation-and-birthing: after all,
since Walter had all along been planning to restore Griselda as his wife and
Griselda by now is past the age of child-bearing, or at least past that age
which back then would have seemed safe for child-bearing, the only chance
Walter has of begetting an heir with Griselda is to reinstate the children they
have.[40]

So far, I have said very little about the teller of the *Clerk's Tale*.
Dinshaw has made the following observation on the relationship between the
Clerk as the teller of the story and Griselda:

> Throughout his performance [the Clerk] condemns Walter's actions
> with unequivocal statements and indignant outbursts . . . Explicitly
> opposing himself to other clerks, he celebrates what he identifies as
> Griselda's specifically womanly strength . . . ; and in his "threadbare"
> (1:290) cloak and poor-scholar aspect, he even looks a bit like
> Griselda, that "povre creature" (232), in her old, threadbare gar-
> ments—a similarity that, given the sartorial preoccupation of the tale, is
> significant. Even before the Clerk speaks, the Host picks up this
> something about him, his resemblance to or sympathy with the female,
> so that Harry identifies him proleptically with the newly betrothed
> heroine of his tale—" 'Sire Clerk of Oxenford,' oure Hooste sayde,/
> 'Ye ryde as coy and stille as dooth a mayde/Were new spoused . . . ' "
> (1-3) . . . The Clerk responds to the Host by putting himself under the
> Host's "yerde": "Ye han of us as governance,/And therfore wol I do
> yow obeisance" (23-24), that "obeisance" echoing Griselda's "obei-
> sance" to Walter . . . The Clerk is in a Griselda-like position . . . vis-
> à-vis the burly Host (a would-be Walter, perhaps: he wishes his wife
> had heard this tale . . .).[41]

I will go beyond Dinshaw's argument that the Clerk is in a Griselda-
like position and submit that the poet is actually performing a gender-identifi-
cation between the male teller of the *Clerk's Tale* and that tale's female heroine. While in Dinshaw's argument Harry proleptically identifies the Clerk with
the heroine of his tale, I would argue that this identification operates the other
way around: it is in reaction to what the Clerk feels is an insulting sissifi-
cation by the macho Host that the Clerk tells not only a story in which
Dinshaw's potential "would-be Walter" indeed becomes the Marquis Walter,

but also a story through which by identifying with Griselda the Clerk acts out the feminization which Harry had assigned to him. Thus it is partly in reaction to the Host's remarks that the Clerk changes Petrarch's romance into a feminist *Schwank*.

In other words, through his tale the Clerk becomes the Host's own Griselda—and he becomes so in a sexually symbolic sense. The Clerk is giving expression to that idea when he says, "Hooste, . . . I am under youre yerde" (IV 22). In *Chaucer's Bawdy* Ross had first demonstrated in detail that Chaucer on several occasions used the word *yerde* in the meaning of penis, but then Ross commented: "Let me list a few more occurrences where the word means 'rod, rule,' so that the unwary may not be tempted to see penises in innocent lines: 'Clerk's Tale' (E 22) where the Clerk says he is under the Host's 'yerde'."[42] I quite warily succumb to what Ross called the temptation to see penises. I do so because back in 1972 Ross probably could not have thought of the Clerk as being in the position of Griselda—and in my view the Clerk tells the tale precisely because he wishes to present himself vis-à-vis the Host as that which Ross calls Griselda, as a "sexless puppet."[43] Ross' sensitivity to gender issues in 1972 was not the same as Dinshaw's in 1989 and my own at the time of this writing. In fact, I was surprised that in *Chaucer's Sexual Poetics* Dinshaw made no reference to Ross' book, for Dinshaw could have strengthened her argument that the Clerk is in a Griselda-like position by refuting Ross' caution concerning the "yerde" in the *Clerk's Tale*.

I had of course read *Chaucer's Bawdy* long before I read *Chaucer's Sexual Poetics*, but even before the appearance of Dinshaw's study I had a feeling that, in his description of the Host's treatment of the Clerk, Chaucer was doing more than just illustrating the contemporary axiom that "A maidenly simplicity is fitting for clerks."[44] I had the feeling that the macho Host was expressing his dislike for males whom he considered effeminate or at least in

some sense 'unmanly'—as he does in his "What man artow?" address to the
elvyssh-seeming Chaucer-the-pilgrim in the Prologue to Sir Thopas.   As I
discussed in Chapter III, Chaucer-the-pilgrim repays the Host by telling a tale
about *elvyssh sire Thopas*, i.e., by surprising Harry with a story about a man
who is not a man sexually. I would argue that Chaucer-the-poet is doing
something similar in the *Clerk's Tale*: he has the belittled teller repay the
Host by surprising him with a story in which the allegedly less-than-manly
Clerk identifies himself with the submissive heroine—and also identifes the
Host with Walter.   Through this double-identification the Clerk poetically
inflicts severe damage on the Host: just as during the divorce spectacle
Griselda psychologically castrates the oppressive Walter, so the Clerk reduces
to a crawling "worm" the Host's "yerde" to which he had submitted.[45]

Does the Host understand what the Clerk is doing to him? The following stanza appears after the Envoy in most of the manuscripts which preserve
the Envoy:[46]

> *Bihoold the murye words of the Hoost.*
> This worthy Clerk, when ended was his tale,
> Oure Hooste seyde, and swoor, "By Goddes bones,
> Me were levere than a barel ale
> My wyf at hoom had herde this legende ones!
> This is a gentil tale for the nones,
> As to my purpos, wiste ye my wille;
> But thyng that wol nat be, let it be stille." (IV 1212a-1221g)

Are the Host's words really "murye"? Maybe they are, *if* the Host is not a
poor loser but, instead, can take a joke directed at himself. But then the
murye could also be meant ironically by the poet. In any case, the Host does
praise the Clerk's contribution—and he also does something which strongly
suggests that he understands what the Clerk has just done to him. When Harry says that he would be willing to forfeit a barrel of ale if his wife at home
could have heard the legend of Patient Griselda, he is letting his fellow pilgrims know that his own wife doesn't always allow him the *governaunce*.

Such an admission from the macho Harry suggests that he has learned something from the Clerk who, as Chaucer had told us in the General Prologue, "gladly wolde . . . lerne and gladly teche" (I 308). Perhaps Harry has learned to be less bossy, and the 'feminized' Clerk has certainly taught him what supposedly is a womanly quality, acceptance. The Host is acknowledging that lesson when in his final comment on the Clerk's contribution he says, "thyng that wol nat be, lat it be stille."[47]

Harry's final statement palimpsestically interacts with the words in which the Marquis first said he was turning his position as monarch and husband over to God's will and then insisted that his own will be done, and the statement adds to the "sentence" of the feminist *Schwank*. Since in one sense the Clerk identifies the Host, the master of ceremonies, with the Marquis Walter, the Clerk is establishing some kind of equivalence between Harry's and Walter's respective types of *masculine willfulness*. However, while Chaucer punishes the Host for his androcentricity merely with a slap on the wrist, the punishment he metes out to Walter is more severe. It *has* to be more severe because in his androcentricity Walter not only abuses a woman—something which, despite his machismo, we are in no position to accuse Harry of—but he also allows his androcentricity to abuse, or at least to offend, God, and to abuse God's representative on earth. Therefore the Clerk's envoy is not so much the song for the Wife of Bath which he announces it to be as it is an attack on males abusing females. As Dinshaw notes, "the triumphant females whom the Clerk thus celebrates are directly derived from the clerkly antifeminist literature he has disavowed earlier (932-38), and the song . . . paints a grotesque picture of wives and marriage."[48]

The Clerk, then, drives home his point against antifeminist literature by playing off that kind of literature against his preceding portrayal of a monstrous abuser of women. And the poet is using the Host's response to the Clerk's feminist *Schwank* for yet another palimpsestic interaction with his preceding portrayal of the woman-abuser. The Host's final line organically interacts with the scene in which Griselda psychologically castrates the Marquis, the scene involving the smock:

> "The smok," quod [the Markys], "that hast on thy bak,
> *Lat it be stille*, and bere it forth with thee."
> But wel unnethes thilke word he spak,
> But wente his weye, for routhe and for pitee. (IV 890-93, italics added)

Once Griselda has demanded the smock in recompense for the virginity she had brought to Walter, the Marquis has no choice but to say, "Lat it be stille" —and crawl away like a worm. In other words, the poet adds to his own teller's feminist *Schwank* by recalling Walter's humiliation in the "open audience" which the Marquis had convened for the purpose of humiliating the woman.

On the other hand, I argued earlier that Walter's mistreatment of his wife is an act of revenge against a social system which had forced him into the "servage" of marriage. I will now add that the social system forces the Walter who would rather be out hunting into becoming a *breeder*. Chaucer is making the notion of Walter as breeder all but explicit when in his description of the people's reaction to the Marquis' putative new bride he adds two lines which I italicize in the following quotation:[49]

> For she is fairer, as they deemen alle,
> Than is Grisilde, and moore tendre of age,
> *And fairer fruyt bitwene hem sholde falle,*
> *And more plesant, for hire heigh lynage.* (IV 988-91, italics added)

As I have discussed, Walter's relationship with Griselda is devoid of any eroticsm; I will now ask: how *can* there be any eroticsm if the Marquis is forced into a breeding relationship? Furthermore, since the breeders will eventually have to come up with the "fruyt" of a boy, their sexual relationship is hampered by performance anxiety—on the part of *both* Walter *and* Griselda. This performance anxiety may not initially have impeded Walter—he does get

Griselda pregnant shortly after their wedding—but the Clerk makes clear that she would have preferred a boy:

> Nat longe tyme after this Grisild
> Was wedded, she a doghter has ybore,
> *Al had hire levere have born a knave child.*
> Glad was this markys and the folk therfore,
> For though a mayde child coome al bifore,
> She may unto a knave child attayne
> By liklihede, syn she nys nat bareyne. (IV 441-48, italics added)

Griselda would have preferred a boy because she knows the requirements of the patriarchal system. Walter, however, since he now knows she is capable of bearing children, is not unduly worried—or is he?

Of course he is worried, and he immediately turns the screws on his wife. The Clerk tells us that, although Walter had "assayed her ynogh bifore" (456), the Marquis has "This merveillous desire his wyf t'assaye" (454). In my earlier discussion of those lines, I noted that Chaucer dissociates himself from the perfect-wife exemplum of the original Patient Griselda legend by having the Clerk indignantly make the following addition to Petrarch's version: "I seye that yvele it sit/To assaye a wyf whan that it is no nede,/And putten hire in angwyssh and in drede" (460-62). I have also discussed the significance of Walter being overcome by this strange desire when the "mayde child . . . had souked but a throwe," and I have also interpreted the Marquis and his subjects as considering the birth of the girl merely a trial run. I will now add that the first of Walter's tests of his wife's obedience and constancy which is *actually recounted* in the tale—aren't we curious as to what the occasions had been when he "assayed her ynogh bifore?"—is Walter's announcement that in accordance with their nuptial agreement he will have to have *her* daughter (489) disposed of.[50] Especially if we re-read the *Clerk's Tale* in the light of the birth-reversal image in the *Prioress' Tale*, Walter's act is a case of putting the baby girl back into Griselda's *pryvetee*. Griselda will highlight his perverseness during the "*open* audience"—isn't that term beginning to take on an unpleasantly voyeuristic meaning?—when she reminds him that she had carried his children in her womb.[51] Let us therefore return to Walter's reaction to her delivery of the girl.

Walter conducts the first "test" recounted in the tale because he feels that he has failed, and therefore indirectly accuses *Griselda* of having failed, the patriarchal system by not producing the male heir needed for the continuation of his dynasty. This instance of Walter's scapegoating also explains the belated birth-reversal of his son. Since Walter's stated reason for the postnatal destruction of the daughter is the low social status of the human incubator, he is able to give the same reason for disposing of their son: after all, now that Walter and Griselda have produced a son no more testing of her should be needed. But "testing" her is not really what the Marquis has been doing. He has a sister in Bologna one of whose descendants could eventually carry on his dynasty—*if* the system weren't strictly patriarchal: Walter's intent throughout is to make a mockery of the institution of marriage which the patriarchal system has forced him into.

Walter does an excellent job of mocking the institution of marriage until during the "open audience" divorce Griselda reduces him to a "worm." He still does a passable job of it until the recognition scene when Griselda unknowingly reminds him that his "testing" game with her has been an attempt to avenge himself on fate for having forced him to be a patriarchal breeder. At that point Walter realizes that he has been victimizing Griselda because he himself had been victimized by a social system which requires him to do what the prolifically potent Hebrew patriarchs had done. Although Walter is a Christian and as such subscribes to the New Law, he is subject to the Old Law which commanded "multiplication."

Perhaps the *Clerk's Tale*'s greatest *solaas* is the manner in which the Clerk's *sentence*, namely the advocacy of a Job-like acceptance of what life has in store for us, is repeated by the Host:

Me were levere than a barel ale
My wyf at hoom had herd this legende ones!
This is a gentil tale for the nones,
As to my purpos, wist ye my *wille*;
But thyng that wol nat be, lat it be *stille*. (italics added)

The Host is deploring either that his wife couldn't hear the legend of Patient Griselda or that she is unlike the Patient Griselda—or, as I would argue is the case, *both*. But Harry acknowledges that there is no point in fretting over what can't be changed. Here Chaucer is using the Host to remind us that Walter had preached to Griselda, "With evene herte I rede yow t'endure/The strook of Fortune or of aventure," but had failed to practice what he preached. Chaucer, then, is employing a stark-collocation rhyme to convey the following *sentence*. The Marquis should have accepted his fate, but he couldn't just let "thyng . . . be stille" because he was reluctant to subject his will to Him whose will his religion tells him comes first. Since Walter could not in the final analysis negate the will of the Father, he subjected to his own will a mother, or more precisely, a woman whom he made into a mother because it was his social duty to become a father.

Griselda is pointing to this connection between father, mother, and God the Father when after the denouement she addresses her children:

"O tendre, o deere, o yonge children myne!
Youre *woful mooder* wende stedfastly
That crueel houndes or some foul vermyne
Hadde eten yow; but *God of his mercy*
And youre benyngne fader tendrely
Hath doon yow kept"—and in that same stounde
Al sodeynly she swapte adoun to grounde.
And in hire swough so sadly holdeth she
Hire children two, whan she gan hem t'embrace,
That with greet sleighte and greet difficultee
The children from hire arm they gonne arace.
        (IV 1093-1103, italics added)

When, in a scene in which Chaucer has considerably expanded the original,[52] Griselda credits her children's miraculous survival in one breath both to God's mercy and to the "benyngne fader," the Clerk is giving us his definitive comment on the man whom throughout his tale he has presented not only as playing God with his wife but also as hubristically identifying God's will with his own.   If we take Griselda's God-and-benign-father statement at face value as we would have to do if we read the *Clerk's Tale* as an allegory in which the wife's absolute obedience to her husband is an integral part of an exemplum which preaches man's obedience to God,[53] then Griselda's statement is not only a case of hypocrisy, but, more importantly, it is downright blasphemous in its near-apotheosis of Walter the Benign.   I read these lines in a manner similar to that in which I interpreted Griselda's statements in the "open audience" spectacle: Griselda is sarcastically cutting Walter down to size and putting him in his place.

I disagree with the interpretation which Salter has offered for the application of the term "benyngne" to Walter: "The term is clearly intended to display all the positive Christian associations it has collected over the poem: it is a verbal climax."[54] And Salter proceeds to interpret Griselda's phrase as a "joyful acclamation of [Walter's] loving provision for her and the children."[55] To me, both Chaucer's and Griselda's application of the term "benyngne" to Walter is a *satirical* climax.[56] In imitation of the often-asked question, quoted earlier, concerning the Prioress, "Love of *what*—dogs?", I will ask, "*What* loving provision did Walter accord to the woman whom he has not only tortured but also deprived of the prime years of her life, and *what* loving provision for the children?"

I deliberately echoed a question asked about the Prioress' putative loving nature because I interpret the "merveillous" behavior of both Walter and the Prioress as the results of their having been forced to act against their own desire by the patriarchal system.   In Walter's case the "merveillous" behavior manifests itself in gruesome actions, in the Prioress' case in the account of a gruesome abreactive tale.   I can now redirect that question from an unequivocally presented victim, from a female member of the clergy, to a male who, while he likewise is a victim, is also an active representative of the oppression practiced by that system. Or more precisely, Chaucer has the female victim Griselda in lieu of the reader direct that question at her male oppressor when the poet has the woman establish a sarcastically parodic equivalence between her children's ''benyngne'' father and the merciful Heavenly Father.

The equivalence is sarcastically parodic in the sense that from the perspective of the mother a merciful God has not merely kept the children alive but, since she had presumed them to be dead, actually (pro-)created them. Thus, at the point of her reunion with the children Griselda, instead of re-begetting the children with her husband, begets them in a kind of cosmic union with the Heavenly Father which another victim of the patriarchal system, the Prioress, fantasizes about. Whether or not Chaucer's characterization of the Prioress as desiring to be *plena gratia Dei* palimpsestically allows us to interpret that, because of the unexpected reacquisition of her children thanks to a merciful Heavenly Father, Griselda indeed is in one sense *plena gratia Dei*, Chaucer is introducing the following idea. When Griselda credits the truly ''benyngne fader'' with the existence of her children, she is repeating, and repeating for good since she is now past the age of childbearing, the psychological castration which she had inflicted on the Marquis in his ''open audience.'' But let us take another look at the divorce spectacle.

It is precisely because of Walter's intention to reunite the family that he divorces Griselda in that ugly ''open audience.'' There is the irony that what causes Walter in the first place to stage the divorce spectacle in which he will be psychologically castrated is that he feels ''im-potent'' in the sense of ''power-less.'' The Marquis realizes that he has his back against the wall because his subjects believe he has murdered his children and therefore have come to hate their monarch:

> To been a mordrere is an hateful name;
> But natheless, *for ernest ne for game,*
> He of his crueel purpos nolde stente;
> *To tempte his wyf was set al his entente.* (IV 732-35, italics added)

In the portions I italicized, Chaucer is using two of his characters, the teller of a tale and a character within that tale, for a dazzling example of what it means both to make earnest of game and to make game of earnest. While "for ernest ne for game" on the surface simply means something to the effect of "not for any consideration" or "not under any circumstances," Chaucer here is using that common phrasing—he had used "in ernest nor in game" in line 609—for a special purpose. He is trying to communicate to us the Clerk's ironic stance within the tale the Clerk is telling. The Clerk is letting us know that Walter's "entente" can no longer be, as it supposedly had been, "To tempte his wyf": instead, Walter is "ernest," i.e., dead serious, in staging a "public audience" *game* which will eventually show his subjects that he is not the murderer they believe him to be. In other words, Chaucer is telling us that the Clerk knows, and that the Clerk knows that Walter himself knows, that the Marquis' "game is up," as it were.

What makes Walter's divorce game so despicable is not only that the Marquis uses it in an attempt to humiliate his lower-class wife, but even more so that he tries to humiliate her in order to compensate for his feeling of "impotence" vis-à-vis his subjects. In a sense, Walter's reaction is the same as it had been when his subjects twisted his arm and subjected him to the "servage" of marriage: Walter is taking his feelings of impotence out on his wife. While the Marquis is staging as earnest something that he hopes his subjects, as well as his family, will later perceive and appreciate as a game, he deludes himself, although he does not delude the Clerk or the reader, by trying to make a game of the serious issue of his state of impotency.

In talking about Walter being in a state of impotency, I have not had any sexual associations in mind—not yet, that is. But reading palimpsestically in the light of the Pardoner's use of papal bulls the account of how Walter uses forged papal bulls to achieve his purpose, I cannot help suspecting that Chaucer had socio-religious satire in mind as he was writing about the forged bulls. However, in contrast to the interpretation I offered in Chapter III, namely that Chaucer was fiercely satirizing not only some of the individuals who handled the papal bulls but also the pope himself, I do not think that in Walter's dealings with the Vatican Chaucer is trying to implicate this particular pope as an individual. The text makes it clear that Walter's dealings are with the court of Rome, not with the pope:

> He to the court of Rome, in ful subtil wyse
> Enformed of his wyl, sente his message,
> *Comandynge hem* swich bulles to devise . . . (737-39, italics added)

The *hem* indicates that several members of the court of Rome are involved in Walter's machinations. Whether or not the use of the plural, which is syntactically confusing because the referent seems to be "the court of Rome," is intended to suggest that the institution of the papacy is subject to "commanding" corruption, the point, as I argued earlier, is that Walter is trying to impose his own will on the pope. But then, what does it mean that a man who feels impotent alias "powerless" tries to impose his own will on a man who is much more powerful than himself—a man who, as the *pater orbis terrarum*, is the earthly representative of the Heavenly Father?

This is an oedipal power struggle, and it is oedipal also in a specifically sexual sense. While the Marquis as son strictly speaking is not trying to take the wife away from the father, he is trying to marry a woman against the father's wishes in the sense that he steals the father's permission for the divorce and the remarriage—not to mention the fact that the woman he will announce as his bride is his own daughter. But then, since the announced divorce-and-remarriage is merely a game on Walter's part, we can say that the son is playing a sick game with his father, a *merveillous game* in which a lower patriarch steals the power from the much higher patriarch, the highest patriarch in Chaucer's *Weltanschauung*. And the Marquis plays this game in order to regain what I will call patriarchal potency.

Whether or not the notion of Walter trying to regain patriarchal potency by stealing the power from the pope already carries sexual associations, it will do so after we reexamine Walter's arrogation of papal bulls in the light of Chaucer's characterization of the Pardoner. As Dinshaw, whom I quoted in my third chapter, notes, the Pardoner "emphatically declares that these [papal] bulls validate his body, make it legitimate and unquestionable. Exhibitionistically he brags: 'my bulles shewe I, alle, and some./Oure lige lordes seel on my patente,/That shewe I first my body to warente'." I earlier added to Dinshaw's line of argument that, the moment Chaucer correlates the Pardoner's nonexistent *coillons* to the fake relics with which the Pardoner tries to cheat people out of their money, the poet is retroactively implying that there is something phony also about the bulls which the Pardoner uses to declare the validity of his body. I then observed that by my addition to Dinshaw's argument I didn't mean that Chaucer is implying that the pardons are *not* "comen from Rome al hoot," but that, on the contrary, there is no reason to doubt the veracity of the Pardoner's statement about "Oure lige lordes seel." I will now add that the Pardoner makes something phony out of the authentic papal bulls, not only by abusing them in the sense that he doesn't care whether his pardons will save anybody's soul, but also by putting them to his personal use as substitutes for his nonexistent testicles. And I wish to argue that in his characterization of Walter Chaucer is presenting a scenario which is obliquely analogous to the scenario in which the Pardoner uses the papal bulls, and that this analogy can help us with our understanding of Chaucer's portrayal of the Marquis.

It is interesting to note that, while Walter of course is no eunuch, he uses papal bulls in his attempt to re-beget the children who are believed to be dead, believed to be as nonexistent as the Pardoner's *coillons*. Doesn't this interrelation between Chaucer's portrayals of the Marquis and the Pardoner introduce the idea that Walter tries to use the papal bulls much in the manner in which the Pardoner does, i.e., that Walter has them perform the functions of the testicles? Such an association is all the more warranted if we take into account that, whereas the Pardoner substitutes his phony *coillons* with genuine papal bulls, Walter uses phony papal bulls in his effort to re-sire his children. In fact, doesn't the connection between the use of phony papal bulls and the abuse of genuine ones seem to place the Marquis morally in the vicinity of the Pardoner? At any rate, I would argue that Chaucer is presenting the Marquis as a spiritual eunuch—even before Griselda psychologically castrates him in the "open audience." Actually, Walter's act of cheating the pope makes Walter even more deserving of the second psychological castration which Griselda subsequently inflicts on him.

On the other hand, we have to remember that in his "merveillous" treatment of his wife the Marquis avenges himself on a patriarchal system which "sowded" him into marriage: Walter is a husband with a vengeance. Here we have another parallel between Walter's and the Pardoner's respective situations: like the Pardoner who feels God has short-changed him by sending him into this world as a eunuch, and who therefore is what I will now call an ecclesiastic with a vengeance, the Marquis too feels cheated by life, perhaps even cheated by God himself. Walter therefore decides to quite literally cheat, if not the Heavenly Father Himself, then at least God's representative on earth. And when nothing would make Walter desist from his cruel plan, "for ernest ne for game," he is playing a game not only with his wife, but also with the pope. Perhaps Walter feels the pope *deserves* to be played with in such a manner, since the pope after all heads the system which has Walter "bounden to a stake." When Walter arrogates the pope's permission for his divorce and remarriage, perhaps he is trying to beat the pope at his own game of arbitrarily granting divorces, of granting dispensations just "as hym leste."

Let me offer another possibility for interpreting the context about Walter's treatment of the pope. When Chaucer first tells us about Walter cheating the pope unimpugned but then refrains from telling us how that awkward political situation is eventually resolved, couldn't the poet himself be telling us that he actually condones Walter's game with the pope while he disapproves of the games with his wife? Chaucer uses his portrayal of the Pardoner to satirically attack the Church's practice of selling forgiveness of sin, a practice in which the pope plays a game with the lives of people which is no less reckless than the games which Walter plays with his wife and his children. Therefore, do we believe that Chaucer would approve of a practice in which the pope can grant divorces to those husbands who are capable of contributing to the coffers of the Church—and thus is able to treat as fair game the lives of defenseless wives?

I would argue that Chaucer is combining his anti-male-supremacist satire in the *Clerk's Tale* and his portrayal of the Pardoner as an extension of the pope into a fierce attack on a "benyngne fader" of sorts. I earlier discussed how Griselda refers to the Marquis as "benyngne fader" in order to sarcastically cut Walter down to size. The poet himself extends that sarcastic application to the head of the patriarchal system in which Griselda has become a defenseless wife: in what I have called the *Clerk's Tale's* satirical climax, Chaucer ironically presents the pope who plays cruel games with helpless wives as a benign father. And since on the one hand I have placed Griselda's act of cutting Walter down to size in the vicinity of what she had done to Walter in the "open audience" spectacle, and since on the other hand I have posited an analogy between the Marquis and the pope, I am now ready to suggest that Chaucer is poetically doing to the pope what Griselda does to Walter. That is, if we believe in the magical punishing power of satire, Chaucer punishes the "benyngne fader" alias generously divorce-granting pope by poetically reducing him to the physical status of the Pardoner.

Chaucer is matching *solaas* with *sentence* when he parodically plays two not so benign fathers off against the truly "benyngne fader," against the merciful God with whom Griselda re-begets the children at the point of their reunion. Yet the Clerk's adaptation of the story of Patient Griselda has to end with a putdown for the game-playing husband. Not only does Griselda, who after the kidnapping and presumed murder of her daughter would have been ethically justified in making Walter sleep on the couch yet had sworn not to *grucche*, repeat the psychological castration which she had inflicted on Walter during his divorce spectacle, but she is also doing something else to her husband. In her "youre benyngne fader" speech Griselda is putting Walter in the category of the "crueel houndes" which she believed had devoured her children.

In her mention of "crueel houndes" Griselda is referring to the hunting dogs Walter used to be surrounded by when he was first stalking after her, but she is also referring to this hunter as having stalked after her children. Chaucer is conveying this idea when, as she faints for the second time, he describes her as pulling the children to the ground as if to protect them from the hunter and his dogs.[57] Thus even the happy ending of the *Clerk's Tale* is an integral part of Chaucer's feminist *Schwank*, not only because Griselda instinctively wishes to protect her children from Walter, but also because they presumably had experienced a healthy childhood—since they were away from their patriarch father, growing up with his sister instead.[58] The stage is set for the more openly comical pronouncements of the anti-male-supremacist Envoy.

CHAPTER V

Comedy versus Satire:
The Merchant, the Parson, and Other
Games with Augustinian Theology

In the preceding chapter, I dealt with Chaucerian feminist jokes mainly in the *Clerk's Tale*. However, while I began and concluded the chapter with an examination of the Clerk's adaptation of the story of Patient Griselda, I unearthed anti-male-supremacist jokes in other parts of the *Canterbury Tales*, especially as they address the Church's patriarchal system in general and the practice of popes playing *games* with women by "benignly" granting divorces to husbands who are benign toward the coffers of the Church. The Clerk's presentation causes the Host to make his husbandly presence felt by putting in a brief and relatively moderate lament about his own marriage, which in turn elicits from the Merchant a lengthy and vehement diatribe about his marriage that enables the master of ceremonies to call on the Merchant to tell a story. Let me then continue my combination of sexual and religious interpretations of the *Canterbury Tales* with an examination of the *Merchant's Tale*.

About halfway through the *Merchant's Tale*, the teller makes the following comments about January's lovemaking:

> But lest that precious folk be with me wrooth,
> How that he *wroghte*, I dar nat to yow telle,
> *Or wheither hire thoughte it paradys or helle.*

But heere I lete hem *werken* in hir wyse
Tyl evensong rong, and that they moste aryse.
    (IV 1962-66, italics added)

Ross has suggested that the phrases *wroghte* and *werken* are more than just the
rhetorical figure of *occupatio*, i.e., the "feigned inability to describe something," and Ross has noted that the reader savors the suggestion of effort
elicited by the *werken*.[1] I have already gone beyond what is for Ross merely
an item of *solaas* by discussing how Chaucer elaborates the suggestion of
effort in the consummation scene where January "laboureth . . . til that the
day gan dawe," in a scene where Chaucer is alluding to St. Augustine's theory
that after Original Sin the sex act became a typical postlapsarian activity which
had to be carried out in the sweat of man's brow.

    Yet why would Chaucer want to describe the lovemaking of the *senex*
amans in the terms of Augustinian sexual theology? A key to the answer lies
in the Merchant's tongue-in-cheek remark, "Or wheither hire thoughte it
paradys or helle": obviously May does not consider her marital sex life
"paradys," but what is more important is that the word *paradys* sends us back
to January's definition of marriage as a paradise in this world:

    "Noon oother lyf," seyde he, "is worth a bene,
    For wedlok is so esy and so clene,
    That in this world it is a paradys."
    That seyde this olde knyght, that was so wys. (1263-66, italics added)

When Chaucer presents January's marital sex life as a postlapsarian activity in
accordance with St. Augustine's sexual theology, he is poetically punishing the
"olde knyght, that was so wys," for his definition of marriage as a wordly
paradise: Chaucer is making the substance of January's marriage the exact
opposite of January's definition.

    Yet why would Chaucer want to punish January for his definition of
marriage? After all, as Richard Neuse elaborates in his article on "Marriage
and the Question of Allegory in the *Merchant's Tale*,"[2] the idea of marriage

as a paradise was widely spread in Middle English poetry. Neuse notes that "January himself is in no doubt that marriage is an altogether holy institution."[3] In fact, I wish to argue that January's problem lies precisely in the fact that he knows that marriage is a holy institution, for January is abusing that institution. That January is abusing the sacrament of marriage becomes clear from the manner in which he announces his plan to get married:

> Freendes, I am hoor and oold,
> And almoost, *God woot*, on my pittes brynke;
> *Upon my soule somwhat must I thynke.*
> I have my body folily despended;
> Blessed be God that it shal been amended!
> For I wol be, certeyn, a wedded man,
> And that anon in al the haste I kan,
> Unto som mayde fair and of tendre age . . .
> (1400-1407, italics added)

The irony here is the fact that January, whom the Merchant sarcastically refers to as "this olde knyght, that was so wys," is trying to outwit God by having his lifelong lechery, almost *post mortem*, sanctioned by the holy institution of marriage. The Merchant had been talking tongue-in-cheek when in a parenthetical statement he commented on January's intention to get married, "Were it for hoolynesse or for dotage/I kan nat seye" (1253-54): of course January is marrying "for dotage," but he is cloaking his lust in the "hoolynesse" of the institution. And when January first admits that he has wasted his body on lechery but then, since he "somwhat must" think about his soul, turns to God for a quick fix, God *knows*—"God woot"—that January is seeking an easy way out.[4]

The reason Chaucer metes out to January the Augustinian punishment of sexual intercourse as labor, then, is that January creates for himself "in this world . . . a paradys" in an attempt to save his soul so that he would be able to go to Heaven—i.e., January enters into the paradise of marriage out of wrong motives,[5] although two of his stated reasons for getting married seem legitimate enough: to pay the marital debt and thus honor God above by con-

tributing to the flock of His children. But then, there is the irony that January
links the two concerns about the marital debt and about the flock of God's
children to the Apostle's pronouncement that it is better to marry than to burn:

> I dote nat, I woot the cause why
> Men sholde wedde, and forthermore woot I
> Ther speketh many a man of mariage,
> That woot namoore of it than woot my page
> For whiche causes man sholde take a wyf.
> *If he ne may nat lyven chaast his lyf,*
> *Take hym a wyf with greet devocioun,*
> By cause of leveful procreacioun
> Of children to th'onour of God above,
> And not oonly for paramour or love;
> *And for they sholde leccherye eschue,*
> *And yelde hir dette whan that it is due* . . . (1441-52, italics added)

January is protesting too much when he at great length explains that he will
eschew lechery, and Chaucer highlights the Lombard knight's insincerity in his
undertaking through the *eschue/due* rhyme: January rationalizes that whenever
he is unable to eschew lechery it is because he has to fulfill his marital debt.
And for trying to present his lechery as fulfillment of marital debt, January is
poetically punished when Chaucer makes it clear that January is delinquent in
his payments.

The poet is conveying the idea of January's delinquency already before
the Merchant's "Or wheither hire thoughte it paradys or helle," namely in his
description of of the wedding night:

> Thus laboureth he til that the day gan dawe;
> And than he taketh a sop in fyn clarree,
> And upright in his bed thanne sitteth he,
> And after that he sang ful loude and cleere,
> And kiste his wyf, and made wantown cheere.
> He was al coltissh, ful of ragerye,
> And ful of jargon as a flekked pye.
> The slakke skyn about his nekke shaketh
> Whil that he sang, so chaunteth he and craketh.
> But God woot what that May thoughte in hir herte,
> Whan she hym saugh up sittynge in his sherte,
> In his nyght-cappe, and with his nekke lene;
> *She preyseth nat his playing worth a bene.* (1842-54, italics added)

As I discussed earlier, Chaucer is presenting January here as a typical postlapsarian sex partner who has to labor to reach orgasm. I will now add that January is celebrating the success of his labor: he is happy that he has finally achieved his *descensus*.

That January's postcoital celebration includes singing is a device which Chaucer uses to refer us to the opening lines of the General Prologue, where the mating birds had been singing: this croaking magpie with his slack skin shaking around his neck is placed in pointed contrast to the melody-making amorous birds in the General Prologue. May is of course disgusted by January's antics. However, when the narrator says that "She preyseth nat his pleyyng worth a bene," the *playing* refers less to January's postcoital singing than to his sexual performance, which a few lines earlier had been described, ironically by January himself, as playing: "For we han leve to *pleye* us by the lawe" (1841). In other words, although January supposedly had played "by the lawe," i.e., in the "hoolynesse" of the institution of marriage, he had been unable to pay his wife the debt of sexual gratification.

It should be noted that after the celebration of his *descensus* January goes to sleep:

> Thanne seide he thus, "My reste wol I take;
> Now day is come, I may no lenger wake."
> And doun he leyde his heed, and sleep til pryme. (1855-57)

Chaucer here is for the purpose of contrast alluding to St. Augustine's characterization of the prelapsarian sex act:

> Atque inter se coniugum fida ex honesto amore societas . . . et mandati sine labore custodia. Non lassitudo fatigabat otiosum, non somnus premebat invitum.

> Between husband and wife there was a loyal partnership springing from honest love; there was . . . an effortless observance of God's command [of reproduction]. No one suffered weariness in his leisure, no one was overcome with sleep against his will. (*City of God*, XIV, 26)

Chaucer is alluding to this Augustinian passage in order to point to the following aspect of his presentation of January's lovemaking as typically post-lapsarian: the January who is unable to stay awake after the celebration of his orgasm is a victim of the phenomenon of postcoital depression, a phenomenon which had not existed before the Fall. More specifically, Chaucer presents January as succumbing to postcoital depression in his wordly paradise in order to further highlight the nature of January's marriage: his marriage is anything but a *fida ex honesta amore societas*, anything but what before his laboring he had assured his wife was "trewe wedlok" (1836). January's "trewe wedlok," then, is not "worth a bene." It is in yet another sense that January's love-making is worthless. When May "preyseth nat his pleyyng worth a bene," her assessment ironically is correct in a sense she is not yet aware of: Chaucer is using the word *bene* also in its literal botanical sense. The symbolism in a poem which describes the mismatch of January, the Old Man Winter,[6] with May as well as the interaction between the ritual aspects of the *Merchant's Tale* and the opening lines of the General Prologue, which set the stage for a springtime ritual[7] by describing how the spring rain impregnates the winter earth, tells us that January fails to do to May what April does to March. January, then, fails not only as a marital debtor but also in his announced plan to honor God, in the "*leveful* procreacioun/Of children to th'onour of God above" (italics added). Since January married out of wrong motives, he was bending the truth when he said to May that they were playing "by the lawe" —and his inability to impregnate May is presented as part of his punishment for abusing the holy institution of marriage.[8]

This type of punishment is important not only for the tale's *sentence*, i.e., for the exposure of January's marriage as "hoolynesse"-cloaked lechery, but also for the tale's *solaas*. Whereas in the terms of medieval theology January is guilty of the fourth category of marital intercourse and thus guilty of a mortal sin, there is the irony that despite his lechery he does not even qualify for that category which is automatically free of sin.   As Malcolm

Andrew has put it,

> The possible motives for married people engaging in coitus are tradi-
> tionally divided into four categories: (1) the procreation of offspring;
> (2) the yielding of the marriage debt; (3) avoiding incontinence (i.e.,
> using marital intercourse to obviate the risk of adultery); and (4) the
> pursuit of pleasure . . . This formulation is specified by the Parson in
> his tale (X [I] 938-942).   Of these four motives, *the first is always
> regarded as free from sin* . . . indeed, in the writings of the earlier
> Church Fathers, the intention of married people to procreate is often
> bluntly specified *as the only legitimate reason for engaging in inter-
> course.*[9] (italics added)

Chaucer uses the *Parson's Tale* to make it clear that January does not even

qualify for the category which would automatically make his lovemaking free

of sin. January is losing his eligibility for the first category when, even before

he can begin the pursuit of what he had earlier termed ''leveful procreacioun/

Of children to th'onour of God above,'' January, as Joseph Mogan has pointed

out, declares that he intends to procreate ''solely to get an heir to save his

possessions (1272; 1437-40) . . . [instead] of having offspring to raise them

religiously in order to honor God.''[10] While I agree with Mogan's purpose-of-

offspring argument, I would like to add that January's economic considerations

might reflect the concerns of the General Prologue's presumably wisely-invest-

ing Merchant himself—concerns which we will see are thematically significant.

When Chaucer first says in the General Prologue about the shrewd

Merchant,

> This worthy man ful his wit bisette:
> Ther wiste no wight that *he was in dette,* (I 279-80, italics added)

and then has the newly-wed Merchant tell a story about a newly-wed rich

aristocrat, i.e., a about a man who possesses inherited wealth rather than

wealth acquired through clever money-management, a story about a newly-wed

who is unable to pay his marital debt, couldn't Chaucer be palimpsestically

trying to tell us something about the Merchant? That is, couldn't Chaucer be insinuating that the teller of the *Merchant's Tale* may be delinquent in paying his own marital debt? My answer is "yes." I will elaborate my answer later in this chapter; suffice it for now to say that the Merchant has January give priority to passing on his material possessions to his hoped-for heir, in Mogan's words, "[over] having offspring to raise them religiously in order to honor God": obviously, I will have to confront the perennial question of to what extent we may identify the Merchant with the knight January—and I hope I will be able to resolve what Donald R. Benson has called "a Chaucerian crux."[11] At this point in my chapter, I am more concerned with Chaucer's characterization of January.

I have already stated that because of his "hoolynesse"-endowed lechery January is guilty of a mortal sin. When right in the middle of the Augustinian "labor" context of the consummation January tries to reassure May that, no matter how long it takes this *werkman* to complete his job,

> in oure actes we mowe do no synne.
> A man may do no synne *with his wyf,*
> *Ne hurte hymselven with his owene knyf,*
> For we han leve to pleye us by the lawe, (1839-41, italics added)

Chaucer is setting January up to be judged by the Parson's pronouncement that marital concupiscence, i.e., the fourth category in the motives for intercourse, is a mortal sin:

> And for that many man weneth that he may nat synne for no likerous-nesse that he dooth with his wyf, certes, that opinion is fals. *God woot,* a man may sleen hymself with his owene knyf, and make hym-selve dronken of his owene tonne. (X 858, italics added)

As Andrew notes, the "Parson's statement serves as an authoritative Christian moral judgment on January's willfully erroneous view."[12] I have been elaborating on January's willfully erroneous view of marriage, but here I would like to add what Ross, almost a decade prior to Andrew's study, had said about Chaucer's use of the proverb concerning a husband's knife:

> consider the "Merchant's Tale" (E 1840) where January tells his young
> wife on their wedding night that a man [can] do no sin with his wife
> "ne hurte hymselven with his owene knyf." January perhaps means his
> own penis. He is obsessed with it and the sex act generally, *though his
> performance is pitiful* . . . The Parson (I 858) shows how the connec-
> tion between intercourse and knife was made. The good padre uses
> homely language to drive his point home . . . (knife=penis,
> tun=scrotum?).[13] (italics added)

I have provided a reason for Chaucer's presentation of January's performance
as pitiful: the lecher's willfully erroneous view of marriage. January is quite
literally "slaying" himself with his own penis because he gets married for the
sake of his "knyf."[14] His marriage is the result of his hormones: I indeed
read Chaucer's use of the word *tonne* in the meaning which Ross has offered
only tentatively. In fact, I would argue that it is precisely because January
marries in compliance with the urges of his scrotum that his "tonne" lets him
down, or—to express it in the terms of St. Augustine's sexual theology—
January's own servant becomes insubordinate. Owing to that servant's insub-
ordination, January performs pitifully, not only as a marital debtor but also in
his grandiosely announced intention to add to the honor of God above: his
descensus is not "worth a bene."

Chaucer is also poetically punishing January for the phallic bragging he
had engaged in when, immediately following his announcement that he would
avoid lechery, enter into the marital-debt relationship, and procreate for the
honor of God above, he thanked God for having preserved his sexual virility:

> God be thanked!—I dar make avaunt
> I feele my lymes stark and suffisaunt
> To do al that a man bilongeth to;
> I woot myselven best what I may do.
> Though I be hoor, I fare as dooth a tree
> That blosmeth er that fruyt ywoxen bee;
> And blosmy tree nys neither drye ne deed.
> I feele me nowhere hoor but on my heed;
> Myn herte and alle my lymes been as grene
> As laurer thurgh the yeere is for to sene.   (1457-66)

January's speech is a display not only of phallic bragging but, actually, of phallic *pride*. Whereas a little earlier he had admitted, "I am hoor and oold,/ And almoost, *God woot*, on my pittes brynke" (italics added), he now is singing a different tune: "*I woot myselven best* what I may do" (italics added). While January had earlier decided to get on God's good side by legalizing his lechery, he here snubs God by claiming that he himself knows best his sexual capabilities. Chaucer may or may not have intended an interaction with the preceding and, as far as the Host is concerned, response-demanding *Clerk's Tale*. However, January's claim is comparable to and affects us in the same manner as Walter's announcement that he would let God govern his marriage just "as hym leste": each man is trying to impose his will upon God.

But then, January also snubs God by claiming to know all about the wordly paradise of marriage—just as another *senex amans*, the carpenter John, had insulted God by proudly claiming that he was a better Christian than *queynte Nicholas* because he knew, and knew *only*, the teachings of his religion. When January claims that he knows all he needs to know for a successful marriage, Chaucer is establishing a connection between John's religious pride and January's phallic pride, thereby underscoring the idea that January's phallic pride is a *religious* pride—and in analogy to the question I asked in discussing the *Miller's Tale*, "How well has John known his wife?", I will now ask: "How well will January 'get to know' his wife?" As in the case of the carpenter guilty of pride, it is poetic justice that the man who compares himself to a blossoming tree will learn, if only for the duration of a few moments, from a tree what his worldly paradise is all about. Significantly, the tree from which he learns the truth about his worldly paradise is a forbidden tree of sorts: January's comparison of himself to a tree is the main point where the *Merchant's Tale*'s season-ritual aspects and Chaucer's comic use of Genesis 1-3 intersect. The pear-tree scene is the culmination of Chaucer's satire on the *senex amans* in that tale.

In fact, I wish to argue that the pear-tree scene is satire in its original ritual-form. As Robert Elliott has elaborated in *The Power of Satire: Magic, Ritual, Art*, satire had developed out of phallic springtime ritual, where the participants would carry a phallic effigy. This phallic effigy later became the Maypole. The entire ceremony was magical; "its purpose was to stimulate fertility, the sacred energy of life."[15] The pear-tree scene is such a phallic ritual. The ritual as described by Chaucer combines the tradition of the Phallic Maypole with that of Priapus, who is mentioned as a tutelary deity of gardens (2034-35). As Ross notes, Priapus is "particularly appropriate to *this* garden, since he is always portrayed with an immense phallus, no doubt as an encouragement to the fertility of the flora . . . There is at least a flourishing pear tree in the garden, strong enough to bear the 'struggling' bodies of two adults, but the presence of the god encourages not horticulture but copulation."[16]

The pear-tree scene, then, is a phallic ritual or, more precisely, a phallic mock-ritual. For although old January certainly is in need of sexual rejuvenation, he unknowingly uses the pear tree for a different purpose: to recover his eyesight. Yet he attains this different kind of rejuvenation in the form of the ancient phallic ritual: he has his arms around the trunk of the pear tree in the fashion in which the phallic effigy was carried in fertility processions. Ross identifies the pear tree as a commonplace symbol for the penis but then goes on: "It is not completely clear how this works in the 'Merchant's Tale' (E 2217) where Damian sits 'upon the pyrie', but like the tree his penis is erect and ready. May expresses an uncontrollable desire for the 'peres' (E 23-33)—testicles?—climbs the tree, and soon is in Damian's arms."[17] I would argue that Elliott's account of the origin of satire makes clear *how* the pear-tree symbolism works. In fact, Damian is an integral part of Chaucer's presentation of the pear-tree scene as satire in its ritual-form, since Damian is the namesake of both a patron saint of healers and a patron saint of generative power who was worshipped with phallic effigies.[18] Holding his arms around the tree/phallus-effigy/Damian, and in effect unknowingly worshipping Damian as well as St. Damianus, January becomes the participant in an ancient ritual where the performance of the sexual union was part of the fertility rites.[19] Only, January is not a participant in that union. Instead, helping May climb the Phallic Maypole in his own springtime paradise,[20] January serves her as a ladder to the forbidden fruit of adultery.[21] In a fertility ritual, or rather a mock-fertility ritual for January himself, Chaucer satirizes and poetically punishes the knight for his abuse of the sacrament of marriage.

The branches that seem to spring from January's head like horns are the branches in which he is being cuckolded or 'put the horns upon';[22] in fact, the branches *are* January's horns in that he is cuckolded not only *in* the branches but also by that which the branches symbolize, i.e., by Damian's phallus plus "peres grene." This situation lends a bitter irony to January's earlier contention:

> I feele me nowhere hoor but on myn heed;
> Myn herte and alle my lymes been as grene
> As laurer *thurgh the yeere is for to sene.* (italics added)

It is January's hoary head that during his performance in the phallic ritual undergoes a springtime rejuvenation and turns green. This symbolic change comes to January as unexpectedly as does his actual physical rejuvenation when he regains his eyesight. Yet he becomes able to see again at the very moment he is being cuckolded in the pear tree. Part of Chaucer's irony here is that in his passage of satire in its original ritual-form he is employing Damian simultaneously in the latter's symbolic roles as phallic agent and as healer. At the moment January says that all his "lymes been as grene/As laurer thurgh the yeere is for to sene," Chaucer is setting him up for the physical blindness that will render him unable to visually follow the evergreen status of some of the plant growth in his garden. Yet wouldn't it be even more ironic if Damian, the namesake of the Phallic Healer, endowed the foolish knight also with a vision that eventually will pay attention to a different kind of growth? Suffice it for now to say that for January the archetypal Phallic Tree of Life, the pear-tree in his paradise, has for him become a tree of knowledge.

Chaucer is playing the two Biblical notions of the Tree of Knowledge and the Tree of Life against each other. Having eaten from the Tree of Knowledge, Adam and Eve were evicted from Paradise lest they also eat from the Tree of Life and regain the immortality they had lost by eating from the Tree of Knowledge. The chronological order is inverted in the *Merchant's Tale*, where the wordly paradise does not have a tree of life but where Pluto, the pagan *deus ex machina*, freely grants January access to a tree of knowledge. But the knowledge which the mock-Adam January gains from the pear tree is only temporary, as with the help of Proserpina, the pagan *dea ex machina*, the mock-Eve May persuades January not to believe what he actually knows. Always deceiving himself, January rejects the information he had gained from the mock Tree of Knowledge.

When Chaucer combines the folkoric motif of the Phallic Ritual with the Biblical Tree of Knowledge motif, he also is giving a new twist to the Biblical concept of temptation. Whereas in Genesis Eve is seduced by the Serpent, in the *Merchant's Tale* January's Eve is seduced by a young man. Chaucer has replaced the Serpent with what the serpent symbolizes, namely the phallus or, in the terms of our plot, with an amorous man who has his phallus erect: that amorous man, in turn, has a name which in itself carries a phallic symbolism—so that one could argue that Chaucer is conflating two phallic symbols into one and thus endowing May's partner in the adulterous act with enormous generative power. In fact, it should be noted that Chaucer

is explicitly comparing Damian to a serpent when he has the Merchant comment:

> O perilous fyr, that in the bedstraw bredeth!
> O famulier foo, that his servyce bedeth!
> O servant traytour, false hoomly hewe,
> Lyk to the naddre in bosom sly untrewe,
> God shilde us alle from youre aqueyntaunce! (1783-87)

Some of the sexual undertones of these lines, which follow the description of Damian's desperate amorousness, are obvious, e.g., the bed metaphor.
Yet these lines are ambiguous; they present Damian as offering his "servyce,"
which does not exclusively refer to Damian's master January but also to May.
Ross, who discusses in detail the sexual connotations of "servyce" and
"serve," interprets the word "foo" to mean the penis which is offering its
service (in a passage where "bedeth" seems to be a pun on "bed").[23] Yet
what is even more important for Chaucer's use of Biblical notions is the identity between the phallic serpent and the Satanic Foe in combination with the
warning, "God shilde us alle from youre aqueyntaunce." We already know
from our discussion of the *Miller's Tale* the sexual meaning of "aqueyntaunce." Chaucer is playing the idea of Damian's becoming "acquainted"
with and gaining "knowledge" of May's *queynte* against the warning about the
Tree of Knowledge. January is warned against the serpent Damian, but he is
also warned against the pear tree both as the place where he will be cuckolded
and as the tree of embarrassing knowledge—the knowledge that his wife has
come to know the forbidden fruit of adultery with the serpent Damian.

When before the pear-tree episode Pluto announces that he will restore
January's eyesight at the moment of May's adulterous act, Proserpina proclaims her countermeasures:

> I shal yeven hire suffisant answere,
> And alle wommen after, for hir sake . . .
> For lak of answere noon of hem shall dyen. (2266-71)

With May being Eve's analogue, Proserpina's words are parodically analogous to the prophecy God gave to Adam and Eve when He evicted them from Paradise. Whereas on account of their ancestors Adam's and Eve's descendants will be mortal, the future Mays at least will not have to die for lack of an answer: they will survive "for hir sake." Whereas Adam will have to work in the sweat of his brow and Eve will have to bear children in pain, the relationship between the future Mays and their men will be one where the man has to live with the constant fear that his wife will cuckold him before his own eyes and then bold-facedly deny everything. According to Genesis, one of the consequences of Original Sin is that man will rule over woman. In the *Merchant's Tale* we learn the opposite: woman will be permitted not only to enjoy the forbidden fruit of adultery, but also to wind man around her finger.

Chaucer, then, is not merely treating us to a parodic inversion of the Genesis account of Original Sin where an aged Adam is cuckolded by Damian, who is compared both to Satan and to a serpent: January had committed that which is parodically analogous to Original Sin *before* the "naddre" Damian seduces May. January is an Adam who falls before Eve does, i.e., before the Satanic Damian enters his "paradys." To January the tree of knowledge in his wordly Eden will mean nothing because he has already fallen, fallen to the point where he rejects the knowledge which could actually purge him of his 'Original Sin' in that it would purge him of his willfully erroneous ideas about marriage: Justinus had sarcastically suggested that January's marriage might prove to be his "purgatorie" (1620), and he might shoot straight up to Heaven, when January voiced his fear that having Heaven on earth in the form of his marriage might perhaps spoil his chances of going to Heaven. Rejecting what he learns from the terrestrial tree of knowledge, January rejects the benefits of Purgatory which God has set up to cleanse souls in preparation for their eventual ascent to Heaven.

In addition to reversing the chronology of the Genesis account, Chaucer parodically inverts the distribution of punishments: while Eve will have to labor in childbirth, January after his 'Fall' has to labor in the consummation of the reproductive act. As I have discussed, January is punished in the very manner in which according to St. Augustine man was punished for Original Sin. The Saint hypothesizes that had it not been for Original Sin the act of generation would be performed without any effort, *sine labore*, because the reproductive organs would be subject to man's will and therefore function perfectly:

> In tanta facilitate rerum et felicitate hominum, absit ut suspicemur non potuisse prolem seri sine libidinis morbo; sed voluntatis nutu moverentur membra illa quo cetera . . .

> In such facility of living and such felicity of mankind, far be it from us to suspect that it was impossible for the seed of offspring to be sown without the infection of lust; rather the sexual organs could have been set in motion by the same authority of the will as the other bodily members . . . (*City of God*, XIV, 26)

Once we realize that January's lovemaking is presented as a typical postlapsarian act where the man has to take aphrodiasiacs "t'encreessen his corage," as an act where the Biblical punishment of woman's labor in childbirth has been parodically replaced with the punishment of *impregnation* as labor, we are confronted with the question of whether May is really pregnant when she says a woman in her state must die if she cannot eat of the small green pears (2328-37)—a question which I have already answered.

While May knows that January's efforts have not been "worth a bene," she expects to be impregnated by Damian in the pear tree. Scores of scholarly analyses have been written on the question of whether Damian succeeds. Usually the answer has been negative, e.g., in Emerson Brown's study, "*Hortus Inconclusus*: The Significance of Priapus and Pyramus and Thisbe in the *Merchant's Tale*," an analysis which is grounded on allusions to classical mythology (with *Hortus Inconclusus* itself being a punning allusion to *coitus interruptus*).[24] I would argue that Chaucer provides the answer in the text—to the extent that the consummate ironist is willing to give us an answer at all. Immediately after the Merchant's graphic description of Damian's acquainting penetration, Pluto restores January's eyesight, who

> Up to the tree . . . caste his eyen two,
> And saugh that Damyan his wyf had dressed
> In swich manere it may nat been expressed,
> But if I wolde speke uncurteisly;
> And up he yaf a roryng and a cry,
> *As dooth the moder whan the child shal dye* . . .
>   (2360-65, italics added)

What is the function of the line in which Chaucer compares January's screams to those a mother utters when the child—note "*the* child" (italics added)—is about to die? While a fabliau may not be subject to the same criteria with which we judge an epic, we are dealing here with a simile describing an event which has been caused by the intervention of something like an epic machinery, i.e., with a simile describing an event which must be of great importance. When Virgil says in the famous simile that after Dido's suicide the Carthaginians are screaming as if Carthage were falling to the enemy, he is foreshadowing Carthage's destruction which was fated to take place in the future as a result of Dido's dying curse, a simile which Chaucer alludes to in the *Man of Law's Tale*.[25] Through his own simile Chaucer is implying the impending death of a child—the child which the mother knows is doomed not to live.[26] Chaucer is using what I will call a mixed simile because the screaming parent is the father—or more precisely, the would-be father, for May has led January to believe that he has impregnated her. January has not succeeded, but she hopes that Damian will do the job for him—yet the hoped-for child, officially or at least as far as January is concerned, would be January's. Thus, when through the intervention of an epic machinery January regains his eyesight and interrupts the act of adultery before Damian's *descensus* alias ejaculation can occur, January ironically is killing not only May-the-mother's but also his own child. Moreover, not only is he killing his heir, but he is also preventing the contribution to God's honor which he had so grandiosely announced.[27]

Damian, then, is Satanic not only because he seduces May, but also because he causes May's death just as Satan had caused Eve's. For May's statement that she will die if she does not get to eat of the fruit ironically is true in a sense not intended by her, i.e., if she does not obtain the contents of what is symbolized by the small green pears, Damian's testicles.[28] She was speaking her own potential death sentence when she told the jealous January to put her in a sack and drown her should she ever be unfaithful (2197-2201). When January does catch her in the act of adultery, May persuades him with the help of Proserpina not to believe what he had seen with his own eyes, so that as far as May is concerned the *Merchant's Tale* seems to end with the Spring of Comedy absorbing the Winter of Satire. However, the season-ritual aspects of the tale suggest that there might be another Winter of Satire. Chaucer had intended to have each pilgrim tell four stories; perhaps the next time around the butt of the Merchant's satire would have been May herself. In fact, doesn't the Merchant's conclusion,

> Thus endeth heere my tale of Januarie;
> God blesse us, and his mooder Seinte Marie, (2417-18)

where the *Januarie/Seinte Marie* rhyme—a stark-collocation rhyme?—seems to place a curious emphasis on January, invite the speculation that the Merchant is already thinking of a tale about May?

To continue this line of speculation: it is possible that the Merchant is indicating that one of his later tales will focus on the dilemma of May when he concludes the story by describing January's proud joy at the thought of having made May pregnant: the old man on May's "wombe . . . stroketh hire ful softe" (2414). Since the union between May and Damian is interrupted before Damian reaches climax, January will realize that she had lied about being pregnant—and he will be able to see what Pluto had wanted him to see. May, having been unable to obtain the fruit from what would indeed have been a tree of life for her, will have to die a disgraceful death—and her caution concerning January's supposedly still dazed vision, "He that *mysconceyveth*, he mysdemeth" (2410, italics added), is a splendid piece of irony as well as a meaningful sexual pun by Chaucer. Damian likewise will die: in an inversion of Genesis, where God announces that the woman's heel will bruise the serpent's head, the serpent Damian will be put to death by the mock-Adam himself. Of course, January will not know the facts until several months hence—in the season of winter. This will be *her* Winter of Satire, and January will have his Purgatory in that he will accept the information he had gained about his marriage from the tree of knowledge.

Even if Chaucer did not intend to write a follow-up story, speculation such as in the preceding two paragraphs is invited by the open-ended conclusion of the *Merchant's Tale* and suggested by the season-ritual aspects that govern the tale: the reader has a feeling that 'the story doesn't quite end here,' i.e, he asks himself, 'What will eventually happen to January and May?' I would therefore argue that we have an implied conclusion to the January-May relationship that expresses poetic justice on the part of Chaucer. It would be in keeping with the spirit of the Christian pilgrimage during which the tales are told if the old man, who after all had confessed that his premarital life had been sin, were eventually given the Purgatory to which he had been so close, i.e., if his marriage eventually redeemed the mock-Adam from his 'Fall.' January, having full rule over his mock-Eve, would then be in a position to reverse Proserpina's two predictions—predictions which parodically invert God's two verdicts in Genesis—that woman will rule over man and never die for lack of an answer. In her Winter of Satire May will *not* have an answer because the queen of the underworld, who during that part of the year is confined to subterranean regions, will not be present to help her[29]—and, in a meaningful combination of Christian and pagan elements,[30] Chaucer would have reconverted the Genesis inversion into something that is closer to the Biblical account, meaningfully absorbing the *solaas* of the parody into the *sentence* of expressing his belief in the teachings of his religion.[31]

In the present chapter, I have been discussing the *Merchant's Tale* as a satire in its original ritual-form, as a satire in which Chaucer poetically punishes a *senex amans* for his abuse of the holy institution of marriage.   However, I have also suggested that there is hope for the target of Chaucer's satire in the *Merchant's Tale*, in contrast to the *senex amans* in the *Miller's Tale*. I will now continue to do in greater detail what I began ten pages ago and examine the two fabliaux in light of each other, first by viewing the *Miller's Tale* against the Phallic Ritual background of the *Merchant's Tale*.

At the outset of my first chapter, I answered with an unqualified "yes" Kendrick's somewhat cautious question concerning a thematic function of the installation of the kneading tubs in the *Miller's Tale*: "Might the carpenter's installation not look like the crude figure of male genitals in erection, a burlesque, carnivalesque version of 'Goddes pryvetee'?" At this point in my study, I would like to argue that the ritual-aspects of the *Merchant's Tale* palimpsestically also transform the *Miller's Tale* into satire in its original ritual-form—but that Chaucer strips the effigy of "Goddes pryvetee" in the *Miller's Tale* of the fertility-magic which had been ascribed to the pagan effigy.

It is for the following reason that the phallic effigy in the *Miller's Tale* cannot carry the fertility-symbolism which the pear tree does in the *Merchant's Tale*. Whereas January helps May climb the tree because he believes that he is helping to contribute to "th'onour of God above," John has built his installation in an attempt to actually defy God, to defy His "pryvetee" of another flood. The irony here is not only that John goes to all this trouble because he has been cheated just as January has been cheated, but also that, whereas

January finally learns about his marriage—and learns that he was wrong in claiming, "I woot myselven best what I may do"—the carpenter who has prided himself on knowing, and knowing *only*, his "bileve" has placed himself beyond the point of being able to learn anything.

The finality of John's fate is illustrated by the contrast between the open-ended conclusion of the *Merchant's Tale* and the finality with which the Miller summmarizes his tale:

> Thus swyved was this carpenteris wyf,
> For al his kepyng and his jalousye,
> And Absolon hath kist hir nether ye,
> And Nicholas is scalded in the towte.
> This tale is doon, and God save al the rowte!   (I 3850-54)

I noted a moment ago that while the season-ritual aspects eventually help January, eventually help him reach his "purgatorie," they do nothing for John.   The same type of contrast applies, *mutatis mutandis*, to the various characters who try to cheat the *senex amans* in the *Miller's* and *Merchant's Tales*.   Whereas May is uttering her own death sentence at the very moment she engages January's assistance in climbing into the pear tree, Alison gets off scot-free.   There is the irony, then, that, when we examine the two female characters palimpsestically, May, the woman who represents spring, is survived by Alison.

Alison survives May not so much because Chaucer wants us to perceive Alison as morally superior, but because, as noted in Chapter I, Alison "is the good [which the carpenter, Nicholas, and Absalom] have chosen, as innocent in herself as gold or rich food or drink.   The choice, not the object chosen, is punished." Unlike Alison, May does the choosing, and through her choice May overreaches herself.   What in the final analysis leads to May's and Damian's destruction is that the adulterous May is sexually aggressive in a sense in which the adulterous Alison is not.   In fact, I would argue that through his palimpsestic composition of the *Canterbury Tales* Chaucer is insinuating the idea that the fact of Alison getting off unscathed because she is the object chosen, innocent in herself, requires that the May who chooses is punished. After all, May aggressively and with downright diabolical inventiveness pursues the forbidden fruit of adultery.

If we were to assume that, like Alison but unlike the carpenter, Absalom, Nicholas, and unlike the January whom Chaucer poetically punishes by presenting him as a typical postlapsarian lover, May and Damian will go unpunished, the distribution of *solaas* and *sentence* between these two tales about a *senex amans* would be unbalanced. The Alison whom in my first chapter I interpreted as an *Ur*-female, as a Mother Earth figure who is invulnerable even to the hot colter of a plow, requires a counterpart—that is, an ironic counterpart. An adulteress whose name automatically suggests the Comedy of Spring but eventually experiences the Winter of Satire would provide such an ironic counterpart: as a repesentative of spring, May can be an *Ur*-female, a Mother Earth Figure, only for one half of the year.

The symbol of spring overreaches herself much in the way in which January, the symbol of winter, had overreached himself because of his phallic pride. When May stakes her life on her ability to conceive a child during a tryst in a tree, she becomes guilty of reproductive hubris. Chaucer's religious point here, his *sentence* in the *solaas* of the brief pear-tree copulation, is that May unwittingly attempts to defy Augustinian theology according to which the postlapsarian male is unable to do what the prelapsarian male could have done, i.e., simply will a seminal emission for the purpose of impregnation. Even the sexual powers of a woman who is a symbol of spring are insufficient to cause the phallic Damian to do with his "peres" to May what in the General Prologue April had "with his shoures soote" done to March. In other words, in a poem about a husband's abuse of marriage as a worldly paradise, Chaucer implicitly presents also the adulterous wife and her corespondent as possessing a postlapsarian sexuality.

May's fate as I interpret it to be provides additional irony with respect to other characters in the two fabliaux, irony which is based on an interaction between the two tales. For example, in her attempt to make Damian a biological and January a nominal, official father, May causes the intended biological father to slay himself with his "owene knyf"—a punishment which is endowed with tragic irony by the kind of punishment which the would-be adulterer Absalom, who believes that "ther cometh moore," unknowingly inflicts on the successful adulterer, on *queynte Nicholas*. Conversely, *queynte Damyan* kills himself with his own presumably "hoote kultour" because, although unlike Absalom Damian does obtain the "moore" of sexual intercourse, Pluto, the chief over the pagan nether regions, severely curtails the time the mock-Satan is allowed to plow in January's worldly paradise.

The notion of the chief over the Graeco-Roman version of hell causing an adulterous Satan figure to kill himself with his own "serpent" may well be Chaucer's most dazzling *solaas* in expressing *sentence* in his characterization of adulterers. There is the irony that the Satanic would-be father who, through his contribution to the healing of January's eyesight, administers the venomous bite to himself as well as to the would-be mother is named Damian, which makes him a namesake of both the patron saint of healers and a patron saint of generative power. The irony, then, is at the expense of a character whom Chaucer had artfully built up into the Perfect Impregnator who, in an all-out satire on phallic hubris, eventually self-destructs. Or does the distinction of being the most dazzling instance of Chaucer's irony in his poetic punishment of adultery go to May? After all, now we have the notion of May, a semiannual Mother Earth, having to die because she is thwarted in her hope that "Ther cometh moore" when the extramarital plow she had dispatched into the tree likewise is "nat . . . worth a bene."

The satirical manner in which Chaucer poetically punishes May adds to his portrayal of Alison. For in the discussion of a tale about marriage as a worldly paradise, a tale whose *solaas* as well as *sentence* is largely based on St. Augustine's sexual theology, it might be well to quote what Alfred David has observed concerning Alison's characterization: "In her portrait [Alisoun] is closely identified with the objects of Nature . . . *For Alisoun sex can be enjoyed as though the fall of man had never taken place* . . . Alisoun's response to sex is the most healthy and natural, and I think it is significant that no mention is made at the end of any punishment for her" (italics mine).[32] Concerning the statement I italicized in my quotation from David, I would like to add the following suggestion. It is precisely in order to point to Alison's prelapsarian-like attitude toward sex that Chaucer has her escape the "hoote kultour": Alison is subject only to that kind of "plowing" which God had commanded before the time when, as a result of the Fall, the male was sentenced to plow the field in the sweat of his brow.

Thus, when Chaucer expressly presents his mock-Adam January's intercourse with May in the terms of the man having to plow the field in the sweat of his brow, Chaucer actually is portraying Alison as sexually prelapsarian in the terms of Augustinian theology. But then, to what extent did Chaucer intend the two *senex amans* fabliaux to interact with each other? Isn't it possible that *queynte Nicholas* does to Alison what in the General Prologue April had done to March? It is in accordance with Augustinian theology that the "postlapsarian" January fails at impregnating May, and it is also true that Chaucer presents Alison as sexually "prelapsarian" and describes her lovemaking with Nicholas in terms reminiscent of the mating of the birds in the General Prologue: "Ther was the revel and the melodye," the Miller says (I 3652). This description is palimpsestically informed by Chaucer's comparison of the January who celebrates his labored *descensus* to a croaking magpie, a comparison which in turn, as noted, serves to contrast January's lovemaking to that of the melody-making birds in the General Prologue. If the answer to my tentative question concerning Nicholas and Alison is "yes," the organically composing poet of the *Canterbury Tales* would be adding to the *sentence* in the Merchant's gamy tale about adultery. Let us therefore return to the *Merchant's Tale*.

Once we have discovered how Chaucer endows an extremely bawdy tale with religiously redeeming values, we are in a better position to deal with the perennial question of whether the Merchant is talking about himself. I have earlier answered that question with "yes," and I will now elaborate my answer. I will do so because, while recent critical opinion mostly tends in that direction, I don't think that the proponents of that critical opinion have fully drawn upon the evidence which is available in Chaucer's text. I mentioned earlier that the information which the General Prologue gives us about the Merchant being in debt suggests that the narrator of the tale about January may be delinquent in paying his marital debt. I will now add that it can hardly be coincidental that, prior to telling a story about a husband who is cuckolded by a Satan figure, the unhappily newly-wed Merchant mentions in his prologue the idea of a wife, *his* wife, being coupled with Satan:

> I have a wyf, the worste that may be;
> For thogh the feend to hire ycoupled were,
> She wolde him overmacche, I dar wel swere. (1218-20)

In addition to the evidence I listed earlier, this parallelism should probably be enough to prove that there is a good deal of identification by the Merchant with January, but there is even more evidence. There is the *Verfremdungseffekt*, copiously commented upon but never satisfactorily explained, that the Merchant has his character Justinus mention the Wife of Bath and her feminist argument. Significantly, Justinus mentions the Wife of Bath in the context in which he first states that January's wife may turn out to be his Purgatory and then proceeds to warn January not to be excessive in his devotion to sexual pleasures, that is, warn him against marital concupiscence:

> Paraunter she may be your purgatorie!
> She may be Goddes meene and Goddes whippe;

Thanne shal youre soule up to hevene skippe
Swifter than dooth an arwe out of a bowe.
I hope to God, herafter shul you knowe
That ther nys no so greet felicitee
In mariage, ne nevere mo shal bee,
That you shal lette of your savacion,
So that ye use, as skile is and reson,
The lustes of youre wyf attemprely,
And that ye plese hir nat too amorously,
And that ye kepe yow eek from oother synne.
My tale is doon, for my wit is thynne.
Be nat aghast herof, my brother deere,
But lat us waden out of this mateere.
The Wyf of Bathe, if ye han understonde,
Of mariage, which we have on honde,
Declared hath ful wel in litel space. (1670-87, italics added)

Chaucer is using Justinus to express "ful wel in litel space" the point of the *Merchant's Tale*: in a state of "hoolynesse"-endowed lechery, the husband slays himself with his own "knyf"—with his own "corage . . . so sharp and kene," as January ironically had thought to himself prior to the consummation—in the sense that he commits a mortal sin.

The minor character Justinus, then, holds an important function in the tale's *sentence*. Huppé has suggested that January's brothers Placebo and Justinus are "allegorical embodiments of two aspects of January's mind," with Justinus embodying "the awareness of right conduct."[33] I wish to argue more specifically that Placebo and Justinus represent lust and reason, respectively, and that Placebo and Justinus represent *the Merchant's* lust and reason. This would explain the Merchant's use of the *Verfremdungseffekt* of having Justinus, a character in his own tale, mention the Wife of Bath: in a brief interior monologue, the Merchant is trying to appeal to his own reason.[34]

Chaucer had been using his General Prologue remark about the Merchant,

For sothe he was a worthy man with alle,
But, sooth to seyn, *I noot how men hym calle*, (I 283-84, italics added)

as a narrative device. When Chaucer emphasizes the fact that he doesn't know the Merchant's name—there are many other pilgrims whose names Chaucer does not mention—he is challenging his readers to find a name for him. Let me provide the Merchant's name: no, not January, but Justinus. By this I do not mean that the Merchant's name actually is Justinus. Instead, the Merchant's function as the teller of the story is that of a Justinus ("The One Who Is Right"). Justinus is the opposite of Placebo ("I shall Approve" as well as "I Shall Please"), who not only expresses approval of January's "hoolynesse"-endowed lechery but also is a personification of that Church-sanctioned lechery, of the *plesaunce* for which January selfishly uses his wife, regardless of whether she thinks it is "paradys or helle."

On the other hand, since there is a suggestion that the Merchant is delinquent in paying his marital debt, I would argue that the Merchant sees a little bit of Placebo in himself, i.e., this newly-wed has been, or at least he thinks he has been, selfish in attaining his own *plesaunce*. That would explain the seemingly schizoid irony on the part of the Merchant in the long passage which begins with January's definition of marriage as "in this worlde . . . a *paradys*" and the the Merchant's comment, "Thus seyde this olde knyght, that was so *wys*" (italics added). The *paradys/wys* rhyme—which in this context of ideas can be called a stark-collocation rhyme—expresses the sarcasm which the Merchant feels towards January's willfully erroneous view of marriage. But then the Merchant proceeds to express what seems to be the same view of marriage, not only by repeating January's "in this worlde . . . paradys" definition by calling marriage the husband's "paradys terrestre" (1332), but also by elaborating on January's definition and by bringing in the Adam-and-Eve story. Donald Benson has observed on this seeming inconsistency:

> One of the most problematical passages in the *Canterbury Tales* is the so-called encomium on marriage near the beginning of the *Merchant's Tale* (E 1267-1398). The passage has a prominent place, by both length and position . . . yet scholars have been unable to agree on the

> fundamental question of whether it expresses the thoughts of the teller
> or of his character [concerning the nature of marriage].[35]

One of the critical opinions which Benson quotes is Robert Jordan's argument for an "inorganic unity": "The mock encomium is an independently worked out satire on women which has its lineage in the academic antifeminist tradition. It fits into the Merchant's Tale only because the subject—women and wedlock—is relevant."[36] I disagree with Jordan's argument for an inorganic unity. I see an organic unity between the supposedly independent satire on women and the rest of the *Merchant's Tale* insofar as the mock-encomium lays the foundation for the tale proper with its parodic use of Genesis 1-3, a parodic use which addresses that part of the Adam-and-Eve story which the Merchant had omitted from his mock-encomium: man's Fall. In fact, the encomium does not really become a mock-encomium until the tale itself restores to the Adam-and-Eve story the portion which the Merchant of course had to omit in his encomium on marriage.

This takes us back to Benson's question: whose view of marriage is being expressed in lines 1267-1398? Neuse has observed: "For all its irony, the Merchant's insistence on his wife's usefulness to the husband demonstrates that his view of marriage is fundamentally the same as January's."[37] I would argue that while both the Merchant and January consider the wife as something "useful," there is an important difference between their views. The Merchant considers a wife useful in the sense that she provides the foundation for a stable and orderly life, something which he says bachelors deprive themselves of:

> On brotel ground they buylde, and brotelnesse
> They fynde whan they wene sikernesse.
> They lyve but as a bryd or as a beest,
> In libertee and under non areest,
> Ther as a wedded man in his estaat
> Lyveth a lyf blisful and ordinaat . . . (1279-84)

While we may find the Merchant's argument concerning a *lyf ordinaat* prosaically utilitarian—Paul A. Olson has observed that "[the Merchant's] speech makes a woman as useful as an insurance policy"[38]—the Merchant dissociates himself from, and fiercely satirizes, January's use of his wife: his use of her as a sex object which January also selfishly abuses in order to get on God's good side.

On the other hand, the Merchant is trying to hide something from his pilgrim audience, namely what I have called the Placebo in the Merchant: his having incurred a marital debt while attaining his own *plesaunce*. While the Merchant does not share January's sin of trying to outwit God in an attempt to save his soul—after all, the Merchant seems to be no older than middle-age—and while "no wight" knows that he has incurred debts, marital or otherwise, he knows that God knows he has been delinquent. And he is afraid that his wife might seek payment elsewhere. That is the reason he cites in his marriage encomium Theophrastus' pronouncement that getting married means incurring the risk of being cuckolded (1305-6): he cites the pronouncement in order to be able to reject it—as if he were trying to exorcise a ghost whom he himself had invoked.

For that is precisely what the Merchant is trying to do in the tale proper: when he so graphically describes January's sexual inadequacy and eventually his cuckolding, the Merchant is telling an anxiety-release story. The *Merchant's Tale* is abreactive fiction on the part of the teller. The Merchant's strategy is to exaggerate in imagining the worst-case scenario which might result from his inability to sexually gratify his wife. Imagining himself in January's situation, not only is the Merchant cuckolded, not only does he know about it, and not only does he catch his wife in the act of adultery, but he actually gets a close-up view of that act:

And sodeynly anon this Damyan
Gan pullen up the smok, and in he throng. (2352-53)

There is nothing voyeuristic about the Merchant's close-up view: as the pleo-
nasm in the "sodeynly anon" indicates—these lines are spoken by the Merchant, not by the January who all of a sudden has regained his eyesight—the
Merchant presents himself as unexpectedly being hit with this spectacle.[39] And
he is giving us an even more detailed picture when he has January, in response
to May's explanation about struggling with a man in a tree, protest, "Strugle?
. . . Ye, algate *in it wente!* . . . He swyved thee" (2376-78, italics added): in
his abreactive fiction the Merchant actually watches the other man's penis
enter his wife's vagina.[40]

   Yet what does it mean for our understanding of the Merchant's abreactive identification with January that May succeeds in persuading January to
accept his explanation? That part of the *Merchant's Tale* addresses the teller's
worst anxiety: that his wife might get pregnant by another man but never tell
him the truth, i.e., let him believe the child is his. Such a constellation in
which the official heir would not be the father's biological child would be
anathema to the prudently investing Merchant, and the teller has to invent a
scenario in which his unfaithful wife is prevented from conceiving. This
scenario involves the husband himself interrupting the coitus before the other
man can ejaculate: in his anxiety-produced fantasy the newly-wed husband
forces his wife to disengage from a coital embrace which might have produced
a bastard.

   The Merchant's own participation in his tale reinforces what I suggested earlier: as amorous as the phallic serpent Damian is, he simply does not
have enough time to fill May with the content of the small green pears. There
is of course also the other possibility, a possibility which would add to the
irony of the situation, that Damian is so strongly aroused that after the penetration and subsequent disengagement he experiences an *eiaculatio ante portas*,
which causes the content of the small green pears to go to waste. Instead of
doing to May what in the General Prologue April had done to March, but

literally doing what the April showers had done to the soil, Damian would in a mock cosmic-union be "raining" on the earth in January's garden.   In any case, using his own abreactive fiction as satire with its archetypal killing power, the Merchant poetically kills his bastard heir—so that the pear-tree episode becomes satire in mock-ritual form in more sense than one.

Yet poetically the Merchant not only kills any potential bastard heir of his, but poetically he also condemns to death his wife in the event she should do to him what in his tale May does to January: the Merchant has all his bases covered. The Merchant had shrewdly thought through every possibility, to the point of wisely investing in Graeco-Roman mythology: he is putting Classical mythology to practical use when he makes sure that his "alter ego [January]"[41] will eventually gain the upper hand because of the roles which the Merchant had assigned to Pluto and Proserpina—an epic machinery in a fabliau.[42] And the Merchant's narrative strategy in his tale proper explains a specific crux in his marriage encomium:

> But drede nat, if pleynly speke I shal:
> A wyf wol laste, and in thy hous *endure*,
> *Wel lenger than thee list, paraventure.* (1316-18, italics added)

If the Merchant intends his encomium on marriage to be taken seriously, why does he say that the wife might actually last in the husband's house longer than he *perhaps* ("paraventure") wishes?[43] The answer is that the Merchant is preparing himself for the occurrence of the wife's adultery—and for her punishment.   The Merchant will allow no *paraventure* (note the "endure"/"paraventure" rhyme): he will make sure that the unfaithful wife will *not* "endure." For a couple of lines the Merchant becomes a participant in his own encomium: he becomes a participant in it as a Justinus of sorts just as he will do in his tale when he has Justinus refer to the Wife of Bath. This is a *Verfremdungseffekt* in the Merchant's marriage encomium that will be paralleled by the *Verfremdungseffekt* in his tale proper.

I trust that in my interpretation of Chaucer's portrayal of the Merchant
I have been avoiding a common mistake which Martin Stevens pointed to in a
1972 article:

> Almost all critics have allowed their reading of the [*Merchant's Tale*] to
> be influenced by the man they envision as its teller. Yet this teller, *in
> circular fashion*, is almost wholly characterized by that tale.[44] (italics
> mine)

Among the "circular fashion" critics whom Stevens cited some two decades
ago is Maurice Hussey who, on the second page of a book-length study entitled *The Merchant's Prologue and Tale*, characterizes the Merchant as "a man
of undetermined middle-age, and *now* a disillusioned one" (italics mine).[45]
Hussey's use of the little word *now* typifies the circular-fashion approach to
Chaucer's characterization of the Merchant: it implies that before his recent
marriage the Merchant had some of those illusions about marriage which he
will voice in his (mock-) encomium, but mere two months of married life have
affected him so severely that he is compelled to tell a repugnantly graphic
story about cuckoldry.

In other words, we would have to assume either that the Merchant
knows or at least suspects that his newly-wed wife has sexually cheated him.
In that case, we would also expect the Host who, as we have seen, usually is
quick on the uptake and at times vehemently so, to have picked up such a
message from the *Merchant's Tale*. But while the Host does respond,

> Ey! Goddes mercy! . . .
> Now swich a wyf I pray God kepe me fro!
> Lo, whiche sleightes and subtilitees
> In wommen been! For ay as bisy as bees
> Been they, us sely men for to deceyve,
> And from the soothe evere wol they weyve;
> By this Marchauntes tale it preveth weel,   (2419-25)

that is, while Harry does comment that the Merchant's story proves the deceit-
fulness of women, the tone of the Host's lengthy response (2419-40), which
makes no reference to cuckolding, is so light that we know that the Host does

not identify the Merchant with the cuckolded January. Instead, the Host uses this opportunity to complain about his own wife being a "shrewe" (2428)—which is precisely what, immediately after dangerously associating his wife with the devil, the Merchant had identified as his wife's worst trait:

> She wolde [the feend] overmacche, I dar wel swere.
> What sholde I yow reherce in special
> Hir hye malice? *She is a shrewe at al.*
> Ther is a long and large difference
> Betwix Grisildis grete pacience
> And of my wyf the passyng crueltee. (1220-25, italics added)

As far as his pilgrim audience is concerned, then, the Merchant had in his prologue complained that his own wife was not a Patient Griselda.

On the other hand, after the Clerk had closed the envoy to the story about Patient Griselda by calling on every wife to mistreat her husband—"lat hym care and wepe, and wrynge, and waille" (IV 1212)—why does the Merchant echo the Envoy by beginning his prologue with the following complaints about marriage in general an his own in particular?

> "Wepyng and wayling, care and oother sorwe
> I knowe ynogh, on even a-morwe,"
> Quod the Marchant, "and so doon other mo
> That wedded been . . . " (1213-16)

An answer to my question seems to offer itself in a suggestion which has been made by Stevens:

> Suppose the whole of his speech were spoken with the tongue just slightly in cheek, by a man momentarily freed from domestic confinement? The Merchant . . . . never tells us just exactly what brings on his "wepyng and waylyng, care and oother sorwe" after only two months of marriage. Notice that we know no specifics about his wife. The temptation is there to identify her, *post hoc*, with May. But *there is no textual warrant for the identification.*[46] (italics mine)

It is true that the Merchant himself never tells us his problem—*Chaucer* does, namely when in the General Prologue he writes that "no wight" knows that the Merchant is in debt. *That* is a textual warrant for a certain degree of identification, and we arrive at it not *post hoc* but, instead, *propter hoc*—if we read the *Canterbury Tales* palimpsestically.

This is not to say that the Merchant *has* been cuckolded or that he suspects he has: I have been arguing that the *Merchant's Tale* is an anxiety-release story but also a shrewdly thought-out, calculated attempt to exorcise the ghost of possible cuckoldry. I will now add that while the Merchant is indeed, as Stevens has tentatively suggested, a man momentarily freed from domestic confinement, his very participation in a pilgrimage to the shrine of Thomas à Beckett is such an exorcism attempt. The Merchant's participation in a pilgrimage, in an activity which is supposed to be a quest for physical as well as spiritual healing, is specifically a quest for the ability to live up to the marital-debt relationship which figures so prominently in the *Canterbury Tales*.

The *Merchant's Tale*, then, instead of being a story full of what Howard has called "self-lacerating rage,"[47] is from the teller's point of view an appeal—or perhaps I should say, a prayer—for healing. It is therefore appropriate for the *sentence* of this tale that the culmination of its *solaas*, the scene which is satire in its original ritual-form, presents us with an "in-thronging" Damian. That is, the scene presents us with a live version of St. Damianus, with a live version of the patron saint of the art of healing who was worshipped with phallic effigies. If the Merchant's story has the cathartic effect on its teller which I believe the author of the *Canterbury Tales* implies it has, then there no longer exists any need to have "care" and "sorwe" about the Merchant's *corage* being up to fulfill his marital debt.[48]

As I briefly suggested in my second chapter, Chaucer's narrative move of having the Prioress tell a story in which "the serpent Sathanas" plants the seed of wicked deeds in the "waspes nest" that he has in the "Jues herte" could likewise be seen as satire in its original ritual-form. Let us try to juxtapose the two passages. What is the essential difference between the Prioress' "Up swal the serpent Sathanas" and the Merchant's pear-tree episode, an episode where a Satan figure likewise "Up swal"? The answer is that whereas Chaucer has the Merchant deliberately, and in great detail, describe a phallic ritual, our poet has the Prioress *unconsciously create* a phallic ritual—unconsciously create such a ritual because Madame Eglentyne is both sexually and procreatively frustrated. The "self-lacerating rage" which Howard has ascribed to the Merchant, then, I would ascribe to the Prioress whom her frustrations cause to poetically instigate the murder of a child.

Read palimpsestically in the light of the Merchant's description of a mock fertility-ritual which kills the expected child of January-May-Damian, the Prioress' "Up swal the serpent Sathanas" episode about the murder of a seven-year-old becomes the performance of a gruesome mock fertility-ritual in which the prevention of the conception of a child is performed retroactively almost eight years later. Compared to the Pardoner's and the Merchant's respective fates, the Prioress's fate seems hopeless. But then, as I elaborated earlier, the Prioress' unintentional self-satirizing is actually Chaucer's way of satirizing certain practices and doctrines of the Church, doctrines which had been concocted by self-righteous males. We despise January for his selfish attempt to get on God's good side by legalizing his lust, but at least some readers are also put off by the Parson who on the one hand warns that through marital concupiscence a husband can slay himself with his own "knyf," and who on the other hand preaches the male-conveniencing view that the wife

> hath merite of chastitee that yeldeth to hire housbonde the dette of hir body, ye, *though it be agayn her likynge and the lust of hire herte.* (X 940, italics added)

It would be unfair to Chaucer as a presumably non-sexist male not to point out that the portion I italicized in the Parson's frequently ultra-conservative sermon is palimpsestically debunked by Chaucer's description of January's treatment of May in general and in particular by the Merchant's tongue-in-cheek remark, "I dar nat to yow telle . . . wheither hire thoughte it paradys or helle." The

Merchant's rhetorical figure of *occupatio*, then, carries even more significance than I have assigned to it throughout this chapter: it is another instance of Chaucer satirizing the male-orientedness of the Church.

It is because of the firmness of his Christian beliefs that Chaucer is able to take certain liberties with those beliefs as well as with what he considers distortions of his beliefs and combine the sacred with the profane without doing any damage to the sacred. In this juxtapositon of the profane with the sacred we can distinguish between two stages. The first stage is the open bawdiness of some of the tales and prologues; they are too bawdy—or so it would seem to a modern Christian—to form the topics of conversation during a pilgrimage. The second stage is a bawdy "game" with some of the basic Christian beliefs. While Chaucer's use in the *Merchant's Tale* of St. Augustine's observations on pre- and postlapsarian sexuality actually is a confirmation, although in parodic form, of Augustinian theology, the Wife of Bath holds a different evaluation of the postlapsarian *membres of generacion:*

> Telle me also, to what conclusion
> Were membres maad of generacion,
> And of so parfit wys a [wight] ywroght . . . ?
> I sey this, that they maked ben . . .
>   . . . for ese
> Of engendrure, ther we nat God displese.
> Why sholde men elles in hir bookes sette
> That man shal yelde to his wyf hire dette?
> Now wherwith sholde he make his paiement,
> If he ne used his sely instrument? (III 115-32)

When the Wife of Bath says that certain human organs were made "for *ese*/Of engendrure" ("for the *pleasure* of procreation," italics added), and that this *ese* does not displease God—we should note the (stark-collocation?) rhyme, "ese/ . . . ther we nat God displese"—she is unwittingly replying to St. Augustine who denies the reproductive act the status of *sancta gaudia*, unwittingly because Chaucer would hardly want us to assume that the Wife of

Bath is familiar with St. Augustine's theories. Here is another Augustinian description of the prelapsarian sex act:

> [credendum est] ita tunc potuisse utero coniugis salva integritate feminei genitalis virile semem inmitti, sicut nunc potest eadem integritate salva ex utero virginis fluxus menstrui cruoris emitti. Eadem quippe via posset illud inici qua hoc potest eici.

> [we have to believe] that the male seed could then be introduced into the wife's uterus without damage to her maidenhead, even as now the menstrual flow can issue from a maiden's uterus without any such damage. For the seed could be injected through the same passage as that by which the menses can be ejected. (XIV, 26)

To the lusty Wife of Bath this would *not* be the way in which, obeying St. Paul's teachings, the man "shal yelde to his wyf hir dette." For the man fails to use his "sely instrument"—where *sely* is the Latin *felix*, i.e., expresses the state St. Augustine assigns to prelapsarian sexuality—in the manner postulated by the Wife: the mere act of insemination does not accord the woman any *ese*.

Contrary to the Saint who deplores the postlapsarian state of human genitals and wishes it were different, the Wife claims that postlapsarian sexuality is perfect. In fact, the Wife is downright erasing the Saint's distinction between pre- and postlapsarian sexuality when she says that the reproductive organs as we know them are "of parfit wys . . . ywroght": they are no different from what God had initially created. It is also possible to interpret that St. Augustine's thesis according to which the prelapsarian male would have impregnated his spouse without deflowering her is given a rejoinder in the Wife's vehement defense of defloration (III 62-76). Since the Wife's contention, "The dart is set up for virginitee" (III 75), is a reference to the phallus,[49] she is arguing that contrary to the Saint's hypothesis the "membre of generacion" *was created also* for the purpose of removing the hymen!

Ross has made the following observation under the heading *membres*: "The Wife of Bath (D 116) admires their perfection and the perfection of their Creator—a sentiment of which the Parson would probably not approve though

he does not interrupt her on the Pilgrimage to say so."[50] I would like to add
that Chaucer even has the Parson make comments on Augustinian sexual theology that turn out to be comical. The Parson makes the following observations
on the relationship among sin, God, reason, sensuality, and the human body:

> ye shul understonde that in mannes synne is every manere of ordre or
> ordinaunce turned up-so-doun. For it is sooth that God, and resoun,
> and sensualitee, and the body of man been so ordeyned that everich of
> thise foure thynges sholde have lordshipe over that oother, as thus: God
> sholde have lordshipe over resoun, and resoun over sensualitee, and
> sensualitee over the body of man. But soothly, whan man synneth, al
> this ordre or ordinaunce is turned up-so-doun. And therfore thanne, for
> as muche as the resoun of man ne wol nat be subget ne obeisant to
> God, that is his lord by right, therfore leseth it the lordshipe that it
> sholde have over sensualitee, and eek over the body of man. And
> why? For sensualitee rebelleth thanne agayns resoun, and by that way
> leseth resoun the lordshipe over sensualitee and over the body. For
> right as resoun is rebel to God, right so is bothe sensualitee rebel to
> resoun and the body also. And certes this disordinaunce and this
> rebellioun oure Lord Jhesu Christ aboghte upon his precious body ful
> deere . . . *This suffred oure Lord Jhesu Crist for man . . . so that his
> blood brast out at every nayl of his handes, as seith Seint Augustyn.* (X
> 259-69, italics added)

Robinson notes that the "quotation from St. Augustine," which I italicized,
"is not identified."[51] The quotation never will be identified. In fact, it is
important for Chaucer's intentions in this part of the *Parson's Tale* that the
statement does not exist anywhere in St. Augustine. Chaucer merely has the
Parson attribute the statement about Christ's suffering to the Saint, and I propose that Chaucer does so for the following reason.

In the passage quoted, the topic basically is sexuality. I said
"basically" because the Parson's pronouncement is so long-winded that the
focus on sexuality is easily lost. I would suggest that Chaucer intends the
Parson's statement as an elaboration of St. Augustine's pronouncements on
prelapsarian versus postlapsarian sexuality: if Original Sin had not occurred,
the reproductive act would be subject to man's will, but because man dis-
obeyed his own superior, God, man was punished by losing authority over his

own subordinates, i.e., over his flesh. We remember that the prelapsarian male would have been able to simply will his erection as well as seminal emission, and that the female would have been able by an act of will to expand her birth canal, so that she could have given birth not only without pain but even without losing her hymen. The Saint is so graphic in his descriptions that the Parson feels he cannot repeat them in his own elaboration of St. Augustine's pronouncements. In fact, I would argue that in his modesty, or perhaps in a *pose* of modesty, the Parson does not even dare to mention St. Augustine in conjunction with his own observations on *sensualitee*[52] but then, in an afterthought, commits the Freudian slip of mentioning him in the wrong context, namely in the context of the Crucifixion. And the Parson's long-windedness is a reflection of how uncomfortable he feels about the Saint's outspokenness.

Regardless of whether or not Chaucer here is actually satirizing the Parson, who Ross has observed "seems suspicious of almost everything natural,"[53] I think Chaucer here is at least poking fun at this cleric,[54] whom, as I have discussed, he satirizes in other parts of the *Canterbury Tales* on account of his needlessly harsh pronouncements on matters of sexuality. Not only has the Parson elaborated the Saint's argument concerning the sexual consequences of Original Sin by extending it to postlapsarian sin, but he has also brought into his elaboration of the Augustinian argument the notion of man's redemption through Christ. We chuckle at the awkward situation the Parson gets himself into when he tries to fit the Augustinian argument into the doctrine of man's redemption: the Parson seems to be holding out the hope that Redemption will also restore the "parfit wys" of sexuality. The Parson would have a very legitimate reason for desiring such a restoration, for, as he will elaborate later in his *Tale*, as a postlapsarian celibate the Parson is not exempt from the sin of lechery "that comth in slepynge . . . and this synne men clepen polucioun"—a sin which, it needs to be pointed out, the Parson adds to the sources Chaucer is drawing upon.[55]

In the General Prologue, where Chaucer satirizes several ecclesiastics, he presumably had not satirized the Parson but, instead, had presented him as the ideal cleric. I do find it difficult, however, to imagine how in his addition of the sin of nocturnal emission in his lesson on penance the Parson lives up to the poet's key statement in his idealizing potraiture of the Parson, i.e., lives up to Chaucer's statement that this clergyman first practices what he teaches: "This noble ensample to his sheep he yaf,/That first he wroghte, and afterward he taughte" (I 496-97). For example, in light of the *wroghte/taughte* inrhyme, could Chaucer be suggesting the outrageous notion that preaching about the sin of nocturnal emission is *not* the Parson's job because you cannot teach about something that cannot literally be "worked at," i.e., practiced, since it is involuntary? In that case, Chaucer would be suggesting that the Parson added this special lesson because the Parson felt a need to teach about something *after* that something had happened to the Parson's literally "slepy yerde."

But then, with the help of another cleric, the Monk, Chaucer had already introduced the notion of the purest being, God himself, using His hands to do "work" with His own *yerde*. Thus, when Chaucer has the Parson, who so vehemently castigates the *membrum virile* whose behavior St. Augustine attests to be involuntary, add to Chaucer's own theological sources the "synne" of nocturnal emission, could the poet be suggesting that the Parson is overcompensating? Couldn't the Parson be overcompensating because he knows that, just as in the case where at Jupiter's command Mercury visited Arcite, the all-seeing Lord had caught the Parson, sleepy or not, with his "yerde in hond . . . upright"?

Through such a suggestion the poet would be setting up a "game" much in the sense in which Lindahl uses that term: a game containing, if not solely consisting of, social interaction. The Parson, who makes it clear that he condemns fiction of any sort, would be responding to the Knight's clever adaptation of the Mercury myth. Whatever the answer to my question concerning a possible overcompensation for guilt feelings by the Parson, Chaucer is communicating to those who read the *Canterbury Tales* palimpsestically that he wants his asseveration, "A bettre preest I trowe that nowher noon ys" (I 524), to be taken with a grain of salt.[56] But let us return to what most readers will agree is satire on the clergy.

Whereas in the General Prologue Chaucer had severely satirized the Monk for his worldly ways, his portrayal of him in the *Monk's Tale* is not entirely unsympathetic. After all, it is the time of spring, the time when April and Jupiter, April's analogue in the *Georgics*, are impregnating the earth. We will not, therefore, condemn the Monk for feeling certain urges and giving himself away in his account of the creation of Adam. Besides, since in his brief account of Adam's creation the Monk intends no *solaas*, he ironically provides the *sentence* of demonstrating that all of us humans are indeed God's children—*genealogically*. Nor do we readers, in the final analysis, resent the Parson when the springtime urges cause him to deliver an abreactive sermon on the subject of sexuality. Nor will we condemn the Merchant for telling a bawdy story that reflects his own—and perhaps many a male's—anxieties about his sexual capabilities, a story in which Chaucer represents a man's punishment in the terms of Augustinian theology. We will forgive the Wife of Bath for proclaiming, in the face of what St. Augustine had written, postlapsarian sexuality as perfect and vigorously recommending its practice. We will forgive the Clerk for siding with the Wife of Bath telling a tongue-in-cheek story in which a patriarchal system all but kills any springtime urges, when that system tries to channel them into the purpose of perpetuating itself and its ideological underpinnings, namely male-supremacy.

The Prioress is the primary victim of that male-supremacist ideology, and I have argued that we should support her plea for "multiplied" mercy, especially since she is denied the kind of multiplication that is a natural result of sprintime urges. We forgive the Pardoner for the sins he commits in compensation for any acts his physiological preordination prevents him from committing in response to the stimulus of the cosmic union. The Host deserves forgiveness for the bawdy remarks this "semely man" has uttered, especially since one of his bawdy outbursts aids in the Pardoner's redemption. While I spent very little time discussing the Knight, what I have said about his mention of Mercury's visit to Arcite suggests that the Knight, too, may have to be given the benefit of Chaucer's springtime ritual.[57] After all, we are even willing to forgive the Miller, whose poetic job it is to "quyte" the Knight, for telling an obscene story whose events quite literally surround the crude figure of huge male genitals in erection, a burlesque version of "Goddes pryvetee."

In fact, there is the ironic twist that while the poet is able to and does blame the obscene *events* in the story on the Miller-the-churl, the *mental image* hovering over the events is Chaucer's own—in a tale which is satire in its original form of the pagan springtime fertility-ritual, but which replaces the pagan effigy with the effigy of "Goddes pryvetee." But then, we will not condemn Chaucer, who says he had participated in the pilgrimage, for being under the influence of the cosmic union. In particular, we will not condemn Chaucer for playing certain springtime urges and springtime concerns against the Christian ideas that are associated with the holy occasion of the pilgrimage. On the contrary, while some of Chaucer's parodic manipulations of Christian notions are "ernest" indeed, his account of the pilgrimage *is* a "game"—an exuberant "game" where fierce satire is in the last analysis absorbed by the Spring of Comedy that harmonizingly permeates the *Canterbury Tales*.

NOTES

INTRODUCTION

[1] Laura Kendrick, *Chaucerian Play: Comedy and Control in the Canterbury Tales* (Berkeley, Los Angeles, London: University of California Press, 1988).

[2] If the foregoing puns in the "Acknowledgments of *Corage*" section are are not clear now, they will become clear in the remainder of the Introduction and particularly in Chapter I.

[3] Martin Stevens, "The *Canterbury Tales* for a New Age," *Review*, 11 (1989), 63-64.

[4] There is of course Thomas W. Ross's book on *Chaucer's Bawdy* (New York: Dutton, 1972). Brilliant and essential to Chaucer scholarship as this book is, it is what the title *Chaucer's Bawdy* says: admittedly modelled after although far transcending Eric Partridge's *Shakespeare's Bawdy*, it is not a cohesively interpretive study in the way Kendrick's book is. Unless otherwise identified, Ross citations in my Introduction are from *Chaucer's Bawdy*.

⁵ As some of the footnotes will show, especially with respect to the General Prologue and the *Miller's* and the *Merchant's Tales* I had offered "audacious interpretive moves" which are similar to Kendrick's own. Small portions of the Introduction first appeared in my articles, "Heresy and Springtime Ritual: Biblical and Classical Allusions in the *Canterbury Tales,*" *Revue belge de philologie et d'histoire,* 54 (1976), 823-36, "The *Canterbury Tales*: Anxiety Release and Wish Fulfillment," *American Imago: A Journal for Culture, Science and the Arts,* 35 (1978), 407-18, "Chaucer's Spring of Comedy: The *Merchant's Tale* and Other 'Games' with Augustinian Theology," *Annuale Mediaevale,* 21 (1981), 111-20, and "Reading Chaucer's Earnest Games: Folk-Mode or Literary Sophisticaton?", *English Language Notes,* 29 (December 1991), 16-19.

As especially the dates of my article publications and the publication dates of the scholarship which I incorporate in the present study indicate, the material I previously published constitutes only a small portion of the book.

⁶ Stevens, p. 65.

⁷ Stevens, p. 67. Stevens observes: "Kendrick says very little about the intertextuality [between different parts of the *Canterbury Tales*] . . . Kendrick oversimplifies the voicing of the text at large . . . I find Kendrick's text a refreshing and enlightening reading of particulars . . . but not a book that truly extends our horizons" (pp. 67-68).

⁸ Robert M. Jordan, *Chaucer and the Shape of Creation: The Aesthetic Possibilities of Inorganic Structure* (Cambridge, MA: Harvard University Press, 1965).

⁹ Jordan, *Chaucer's Poetics and the Modern Reader* (Berkeley and Los Angeles: University of California Press, 1987), p. 4.

¹⁰ Carolyn Dinshaw, *Chaucer's Sexual Poetics* (Madison: University of Wisconsin Press, 1989), pp. 156-84. See, however, Glenn Burger's attempt to provide what he considers a corrective to Dinshaw's "Eunuch

Hermeneutics'' approach in his article, "Kissing the Pardoner," *PMLA*, 107 (1992), 1143-66. On the other hand, my objection to Burger's own approach would be that he refuses to examine Chaucer's characterization of the Pardoner as a possible "mare," even though Burger quotes insights of gay criticism. Cf. Chapter III, n. 31.

[11] Carl Lindahl, *Earnest Games: Folkloric Patterns in the Canterbury Tales* (Bloomington and Indianapolis: Indiana University Press, 1987), p. 10.

[12] Stevens, p. 59.

[13] The problem inherent in the folkloric treatment of literature is perhaps best summed up by Bruce A. Rosenberg's review of Lindahl's book in the 1988 volume of *Studies in the Age of Chaucer*. After pointing out that "[literary historians and folklorists] differ in their appreciation of differing arts they study, schooled and elitist, and folkloric and 'spontaneous'," Rosenberg comments:

> The study of folklore had for nearly a century been the province of professors of literature . . . Then about three decades ago a number of talented folklorists, trained mainly by anthropologists, made a declaration of independence for the American Folklore Society. It was no longer to be a satellite of the Modern Language Society. With seeming ease and effortlessness they moved the study of American folklore *away from its text-centered focus in the direction of anthropology. The text, the product, faded* as the folkloric process, the folkloric and communicative event, assumed the spotlight. *Folklorists were not much interested in text literature* . . . (p. 169, italics mine).

The misattribution of the earnest-game pronouncement is not the only time that Lindahl either misreads or misrepresents what Chaucer's text says. Apparently in an effort to support his thesis about the *Clerk's Tale* having been intended as an anti-elitist message, Lindahl states that "[the Marquis Walter] decrees that Griselde shall be sent naked back to her father's house" (p. 150). The Marquis issues no such decree. As I will discuss in Chapter IV, underneath its surface the tale is much more about gender-struggle than it is about medieval pre-Marxist class struggle.

[14] Lindahl, p. 6.

[15] Lindahl, p. 9.

[16] Citations are from *The Riverside Chaucer*, gen. ed. Larry D. Benson (Boston: Houghton Mifflin, 1987), based on *The Works of Geoffrey Chaucer*, ed. F. N. Robinson, 2nd ed. (Boston: Houghton Mifflin, 1957). Explanatory notes which are in Robinson's but no longer in Benson's edition will be identified. Since "solas" rather than "solaas" is the spelling used by the critics I cite most frequently, e. g., in one of Kendrick's chapter titles, I will at times be using that spelling.

[17] Ross, p. 22; see also p. 64.

[18] C. S. Lewis' *A Preface to "Paradise Lost"* (London: Oxford University Press, 1949) laid the groundwork concerning Milton's use of Augustinian sexual theology. I pursue further Lewis' line of argument in my article, "Ovid's *Art of Love* and Augustinian Theology in *Paradise Lost*," *Milton Quarterly*, 21 (1987), 62-65, and other publications listed in that article.

[19] Citations are from the Loeb Edition of *The City of God*.

[20] Latin Virgil quotations are from the Oxford text; translations are my own.

[21] I will be using the term *Iuppiter descendens* throughout my study, although the name which Virgil uses here is *Aether*. For a medieval discussion of the literary-critical importance of the *Georgics*, I refer to a statement made by the English poet and grammarian John of Garland (ca. 1195-ca. 1272) in his *Parisiana Poetica*: "There are . . . three styles, corresponding to the three estates of men. The low style suits the pastoral life; the middle style, farmers; the high style, eminent personages, who are set over shepherds and farmers . . . Virgil composed three works to correspond to these three types, the *Eclogues*, the *Georgics*, and the *Aeneid*" (quoted from *Chaucer: Sources and Backgrounds*, ed. Robert P. Miller [New York:

Oxford University Press, 1977], p. 71). This division into three styles was almost held sacred in the Middle Ages, where it was codified as *rota Virgilii*. For a modern discussion of the *rota Virgilii* tradition see Ernst R. Curtius, *European Literature and the Latin Middle Ages*, trans. W. R. Trask (Princeton: Princeton University Press, 1953), pp. 201, 231 ff. For discussion of the Virgilian cosmic-union picture in English-language literature, see the book listed in n. 24 below, especially Chapter V, "Cosmic Union and the Classical/Christian Tradition from Chaucer to Eliot."

22 For discussion of the authorship of the English translation, see the *Riverside Chaucer*, pp. 1103-1104.

23 In a groundbreaking article on allusion-study, Earl R. Wasserman has made the following observations. Beginning where in 1959 Reuben Arthur Brower ended in his seminal *Alexander Pope: The Poetry of Allusion* (Oxford: Clarendon Press, 1959), Wasserman concluded his 1966 article on "The Limits of Allusion in *The Rape of the Lock*": "the mode of existence of Pope's poetry . . . ought to be defined broadly enough to include a creative act by the reader, [whom the allusion invites] to exercise, within poetic reason, his own invention by contemplating the relevances of the entire allusive context" (*Journal of English and Germanic Philology*, 65 [1966], 443).

24 Carmela Perri, "On Alluding," *Poetics*, 7 (1978), 299. For discussion of the operations of literary allusion, discussion building on but eventually going beyond Earl Wasserman, see my book, *The Mutual Commerce: Masters of Classical Allusion in English and American Literature* (Heidelberg: Carl Winter Universitätsverlag, 1985). The book contains a chapter on "The *Aeneid* in the *Knight's Tale*."

25 Under *priken* Ross has made the following observations concerning the line, "so priketh hem nature in hir corages": "[it] means that nature revives the spirits of the birds in the spring. The juxtaposition of *corage*, however, may to some suggest that something more is happening here, perhaps

the general sexual awakening that many critics sense is part of it" (p. 167). Although Ross had already discussed both the Merchant's and January's use of the word *corage* in its unequivocal sexual meaning, Ross, apparently, did not consider extending the "general sexual awakening" from the birds to the pilgrims.

[26] It is quite possible that, as Muriel Bowden and others have argued, in the opening lines Chaucer is using Guido delle Colonne's *Historia Destructionis Troiae*. Chaucer would be doing this in addition to allusively utilizing the Virgilian passage, which would form the basis not only because of the orgasmic image of the water impregnating earth but also because of the role which—after the replacement in lines 5-7 of Jupiter/Aether by the Aether-like Zephirus—is held by Zephirus.   The lines about Zephirus—"When Zephirus eek with his sweete breeth/Inspired hath in every holt and heeth/The tendre croppes"—do not have a direct analogue in Guido, who does not speak of the deity Zephirus but, using the plural, talks about the zephir *winds* which ripple the surface of the water ("*zephiri crispant aquas*" [quoted from Muriel Bowden, *A Commentary on the General Prologue to the "Canterbury Tales"* (New York: Macmillan, 1949), p. 40)]).   In the General Prologue Zephirus breathes spirit into the vegetation, as he does in the Second *Georgic* where Virgil's imagery is rather physical: the fields open their bosom to Zephirus.

[27] Ross comments on *descende*:   "In view of his years and his need for aphrodisiacs, it would be probable that the meaning here is 'lose erection' " (p. 75). Ross may be right, but if he is, then we are dealing with a splendid case of irony: January would be meaning one thing but the poet, who has him labor all night, would be meaning something else, namely the selfish old lecher's sexual gratification through orgasm—and that January labors all night long does not, of course, mean that he possesses the *corage* of an erection throughout the night.   I will elaborate on this point in Chapter V.

[28] Benson, *Riverside Chaucer*, p. 5.

[29] D. W. Robertson, Jr., *A Preface to Chaucer: Studies in Medieval Perspectives* (Princeton: Princeton University Press, 1962), p. 22.

[30] Donald R. Howard, *The Idea of the Canterbury Tales* (Berkeley, Los Angeles, London: University of California Press, 1976), p. 49.

[31] Howard, p. 49.

[32] Kendrick, p. 30.

[33] A. Leigh DeNeef, "Robertson and the Critics," *Chaucer Review*, 2 (1968), 215.

[34] Francis Lee Utley, "Robertsonianism Redivivus," *Romance Philology*, 19 (1965), 257.

[35] Joerg O. Fichte, *Chaucer's "Art Poetical": A Study in Chaucerian Poetics* (Tübingen: Gunter Narr Verlag, 1980), p. 13.

[36] For discussion of that type of satire, especially in the General Prologue, see Jill Mann, *Chaucer and Medieval Estates Satire: The Literature of Social Classes and the General Prologue to the Canterbury Tales* (Cambridge: Cambridge University Press, 1973).

[37] *A Variorum Edition of the Works of Geoffrey Chaucer*, vol. II, Part 3, *The Miller's Tale*, ed. Thomas W. Ross (Norman, OK: University of Oklahoma Press, 1983). Hereafter I will usually refer to this part of the *Chaucer Variorum* as *Miller Variorum*.

[38] Utley has made this remark about the Robertsonians' treatment of two of Chaucer's ecclesiastics:

> Chaucer's Prioress' "soft, red lips" and Ovidian brooch place her directly among the daughters of Venus, an interpretation which . . . critically cancels out the gentle and throttled increase in satire marking the opening set of portraits in the *General Prologue*. Chaucer's Monk, whose passions for rich clothes, administration, and hunting do not suffice to condemn him, becomes a lecher also, following ambiguous meanings of *priking* and *venerie* and *hunting for the hare*. (p. 258)

It might not be impertinent to mention that Dinshaw not only speaks of Robertson's "disgust with sexuality" in one of her chapters (p. 34), but actually indexes that phrase under *Sexuality*: "sexuality, 157-58; Robertson's disgust with, 34" (p. 309).

[39] Ross observed in *Chaucer's Bawdy*: "when [the Robertsonians] explain Middle English humor, the exegetes sometimes make the jests sound like Sunday School teachers' jokes" (p. 15).

[40] Ross, p. 48.

CHAPTER I

[1] Kendrick, pp. 5-6. Small portions of this chapter first appeared in the *Revue belge*, *American Imago*, and *Annuale Mediaevale* articles listed in n. 5 of the Introduction, as well as in my articles, "The Misdirected Kisses in the *Miller's Tale*," *Journal of Evolutionary Psychology*, 3 (April 1982), 103-108, and "Chaucer's Mercury and Arcite: The *Aeneid* and the World of the *Knight's Tale*," *Neophilologus*, 64 (1980), 307-19.

[2] Kendrick, p. 15.

[3] Kendrick, p. 22.

[4] Jordan, *Chaucer and the Shape of Creation*. The portion up to the bracket is quoted from p. 187, the portion thereafter from p. 196. Unless otherwise indicated, all citations from Robert Jordan are from that study.

[5] Paul A. Olson, "Poetic Justice in the *Miller's Tale*," *Modern Language Quarterly*, 24 (1963), 230-31.

[6] Ross, p. 186. Unless otherwise indicated, all mentions of the name Ross in the footnotes to this chapter refer to the *Miller Variorum*.

[7] For discussion of John's magic charms see the Explanatory Notes in the *Riverside Chaucer*, p. 846, which give an example of a *nyght-spel* (I 3480) that has survived into modern times: "Matthew, Mark, Luke and John/Bless the bed that I lie on."

8   Ross, p. 153.

9   While not every reader will see in my translation the rhyme which puns on *twat*, it at least renders the carnal-knowledge idea. By contrast, the Bantam Dual-Language Edition, which because of its practicality is frequently used in lower-division English courses, provides for the famous *rime riche* the following translation which is not only bowdlerized but downright stultifying: "(these clerks are very subtle and sly),/And privily he grabbed her where he shouldn't" (*The Canterbury Tales by Geoffrey Chaucer*, eds. A. Kent Hieatt and Constance Hieatt, Selected with Translations and Notes by the Editors [New York and Toronto: Bantam Books, 1964], p. 155).

10   Larry D. Benson, "The 'Queynte' Punnings of Chaucer's Critics," in *Studies in the Age of Chaucer, Proceedings, No. 1: Reconstructing Chaucer*, ed. Paul Strohm and Thomas J. Heffernan (Knoxville: University of Tennessee Press, 1985), pp. 23-47.

11   For reasons which soon will become clear, I will cite from the Preface of the *Riverside Chaucer* in n. 29 below.

12   *Riverside Chaucer*, p. 69.

13   Douglas Gray, *Riverside Chaucer*, p. 845. For comments on apparent inconsistencies among the glosses, the Explanatory Notes, and the Glossary of the *Riverside Chaucer* see n. 29 below.

14   Jacqueline de Weever, *Chaucer Name Dictionary: A Guide to Astrological, Biblical, Literary, and Mythological Names in the Works of Geoffrey Chaucer* (New York and London: Garland Publishing, Inc., 1988), p. 255.

15   In 1962 Robertson made the following comment on the "queynte"-passage: "Perhaps the most 'shocking' passage in *The Canterbury Tales* is the description of the wooing of Alisoun by the 'hende Nicholas'; but the technique employed by the young clerk is illustrated without qualms in a fourteenth-century devotional manual, where, of course, it conveys the idea of

lechery. Obscene materials, like classical materials, could become part of 'the theocratic programme of cosmic order' '' (p. 22). As I will attempt to demonstrate especially in my chapter on the Pardoner, the Miller's *queynte* passage is hardly the most "shocking" in the *Canterbury Tales*. What in the pre-sexual-revolution era Robertson thought modern readers might find shocking is Chaucer being so frivolously graphic in his description of Nicholas' sexual advances at Alison. I agree with Ross who, immediately prior to quoting the Robertson statement I have cited, makes a slightly mocking remark about Robertson's reading: "Robertson . . . makes Nicholas' rude act bear the burden of moral significance" (p. 154). I respectfully submit, however, that Ross is mocking Robertson for the wrong reasons. Nicholas' "rude" act *is* morally significant: not as a Chaucerian attack on lechery as Robertson would have us believe but, instead, as satire on self-righteous, anti-intellectual complacency about one's own religious position. In fact, could Chaucer be presenting us with a *"hende* Nicholas" who, as an executor of "the theocratic programme of cosmic order," hands out to John his punishment in the fashion deemed appropriate to describe in devotional *manuals* and *hondbokes*?

16 Ross observes: "it is neither coincidental nor inconsequential that both the narrator and the character John use the same phrase [*Goddes pryvetee*]. By repeating it, Chaucer portrays the *vulgar minds of both Miller and carpenter*; a modern critic of realistic fiction would see the repetition as a flaw" (p. 185, italics mine). The point is that in his pronouncement the naive carpenter does *not* have in mind the vulgar notion which the teller had earlier introduced into the "Goddes pryvetee" context; this is an instance of irony which a modern critic of realistic fiction would be more likely to consider an adroit narrative device than a flawed "repetition."

17 Ross thus could be missing the irony when he comments on the *ful yoore ago*: "It is not clear whether John means that he heard the story long

ago or that the events occurred in the distant past. In either case it is a vacuous remark'' (p. 199). What appears to be a vacuous remark on John's part may on the poet's part very well be a phrase pregnant with meaning.

[18] Kelsie B. Harder, ''Chaucer's Use of the Mystery Plays in the *Miller's Tale*,'' *Modern Language Quarterly*, 17 (1956), 196.

[19] Ross cites a critic who ''refers *(mistakenly?)* to 'old John's building of the tubs' '' (p. 211, italics mine). There is nothing in the text to suggest that the tubs John fetches had *not* been made by the carpenter himself. It would enhance the irony of the situation if we could assume that the *senex amans* himself had built from scratch what Kendrick calls ''the crude figure of huge male genitals in erection,'' in addition to building the ladder which he will climb to his own cuckolding. At any rate, the point here is the anthropocentric pride of the carpenter who with his own hands puts together the installation.

[20] Constance B. Hieatt, ed., *The Miller's Tale by Geoffrey Chaucer* (New York: Odyssey Press, 1970).

[21] John Halverson, ed., *Geoffrey Chaucer: The Canterbury Tales* (Indianapolis: Bobbs-Merrill, 1971), p. 112.

[22] John H. Fisher, ed., *The Complete Poetry and Prose of Geoffrey Chaucer* (New York: Holt, Rinehart and Winston, Inc., 1977), p. 62.

[23] Fisher, p. vii.

[24] *Riverside Chaucer*, p. 71.

[25] *Riverside Chaucer*, p. 1222.

[26] *Riverside Chaucer*, Preface, p. ix.

[27] Robinson, p. 935.

[28] Norman Davis, *A Chaucer Glossary* (Oxford: Oxford University Press, 1979), p. 14. The *Glossary* was compiled Norman Davis, Douglas Gray, Patricia Ingham, and Anne Wallace-Hadrill, with Norman Davis being the General Editor. See the next note.

[29] The *Riverside Chaucer* announced in the Preface: "the contributors have generously provided help to one another in a great variety of ways. The most notable products of this cooperation are the glosses and the Glossary. Larry D. Benson and Patricia J. Eberle have prime responsibility for those, but all the writers of the Explanatory Notes provided glosses for their parts of the text, often with suggestions for other parts as well, and much of the Glossary thus embodies the work of all the contributors" (p. ix). That I have lost faith in the "cooperation" is not the fault of those who have (or claim) primary responsibility for the glosses and the Glossary. Gray doesn't comment on line 3435. According to the *Chaucer Glossary*, in which the General Editor, Norman Davis, explains how "the *initial* [alphabetically distributed] work of compilation was divided" (italics mine), Gray was not responsible for explicating the carpenter's use of the word *bileve*: the Preface announced that "The whole was edited by Norman Davis." But if I had been Gray, who was to offer in the *Riverside Chaucer* his reading of John's *bileve* as "creed," I would have made sure that the meaning "creed" was included in the *Chaucer Glossary* instead of simply relying on the General Editor. And the General Editor of the *Chaucer Glossary* who, by approving of "belief, faith" as the only entry, seemingly expressed disagreement with the standard interpretation as "creed," also served as a contributor to the *Riverside Chaucer*. For additional confusion as to whom to put your stock and faith in, see n. 30 below.

[30] Quoted from the *MED*. While it is clear that Langland had specific formulaic prayers in mind, the *MED* cites *Piers* for the following rather generic definition of *bileve*: "A body of religious doctrines, a religion or faith, a Church; esp. the doctrines of Christianity, the Christian religion or Church." The *MED* is adding to the confusion when it quotes the carpenter's line as the very next example.

[31] Cf. *Riverside Chaucer*, pp. 946-47.

[32] Actually, Ross does mention *faith* as a possible meaning for John's use of the word *bileve*, but he does so only indirectly, namely when he discusses Nicholas' promise in lines 3581-82, "And thanne shal we be lordes al our lyf/Of al the world, as Noe and his wyf," and quotes Robertson's reading of those lines:

> Robertson . . . says, "John the carpenter is duped by Nicholas because the latter is able to take advantage of his extreme avarice. The prospect of being lord of the world with Alisoun, as if he were Noah and she his wife, blinds him to the improbability of the clerk's prediction so that he forgets even the elementary principles of his simple faith [see *bileve*, line 3556]." It might be more accurate to attribute John's duping to his stupidity rather than to one of the seven deadly sins, as Robertson does. Nicholas says that *we* (not *you*) shall be lords all our life; he seems deliberately, and impishly, to confuse the *menage a deux* with his proposed *menage a trois*. (p. 205)

Robertson did not make clear what exactly he meant by "the elementary principles of [John's] simple faith," but since he declared John's forgetting of those elementary principles to be the reason for the carpenter's duping, Robertson must have meant something more than just the *Credo*, which contains nothing about the Covenant.

Since Robertson wasn't "glossing" Chaucer's text—remember what DeNeef said about the Robertsonians' attitude toward the text itself (see n. 33 in the Introduction)—he probably felt no need or perhaps even considered it beneath the dignity of his allegorical reading to correct Skeat et al., *if* he paid attention to textual critics as seriously as he did to allegorical readers. For if, as Utley suggested, Robertson displayed an attitude of superciliousness which put other critics off, such an attitude might also have prevented Robertson from absorbing the opinions of other critics. Let me therefore quote Utley's suggestion in its entirety: "It is Robertson's attitude and results which disturb us. When a scholar declares: 'I have found out something interesting which I would like you to share with me,' we listen. But when a Jungian or a Robertsonian says, 'I have a special and arcane knowledge, though I doubt whether you have the experience or the erudition to follow me,' we are likely to take him at his word and turn away" (p. 251).

I am, of course not "turning away" from the Robertson who found John guilty of one of the Seven Deadly Sins, but I think Robertson (if I may use DeNeef's terms) was "careless" in rigidly-allegorically limiting John's failure to the sin of avarice. I agree that the carpenter is guilty of avarice, but that sin alone does not qualify him for the form of punishment which Chaucer has *queynte Nicholas* mete out to him. As a rigidly orthox Christian critic who doesn't allow himself to simply let Chaucer's *solaas* come to him—as Kendrick notes, to Robertson Chaucer's " 'obscenities' are philosophical, not funny" (p. 23)—Robertson over-eagerly slaps the well-to-do old carpenter who had bought himself a young wife with a verdict of avarice. My guess is that Robertson had found John guilty of that particular sin even before he seriously considered the carpenter's *bileve* pronouncement since, in the terms of the *cupiditas*-versus-*caritas* dialectic in which Robertsonians view Chaucer's writing, that form of *cupiditas* would be best suited to the old carpenter. And I think that Robertson had his *avaritia* argument automatically subsume any other argument which John priding himself on only knowing his *bileve* might give rise to: Robertson's argument that John forgetting "even the elementary principles of his simple faith" caused John's duping was merely a natural afterthought.

I wish I could agree with Robertson's afterthought: I then would be able to argue that John becomes guilty of pride when he claims to be a better Christian than the clerk because he knows and knows *only* the basic teachings of his religion although he doesnt know about God's Covenant with man. However, as I have tried to show, Chaucer is using both-and irony when he makes the reader uncertain, even confuses the reader, as to the meaning of the word *bileve* in line 3456. The kindest statement I can make about Robertson's handling of that line is that, rather than being a careless scholar, Robertson was as much a victim of Chaucer's intended uncertainty or confusion as we are today. What confounds me, though, is that the Thomas Ross who, as noted, is not exactly an aficionado of Robertson's and his disciples' methodology, did not make better use of the Robertson reading he quotes: Ross could have attacked Robertson either by contending that *Robertson* was wrong in interpreting that what John means by "bileve" includes knowledge of the Covenant or by pointing out, as I do, that if John does mean "bileve" in a generic sense *John* is wrong and therefore guilty of pride, a sin much more serious than the one Robertson accuses the carpenter of. Robertson's afterthought interpretation of the *bileve* and Ross' handling of what apparently he didn't recognize as a convenient afterthought combine into an illustration of Chaucer's success in trying to puzzle his readers.

[33] Latin Horace quotations are from the Oxford text; translations are my own.

[34] Ross, *Chaucer's Bawdy*, p. 33.

[35] It is helpful for our understanding of the *Miller's Tale* that, as Ross points out, in "the Old French fabliaux the *clerc amant* usually escapes punishment for his adultery or fornication" (p. 31).

[36] Alfred David, *The Strumpet Muse: Art and Morals in Chaucer's Poetry* (Bloomington: Indiana University Press, 1976), p. 98.

[37] Kendrick, p. 18.

[38] In our discussion of the idea of God having been anthropomorphosed into a Jupiter who punishes sinners with a flood, it might not be impertinent to note that Edmund Spenser would allusively utilize the Virgilian cosmic-union motif in a context in which he anthropomorphoses a Christian God of sorts into a Jupiter who punishes humans he is angry at with a rainstorm, namely, the Redcrosse Knight and Una:

> The day with cloudes was suddeine ouercast,
> And angry *Ioue* an hideous storme of raine
> Did poure into his Lemans lap so fast,

That every wight to shrowd it did constrain . . .
(*The Faerie Queene*, I, Canto I, vii, 50-53 [*The Works of Edmund Spenser: A Variorum Edition*, eds. Edwin Greenlaw et al. (Baltimore: The Johns Hopkins Press, 1932)]

The 'Christian God of sorts' here is the Catholic God's representative on earth, the Pope, whom the Protestant Spenser in fierce satire anthropomorphoses into a Jove, the highest god in ancient Roman religion, who is angry at Protestantism's undermining of the authority of Roman Catholicism. Spenser presents the Pope as angrily raping the earth in a quickie which does not exactly make the earth *laeta*/joyous. I would argue that Spenser took his cue for parody from Chaucer himself when he inverted the Virgilian *and the Chaucerian* procreation picture by presenting the head of the celibacy-commanding Catholic Church as a Jupiter whose 'emission' is explicitly described as *anything but* fruitful—and thus actually can be helpful for our explication of Chaucer's own text: see my article, "Spenser's 'Angry Ioue': Vergilian Allusion in the First Canto of *The Faerie Queene*," *Classical and Modern Literature*, 3 (1983), 162-82, and also my book chapter listed in n. 21 of the Introduction.

[39] Harder, p. 198.

[40] Harder, p. 198.

[41] Olson, p. 229. Tracey Jordan makes the following interesting observation concerning Nicholas' intellectual activities in a recent article entitled "Faerie Tale and Fabliau: Chaucer's *The Miller's Tale*," *Studies in Short Fiction*, 27, (1990), 98: "Nicholas' eager curiosity, his desire to acquire knowledge of the stars—those heavenly bodies—through his study of astrology, is not only an indication of his aggressive, rebellious character (in contrast to the carpenter, who believes 'Men sholde nat knowe of Goddes pryvetee') . . . but an expression of his desire for sexual knowledge as well. The word 'study' carries the connotation of 'eager desire'." Unfortunately, however, Tracey Jordan neither addresses David's point about Nicholas'

sexual triumph versus the triumph of his art nor relates the duality of the
clerk's exploits to the famous identical rhyme.

[42] The pun in "spille" has of course received critical attention.
Howard observes, "a triple pun, it may be" (p. 240), but he does not
elaborate why the pun involving the notion of the little death of orgasm might
be triple. See Ross, p. 155, with whose reservations about "spille" meaning
"to have orgasm" I disagree. In fact, Ross had earlier observed under *spille*
in *Chaucer's Bawdy*: "['To die'] is probably the meaning [here] . . . , but it
is also possible that it meant 'to have an involuntary emission.' In the hot
love affair between Nicholas and Alisoun, such an event is perfectly possible"
(*Chaucer's Bawdy*, p. 208). Why did Ross consider the event of involuntary
emission perfectly possible in 1972 but not in 1983? In 1977 and in 1989
Fisher glossed *spille* as "die (*double entendre*, ejaculate)" (p. 60). I have
faith that my bringing in of Augustinian theology later in this chapter will shed
light on the outcome of the question as to the possibility of such an "event."

[43] Ross' description of the interaction between the two rhymes is
delightfully succinct and understated: "it would not be unfair to suggest that
[the] major role [of *ybleynt*] is to provide a rhyme with *yqueynt* in the next
line" (p. 231). See also Frederick Turner's comment in n. 45 below.

[44] For a discussion of Absalom's lover's malady, see Schweitzer's
article listed in n. 51 below.

[45] Frederick Turner, "A Structural Reading of the *Knight's Tale*,"
Chaucer Review, 8 (1974), 292, makes the following observation: "Absolon
and the Carpenter are both fooled, and both symbolically emasculated
(Absolon's 'hoote love was coold and yqueynt' . . . —the possible pun on
'yqueynt' is significant—and the Carpenter breaks his arm in the fall from the
roof"). If Alison's prank has quenched Absalom's lust in the manner in
which I have suggested, then Absalom has been more than merely
"*symbolically* emasculated": the idea is that Absalom has been traumatized,

possibly to the point of impotence. While Ross quotes Turner but does not comment on Turner's remark about Absalom's symbolic castration, Ross does comment concerning *John's* fate: "A broken arm is not, thank goodness, equivalent to emasculation; however, John's injury may in some way be emblematic of his loss of manhood" (pp. 232-33). I see John's injury as emblematic of a loss of manhoood in the sense that his injury is a direct result of another man "getting to know" the *senex amans'* wife.

[46] Ross, p. 229.

[47] It is possible that in my *vagina dentata* reading of the second window scene I have been influenced—but, I hope, not *mis*directed—by the famous scene in Laurence Sterne's *Tristram Shandy* where, according to the rumor spread by the protagonist's physician, Tristram is unmanned when the maid invites him to urinate out of the bedroom window and she inadvertently has the window 'clap to' on his penis in guillotine-like fashion. Yet I would like to refer to an enlightening comment by John Leyerle, "Thematic Interlace in 'The Canterbury Tales'," in *Essays and Studies* (London: John Murray, 1976)), p. 111: "The Miller's Tale has a poetic nucleus of holes in all their complex conjunctions: windows, doors, tubs, marlpits, rings, eyes, nether eyes, and towts; they reveal the anarchy and chaos of sexual license."

[48] Cf. Janette Richardson's observation: "The man who prides himself upon having the very thing he lacks is a favorite character with Chaucer, as evidenced by . . . the rustic adherent of courtly love in the *Miller's Tale*" (*Blameth Nat Me: A Study of Imagery in Chaucer's Fabliaux* [Den Haag: Mouton, 1970], p. 81). Olson comments: "the biblical Absalom is called by Pierre Bersuire a figure for 'mundi pompam' [i.e., worldly pomp], by Nicholas of Lyra an emblem of 'superbia,' by Gower a representative of 'surquidrie' and 'orguill' [i.e., arrogance and pride], and by Bromyard a figure for those who rejoice in clothing and ornaments" (p. 232). To me Chaucer's Absalom is not guilty of the same degree of *superbia* that John is,

which we could call existential pride (and Absalom's punishment doesn't measure up to John's). The irony is that when Absalom calls himself "a lord at alle degrees," he is getting carried away by his pride in the sexual conquest he thinks he has just secured; I will call it phallic hubris. This phallic hubris manifests itself by the vanity of Absalom's external appearance: as Ross observes, the fact that Absalom's "absurdly extravagant . . . dress . . . is tight-fitting probably has sexual connotations" (p. 33).

⁴⁹ David observes: "In her portrait [Alisoun] is closely identified with the objects of Nature . . . *For Alisoun sex can be enjoyed as though the fall of man had never taken place* . . . Alisoun's response to sex is the most healthy and natural, and I think it is significant that no mention is made at the end of any punishment for her" (pp. 96-97, italics added). Concerning the statement I italicized in my quotation from David, I would like to ask: could Chaucer actually be presenting Alison as sexually prelapsarian in the terms of Augustinian theology? I will try to answer that question in Chapter V.

⁵⁰ Bernard. F. Huppé, *A Reading of the Canterbury Tales* (Albany: State University of New York Press, 1964), p. 85, has made this comment on the *Miller's Tale*: "It is a story which ends in, as it revels in, *the Babylonian confusion* of a world where men seek only their own pleasures. [The Miller's] is *a topsy-turvy world*, where the wife rules, in clear defiance of God's order—with the inevitable result that the Parson proclaims, 'For ther as the womman hath maistrie, she makes to much desray . . . '(X, 926)" (italics mine). I like Huppé's characterization of the Miller's world as one of Babylonian confusion: the idea of such a confusion is precisely what Chaucer is trying to introduce when he first has the Miller give us a *Weltanschauung* which makes "Goddes pryvetee," i.e., God's secrets, into something obscene by linking it to the pudendum of a wife whose faithfulness cannot be predicted, and then has the Miller present the naive carpenter as using the same phrase. We need to bear in mind, however, that it is the men themselves, not the

woman, who make the world topsy-turvy. In the case of Nicholas and Absalom, it is lusting after another man's wife. John becomes a victim of Babylonian confusion first in the sense that his "wit was rude," as a result of which he becomes a *senex amans*, but second, and more importantly, in the sense that, much like the Babylonians whose proud aspirations led them to build a tower with which to reach the sky, John thinks he can outwit God by becoming, with help from another human agent, a self-ordained Noah.

51   Edward C. Schweitzer, "The Misdirected Kiss and the Lover's Malady in Chaucer's *Miller's Tale*," in *Chaucer in the Eighties*, eds. Julian N. Wasserman and Robert J. Blanch (Syracuse, NY: Syracuse University Press, 1986), p. 230. Schweitzer notes Chaucer's changes vis-à-vis his sources:

> Absolon's counterparts kiss the successful lover's rump, not the woman's. For Absolon's fantasy of "sweete Alisoun" to be shattered, however, Absolon must kiss not Nicholas but Alisoun herself. While Absolon's counterparts, accordingly, learn only that they have been tricked, the Miller makes Absolon, kissing Alisoun, learn that and more: Absolon learns the folly of love *paramours*—something about which the Miller himself and all those equally churlish smiths in the analogues can never have had any illusions. (pp. 226-27)

Comparing Absalom's love-sickness to Arcite's eventually fatal love-sickness in the *Knight's Tale*, the tale which is parodied by the *Miller's Tale*, Schweitzer notes that "Absolon is cured of his love-sickness in just the way medieval physicians prescribe for the most extreme cases: shocking the lover with the physical reality of sex in order to destroy the idealized fantasy by which he is obsessed" (p. 227). Schweitzer is of course correct in his interpretation of Chaucer's treatment of the (mock-) courtly lover Absalom, but we must not overlook that Chaucer does eventually bring into play the successful lover's rump, namely in order to imply a parallel between the folly of the idealizing lover and the folly of a clerk named Nicholas who, while being rather down-to-earth as a lover, becomes the victim of his pretentious, ethereal pursuits.

[52] Tracey Jordan, p. 88.

[53] Robert Jordan, p. 195.

[54] Dinshaw, p. 9.

[55] Nicholas being "written" on by Absalom is poetic justice in a tale which reflects Chaucer's sexual poetics in the sense that, in Dinshaw's words,

> literary activity has a gendered structure, a structure that associates acts of writing and related acts of signifying—allegorizing, interpeting, glossing, translating—with the masculine and that identifies the surfaces on which these acts are performed, or from which these acts depart, or which these acts reveal—the page, the text, the literal sense, or even the hidden meaning—with the feminine . . . [T]he significance and value of the masculine and the feminine in such a model of gendered hermeneutics constantly shift and change . . . in Chaucer's poetry; Chaucer plays with the gender associations, hermeneutic values, and power relations this structure suggests. (p. 9)

Dinshaw's observation about literary activity possessing a gendered structure immediately precedes her comment on the denouement of the *Miller's Tale*. The "playful [structure-]reversal" which Chaucer performs in the misdirections episode actually is considerably more complex than Dinshaw has suggested. For we are dealing here with a double-reversal of gender-structures, or perhaps more precisely, with two overlapping reversals of gender-structures, since the structure reversals already begin in the first window scene.

In the first window scene the male thinks he is in the position of the "writer" in the sense that he "pre-*scribes*" the scenario he expects: he thinks that by "writing" a kiss on the surface of the female he can guarantee that "ther cometh moore," i.e., that he will be able to use his *stilus* with the woman serving as the page—and serving as the text which he can interpret. Absalom misinterprets the text because the female turns the page on him, so to speak. *She* is the one who does the "pre-scribing," and when *she* kisses *him* insofar as she motions to his mouth a mouth that is accompanied by a beard she is performing a gender-reversal for both of them. Absalom tries to reverse the reversal by coming back with a colter, the *Ur*-phallus with which to plow (i.e., "write" on) the surface of mother earth. However, Absalom's (eventually successful) enterprise of reversing the reversal is forced to take a step backward, not because of something the targeted surface (woman, page, or text) does, but because another male tries to "over-write" what Alison has done and outdo her in turning the page on Absalom.

Nicholas' problem is that he misinterprets the text, which, as in the case of Absalom's misdirected kiss, he cannot see because it is dark. As the phallic "super-scriptor" who had been in control (or thought he had been in control) all along, Nicholas treats Absalom as a male who intends to "write on" the female. Nicholas does not realize that Absalom, effeminate or not, has undergone a gender-reversal and therefore has no intentions whatsoever of approaching the woman/page/text in the same manner he had before: "the feminized Absolon," in Dinshaw's words, has brought with him a more potent pen than he had before and, again in Dinshaw's words, Absalom " 'writes on' . . . . the naked body of the naked clerk Nicholas."

The plow is mightier than the pen, i.e., mightier than the clerk, part of whose vocation is to handle a pen. Especially since the window scenes would never have taken place if it hadn't been for *hende Nicholas'* manipulations, in terms of Chaucer's sexual poetics justice is being served when Absalom hands out punishment by unknowingly avenging himself on his knowledgeable rival rather than on the targeted text, the woman. Wouldn't it therefore be poetic justice if we could assume that Chaucer is insinuating that Absalom is performing a symbolic cunnification on Nicholas when he hits him with a colter—that is, when the feminized Absalom "plows" Nicholas he is transmogrifying him into into a *queynte*?

⁵⁶ Eric Partridge, *Shakespeare's Bawdy*, rev. ed. (New York: Dutton, 1969), p. 163.

[57] Roy Peter Clark, "Squeamishness and Exorcism in Chaucer's *Miller's Tale*," *Thought*, 14 (1974), 43.

[58] Douglas Gray cautions that the misdirections episode, especially its windy part, "has been the subject of some absurdly earnest . . . moralizing criticism" (p. 848). One of the problems with Clark's moralizing interpretation here is that if we wish to argue that, by replacing Alison and windily improving upon her joke, Nicholas "exorcizes" the "intruder," then the "symbolic buggery" is *preceded* by the act of exorcism—so that the entire exorcism-thesis as proposed by Clark goes out the window. It could perhaps be argued that Nicholas intends an act of exorcism which *unintentionally* transforms the intruder's assault into "symbolic buggery," but in such a case it doesn't seem to make much sense to argue that "the blatant effeminacy of Absalom" makes Absalom's hot-colter operation an act of "symbolic sodomy." While Absalom is indeed portrayed as effeminate, Chaucer's point is that Absalom's act is one of phallic violence intended against a female (which may or may not be out of character with Absalom's presentation as effeminate, but which could actually be seen as an attempt to overcompensate for that effeminacy).

[59] Ross, pp. 125, 229, 233, 241, and 242.

[60] Ross, p. 229.

[61] Ross, p. 242. Ross cites several analogues which present an *in ano* cauterization of sorts (pp. 5-6 and 241), but those analogues do not help us with our reading of Chaucer, not ony because they are post-Chaucerian but also, and more importantly, because the intended as well as the eventually affected victim is the male lover, not the woman.

[62] Ross, p. 242.

[63] Clark, in another article, "Christmas Games in Chaucer's *The Canterbury Tales*," *Studies in Short Fiction*, 13 (1976), 284, speaks of "Absolom's symbolic rape of Nicholas." I'm not sure I can agree with the

rape of Nicholas being "symbolic." Chaucer's idea here is that Absalom had intended to symbolically rape Alison in punishment for the degrading rejection of his advances and is denied the fulfillment of that symbolism when, without the would-be rapist's knowledge, Nicholas replaces the intended rape victim. For the same reason I have to disagree with Tracey Jordan when, after quoting Clark to build up to a phallic-violence argument, she speaks of "confusion of love and violence that characterizes the phallic revenge Absolon *administers* with his hot colter" (p. 90, italics mine), but I likewise find it disappointing that Tracey Jordan, who astutely assesses Alison's role as "eminently female" (p. 91), fails to take what, at least after the accumulation of material on "plowing" in the *Miller Variorum*, would seem to be the natural next step and identify the dandified mock-courtly lover Absalom as a totally misdirected plowman or something of that sort. The parodic aspects of the hot-colter motif, especially as it pertains to Alison, have received curiously little critical attention.

⁶⁴ Ross, p. 231.

⁶⁵ Norman Davis quotes in the "Language and Versification" section in the Introduction of the *Riverside Chaucer* that "The subjunctive in main clauses may be used . . . in a hypothetical conditional sentence: *A clerk hadde litherly biset his whyle* (a scholar would have wasted his time)" (p. xlii). To native speakers of 'purely' Teutonic languages such as German and Dutch (see the citations from J. Kerhof in the next paragraph) the grammatical makeup of Nicholas' promise to Alison is obvious.

⁶⁶ For discussions of the irrealis see J. Kerkhof, *Studies in the Language of Chaucer* (Leiden: Leiden University Press, 1982), pp. 26-28. The quotation is from p. 27.

⁶⁷ Ross, p. 231.

⁶⁸ See Ross, p. 231.

[69] The Glossary of the *Riverside Chaucer* lists neither the *ybleynt* nor the infinitive of the verb it might have come from, but Douglas Gray, the contributor of the Explanatory Notes, is also one of the four contributors to the *Chaucer Glossary*. The 1979 *Chaucer Glossary* explains *ybleynt* as "*p. p.* turned away, ducked," and refers to Absalom's exclamation. Especially since by 1987 Gray must have been aware that in 1963, 1974, and 1977 three major Chaucer editors-scholars had agreed on "abstained" (see *Miller Variorum*, p. 231), one wonders why he didn't feel any need to comment in the *Riverside Chaucer* on what obviously is a controversial line. After all, it was Gray who would point out in the *Riverside Chaucer* that the window episode "has been subject of some absurdly earnest . . . moralizing criticism." It might not be impertinent to note here that in his *Miller's Tale* Explanatory Notes in the 1987 *Riverside Chaucer* Gray does not cite the *Miller Variorum* of 1983, but then the only *Variorum* edition of Chaucer listed in the *Riverside Chaucer* is the 1982 edition of *The Minor Poems* (p. 79).

[70] Ross, p. 228.

[71] Ross, *Chaucer's Bawdy*, pp. 83-84.

[72] Since the *OED* doesn't elaborate on the linguistic development from *ers/ars/arse* to *ass*, let me cite the *Random House Dictionary of the English Language*, which under *ass* explains the development as the "loss of *r* before *s*, as in PASSEL, CUSS" out of *parcel* and *curse*.

[73] The *OED* doesn't list any examples of *arse* with a sexual connotation. See the next note.

[74] The earliest listing the *OED* carries for the sexual connotation of *ass* is "chasing ass" in John Updike's 1961 *Rabbit, Run*. This American idiomatic expression had been in existence long before the publication of Updike's 1961 novel, but at that time the expression seemed to be virtually unknown in the U. K. The ambiguity in Chaucer saying that Alison projected her "hole" and that Absalom kissed her *ers* while encountering a *berd* could

have been highlighted long ago, even before Ross' query as to which hole Absalom kisses, if there had been better communication between British and American Chaucerians. Very few British Chaucerians knew the heterosexual sexual connotation in the Americanism "ass," if they saw any sexual connotation at all, and very few American Chaucerians knew that their British fellow scholars didn't know. As a neutral (foreign) observer who grew up in the international business-and-banking community in Hamburg which included native speakers of both British and American English, I recognize the communicative breakdown between the Brits and their "Colonials" and propose myself as an "interpreter" of the first window scene in the *Miller's Tale*. (I personally witnessed the following illustrative misunderstanding between an American exchange student and a group of our British hosts while at Sheffield University in 1961 or 1962: when the American student bragged about "getting a piece of ass," he was asked whether he was a "bugger.")

[75] Ross, p. 230.

[76] Ross, p. 230.

[77] The reverse order is given by the *Riverside Chaucer*, which glosses "A berd! A Berd!" as "a beard! a trick!" (p. 75). For reasons which I have already offered, I disagree with that order.

[78] Ross, *Chaucer's Bawdy*, p. 96.

[79] Ross observed in Chaucer's *Chaucer's Bawdy*: "when Absolon says to Alisoun, 'Lemman, thy grace, and sweete bryd, thyn oore' (A 3726), what reader would not be reminded that when Absolon bestows the kiss, it is her 'berd' (her 'bottom-grass,' her 'grace') that touches his lips" (p. 97).

[80] Cf. de Weever, pp. 4-5.

[81] *Riverside Chaucer*, p. 69.

[82] Gray, *Riverside Chaucer*, pp. 848-49.

[83] See me quotation from the *Riverside Chaucer* in n. 58 above.

84 Ross had made the following observation in *Chaucer's Bawdy*: "When Absolon has kissed Alisoun's 'nether ye' . . . by misdirection, his once hot love is 'coold and al yqueynte'—i.e., quenched, but surely (there is) a whiff of the pudendum too" (p. 178). Ross' statement seems ambiguous, perhaps even enigmatic, to me, and I wish Ross had elaborated on this point in the *Miller Variorum*.

85 Lindahl, p. 129.

86 Stevens, p. 59.

87 Tracey Jordan, p. 98.

88 Northrop Frye, *Anatomy of Criticism* (Princeton: Princeton University Press, 1973), p. 156.

89 While normally an author employs centripetal ("in-pulling") vectors to import meanings from the alluded-to text into his own work, sometimes an author will employ centrifugal ("out-going") vectors in order to affect our reading of the text alluded to, usually for the purpose of parodying that text. This concept "view[s] a work of literature as located in the center of the circle whose circumference houses all the contexts to which this work alludes" (quoted from my *Mutual Commerce*, p. 2).

90 Quoted in *Riverside Chaucer*, p. 930.

91 Vulgate citations are from the 1959 *Biblia Sacra* edition of the Biblioteca de Autores Christianos.

92 Kendrick, p. 27.

93 Cf. W. Bryant Bachman, Jr., "Mercury, Virgil, and Arcite: *Knight's Tale*, 1384-1397," *English Language Notes*, 13 (1976), 173. Bachman argues that the purpose of Chaucer's allusion to Mercury's dream appearance to Aeneas is to recall for the reader "the melancholy conflict between human desires and human destinies." Bachman is of course referring to the fact that Jupiter had sent Mercury to admonish Aeneas to leave Dido, the woman whom Aeneas loves but is not destined to marry. The allusive

filiations are much more complex, since we have the allusively functional contrast between Mercury admonishing Aeneas to leave the beloved woman but encouraging Arcite to pursue her. See my *Neophilologus* article listed in n. 1 above, and also n. 94 below.

[94]   See my *Neophilologus* article listed in n. 1 above, and the elaboration of that argument in my second *Mutual Commerce* chapter, "The *Aeneid* in the *Knight's Tale*," where I demonstrate how in his presentation of Arcite's life-journey Chaucer allusively conflates, at time playing off against each other, the *Aeneid* and Boccaccio's *Teseide*.

[95]   Ross, *Chaucer's Bawdy*, p. 155.

[96]   Ross, *Chaucer's Bawdy*, p. 240.

[97]   Cf. Lorraine Kochanske Stock, "The Two Mayings in Chaucer's *Knight's Tale*," *Journal of English and Germanic Philology*, 85 (1986), 218, who speaks of Arcite's hope that possession of Emily "will satiate the physical pangs of love he *unwillingly* endures" (italics mine). This spirited article exposes an Arcite who "languishes in a state of aggravated physical desire" (p. 217).

CHAPTER II

[1]   Albert C. Salzberg, "A Jew Teaches Western Literature," *CEA Forum*, 19, nos. 3-4 (1989), 20-23. Small partions of this chapter have appeared in the *American Imago* article listed in n. 5 of the Introduction and in my article, "Sexuality and Self-Recognition in the *Pardoner's Tale*," *Journal of Evolutionary Psychology*, 3 (October 1982), 124-29.

[2]   Salzberg, p. 20.

[3]   Salzberg, p. 20.

[4]   Salzberg, p. 22.

[5]   A *Variorum Edition of the Works of Geoffrey Chaucer*, vol. II, *The Canterbury Tales*, Part Twenty, *The Prioress's Tale*, ed. Beverly Boyd

(Norman and London: University of Oklahoma Press, 1987), p. 42. Boyd's edition will hereafter be referred to as *Prioress Variorum* or simply as Boyd.

⁶ Paull F. Baum, *Chaucer: A Critical Appreciation* (Durham, NC: Duke University Press, 1958), p. 79.

⁷ In a 1981 article entitled "Chaucer's Use of Signs in His Portrait of the Prioress," Chauncey Wood observed: "the judgments of most scholars about the Prioress seem strangely affectionate" (in *Signs and Symbols*, eds. John P. Hermann and John J. Burke, Jr. [University, AL: University of Alabama Press, 1981], p. 100).

⁸ Edward H. Kelly, "By Mouth of Innocentz: The Prioress Vindicated," *Papers on Language and Literature*, 5 (1969), 362-74.

⁹ Kelly, pp. 362-64.

¹⁰ Kelly, p. 364.

¹¹ Kelly, p. 368.

¹² Boyd, p. 153.

¹³ Boyd, pp. 154-55.

¹⁴ In the article listed in n. 28 below, Edward I. Condren seems to be identifying with Kelly's "heartfelt" hermeneutics when he quotes at length the passage in which Kelly had pronounced his verdict and unquestioningly accepts that verdict (p. 213, n. 6). A certain tendentiousness seems to display itself in Condren's statement: "Strongest among the Prioress's detractors is R. J. Schoeck" (p. 213, n. 4). Can one *seriously* speak of a "detractor" of a character in a work of literature?

¹⁵ John Gardner has observed that the Prioress' "veneration of purity rings ironically against her scatological inclination" (*The Poetry of Chaucer* [Carbondale and Edwardsville: Southern Illinois University Press, 1977], pp. 304-306).

¹⁶ Florence H. Ridley, *The Prioress and Her Critics*, University of California Publications: English Studies, no. 30 (Berkeley and Los Angeles:

University of California Press, 1965), p. 4. Ridley citations from this study usually will be identified as Ridley, *Prioress*. Citations from her contributions to the *Riverside Chaucer* will be identified as Ridley, *Riverside Chaucer*.

[17] Instead of summarily dismissing "such . . . criticism," which I assume to mean psychoanalytic criticism, as "warped," Ridley would have been on firmer ground had she simply used the text in her attack on Maurice Cohen, "Chaucer's Prioress and Her Tale: A Study of Anal Character and Anti-Semitism," *Psychonanalytic Quarterly*, 31 (1962), 232-49. For example, Cohen misinterprets and translates the *sterve* (i.e., *to die*) in the Prioress' statement, "With torment and with shamful deth echon/This provost dooth this Jewes to sterve," as *starve*, and adds that "Starving as deprivation suggests also greed for the wealth of the Jews—a motive of great importance in medieval persecution" (p. 243). "To die" would not have fit Cohen's argument, where he uses the Prioress' alleged mention of "starving the offending Jews" to support his thesis about the Prioress' "fantasies of oral sadism" (p. 241), a thesis for which I see little justification (*sterve* and *starve* are of course cognates; cf. German *sterben*, "to die").

However, while the article is over-abundant with psychoanalytic arguments, in fact so over-abundant that some of them seem to contradict each other, I found several of Cohen's observations interesting and helpful, and I would not want to see his article discarded or ignored. I therefore wasn't particularly thrilled when in her Explanatory Notes in the *Riverside Chaucer* Ridley did not list Cohen's article but included my *American Imago* article, which, discussing several characters in the *Canterbury Tales*, had devoted about three pages to the Prioress. Ridley didn't seem to say anything negative about my thoughts on the Prioress—her only comment was that I had interpreted the *Prioress' Tale* as "a pschycotic study" (p. 914)—but the omission of Cohen's seventeen-page article made me feel as though I had been given Cohen's place as the psychoanalytic detractor of the Prioress. Maybe I should take this as encouragement for my examination of Chaucer's portrayal of the Prioress.

[18] Boyd would call Ridley's 1965 study "the most vigorous of the rebuttals of the satirical intention of [the *Prioress' Tale*]" (p. 32).

[19] Ridley, *Prioress*, p. 29.

[20] Ridley observes:

some critics find in the Prioress's treatment of animals and her reaction to their pain not an illustration, but a sardonic rebuttal of the line, "And al was conscience and tendre herte" [I 150]. They say it is designed to show that Eglentine loved animals *instead of* humans. Muriel Bowden finds the Prioress's tears for their suffering evidence of lack of concern for human suffering . . . [Gary] Taylor, citing the Prioress's motto, "Love conquers all," asks bluntly, "But love of what? Dogs? Madame Eglentine loved dogs" . . . [D. W.] Robertson finds [her love of animals] a device of "unmistakable sarcasm" . . . John M. Major [finds it] a means of making the Prioress an object of "deliberate irony . . . powerful at work." (*Prioress*, p. 23)

Ridley attempts to rebut the "hard critics" she has quoted by resorting to an interpretation of the Prioress as "simpleminded; *these dogs are her children, the only ones she is ever likely to have;* and so nothing could be more natural than her tears. It is by those very tears that Chaucer most clearly shows that her religious vocation, while it may have redirected, has not stifled her basic feminine instinct of maternal love" (p. 24, italics mine). One of the problems with Ridley's rebuttal is that, if for the Prioress the dogs are indeed *Ersatz* children, the repression of her maternal instinct (as well as the repression of her sexuality) may have had a serious effect on her mental health—as I will argue is indeed the case.

[21] Ridley, *Prioress*, p. 24.

[22] Ridley, *Prioress*, p. 29.

[23] Cf. Ridley, *Prioress*, p. 7.

[24] Ridley, *Prioress*, p. 1.

²⁵ Concerning the tendency to view the Prioress' prologue and her tale as separate "works," see n. 69 below.

²⁶ Ross, *Chaucer's Bawdy*, p. 48.

²⁷ Kendrick observes: " 'gentil' medieval interpreters would try to react to Mary's bare breast . . . (much like modern Robertsonians) by searching for some Christian 'morality' or 'holiness' therein" (p. 15). As I attempt to demonstrate throughout this chapter, in his characterization of the Prioress Chaucer could hardly be said to be a " 'gentil' medieval interpreter."

²⁸ Edward I. Condren, "The Prioress: A Legend of Spirit, a Life of Flesh," *Chaucer Review*, 23 (1989), 197.

²⁹ See n. 30 below.

³⁰ Compared to the "ravyshedest doun," the Annunciation in the Vulgate sounds rather tame: "Spiritus sanctus superveniet in te" (Luke 1:35). Pointing out that *ravish* derives after all from the Latin *rapere*, Cohen calls that part of the Prioress' hymn a "fantasy of divine rape" (p. 235). Roger Ellis, *Patterns of Religious Narrative in the Canterbury Tales* (London and Sydney: Croom Helm, 1986), notes that "the linguistic game is . . . dazzling (p. 76).

³¹ Condren observes: "the masculine principle of the Holy Spirit (vertu <L. *virtus*, cognate with L. *vir*, man) becomes the actual instrument of coneception: 'Of whos vertu . . . Conceyved was the Fadres sapience' " (p. 216, n. 17). I am encouraged by the fact that a 1989 article in the *Chaucer Review* hardens what I had said in my 1978 *American Imago* article about the Prioress' comments on Mary's conception in general and her use of the word *vertu* in particular (some of the preceding lines in my present paragraph pretty much repeat what I said on pp. 407 and 412 in that article). What stiffens my resolve in this chapter is that all of the coitus-impregnation-conception-birthing-suckling imagery which is essential to Condren's argument in his fascinating article was covered in my *American Imago* article. Was it Ridley's

influence—Condren calls her *Prioress* monograph a "judicious survey of the major views" (p. 213, n. 3)—that caused Condren to ignore studies published in psychoanalytically oriented journals? Especially since Condren elaborates on what he calls the Prioress' "visceral metaphors" (p. 205), one would have expected him to mention Cohen, who has a lot to say on that subject—and whom Ridley had so prominently quoted.

At this particular point I wish to acknowledge that I am indebted to Condren for his unintentional qualified support of my reading that the "ravisher" in the prologue is the Holy Ghost rather than Mary herself. Carefully examining the syntax in the hymn, Condren argues that the relative pronoun *That* in "That ravyshedest . . . the Goost" refers to Mary, and that making Mary the "accusative case, object of the verb *ravyshedest* . . . . would require a tortured shift in direct address from Virgin Mother to Holy Spirit: 'O Mary who [you, O Holy Spirit,] ravished' " (p. 216, n. 26). I will accept the tortured shift in direct address, accept what Condren calls "the tortured syntax of the intervening reflective line" (p. 198), and argue that the tortured syntax is a formal device on the poet's part to insinuate to us how tortured the Prioress is. In fact, the Prioress' tortured syntax here anticipates the syntactical ambiguity in "Of grete God that parfournest thy laude/By mouth of innocentz, lo, here thy might" (VII 607-608) where, as Kelly points out, "It is not clear . . . which mouth of innocence the Prioress refers to, the mother's or the son's, for the boy immediately begins the *alma redemptoris*" (p. 371). What is important for my present argument is the intensity of the sexual imagery regardless of who ravishes whom—in the background there is always the Biblical statement, "Spiritus sanctus superveniet in te"—an imagery which was at least partially rendered by Ridley in 1987 when in her translation of lines 469-72 she rendered *vertu* as *potency*: "Through humility you ravished from God the Holy Spirit which alighted within you, from whose potency Christ, the Wisdom of God, was conceived" (*Riverside Chaucer*, p. 914).

Fisher notes that *vertu* means "potency, the original Latin meaning of *virtus*" (p. 242). The original meaning of Latin "vir-tus" is *not* "[sexual] potency" but, as I have noted, "man-ness": the word usually refers to a person's spiritual-moral qualities. Chaucer is *punning* on the etymology of "vir-tus," and the pun includes a wordplay on "sapere." I will further elaborate on the the *vertu* context over the next few pages.

[32] Thus, whereas Richard J. Schoeck, one of the "hardest" critics of the Prioress and her tale, noted in 1958 the irony of a Biblical preface to an anti-Semitic miracle-tale of the Virgin ("Chaucer's Prioress: Mercy and Tender Heart," repr. in Richard J. Schoeck and Jerome Taylor, eds., *Chaucer Criticism: The Canterbury Tales* [Notre Dame: Notre Dame University Press, 1960], p. 250), we can now say that the Biblical preface itself is already full of irony.

[33] Condren, p. 200.

[34] I first made the points about about the Prioress representing the recital of her tale as poetically giving birth both to the tale and to the little boy in my *American Imago* article, pp. 412-13. Condren has observed since then: "As the white lily flower bore Christ, so the Prioress 'wol do [her] labour' to tell a story . . . childbirth equals literary creation; infant equals story" (p. 197). Condren contibutes to the argument by citing evidence that Chaucer's use of the word *labour* indeed refers to childbirth (p. 215, n. 23).

[35] David, p. 210.

[36] David observes: "Underlying the figures of the little boy and his widowed mother are those of the Christ child and the *mater dolorosa*. The Prioress characteristically conceives of Christ as the infant Jesus as though he had been one of the innocent victims of Herod's massacre (to which there are several allusions) rather than crucified of his own volition for the sins of mankind. In the tale there is no human or divine father figure, only the widow and the Virgin, the great mother figure of the Middle Ages" (pp. 210-

11). What needs to be explained, and I will attempt to do so, is *why* the Prioress alludes to Herod's massacre and *why* there is no human or divine father figure in the tale.

37 Quoted by Ridley, *Riverside Chaucer*, p. 915.

38 My interpretation that poetically speaking the Prioress kills the boy in order to castrate him would seem to answer Condren's question concerning Chaucer's change vis-à-vis most of the tale's analogues: "Elsewhere the young clergeon springs back to life at the end of the story, whereas in the *Prioress' Tale* the removal of the grain ends both his life and his song . . . If the Prioress intends to recreate one of the Virgin's great miracles, why does she diminish the miracle?" (p. 193).

39 "The burning bush here symbolizes the virginity and purity of Mary undiminished in the Incarnation of Christ" (Boyd, p. 122).

40 Chaucer's use of the "nat . . . worth a bene" is much more complex, especially in terms of the poet's use of irony, than it may appear from my brief reference to it here; I will elaborate on that context in Chapter V.

41 Paul G. Ruggiers, *The Art of the Canterbury Tales* (Madison: University of Wisconsin Press, 1965), p. 178.

42 Ridley, *Prioress*, p. 25.

43 Ridley, *Riverside Chaucer*, p. 916. The Prioress' aside had been interpreted as an allusion to the monk in the *Shipman's Tale* at least as early as 1951 (cf. Boyd, p. 157).

44 See, for example, Ridley, *Riverside Chaucer*, p. 916.

45 Douglas Loney, "Chaucer's Prioress and Agur's 'Adulterous Woman'," *Chaucer Review*, 27 (1992), 107-108.

46 My guess is that one of the reasons Loney missed out on this linguistic complexity was that in his 1992 essay he was still using Robinson's 1957 edition instead of the 1987 *Riverside Chaucer*, which, referring to

Skeat's edition, notes that "Jerome has 'amor mulieris' for the Vulgate's 'os vuluae' " (*Riverside Chaucer*, p. 868).

[47] For this point of information I am enebted to Edward Le Comte, *Milton and Sex* (London: Macmillan, 1978), p. 79. Milton, who had studied Hebrew, would pun on the slang meaning of "to eat" in his presentation of the Fall, e.g., in his description of Adam as eating "that fair enticing Fruit" (*Paradise Lost*, IX, 996). Milton citations are from Merritt Y. Hughes' edition of *Paradise Lost* (Indianapolis: Odyssey Press, 1962).

[48] Condren, p. 217, n. 17.

[49] Condren, p. 192.

[50] Wood, p. 82.

[51] As Wood observes, "it is important to note that Chaucer's portrait of the Prioress is *not* like conventional satires on nuns, which regularly accused them of concupiscence. Both in subject matter and in form Chaucer is working out a satiric approach new to his age" (p. 83). Part of the newness of Chaucer's approach is that he combines satire of religious bias with satire of sexual concerns and mores. It is an oversimplification to claim, as George E. Adams does in an article entitled "Sex and Clergy in Chaucer's 'General Prologue'," that "the anger in [the Prioress'] story is that of a well-born lady who dislikes both the religion and the customs of the Jews" (*Literature and Psychology*, 18 [1968], 217).

[52] Condren, p. 208.

[53] Boyd, pp. 143-44.

[54] In light of the fact that the "aleye hadde a privee place," would it be impertinent to play on a modern association and speak of a "pryvetee" which Madame Eglentyne had committed in a back alley?

[55] Joseph A. Dane, "The Prioress and Her *Romanzen*," *Chaucer Review*, 24 (1990), 219-22. The two quotations are from p. 220.

[56] Ellis, p. 77.

57 Ellis, p. 77.

58 Cohen argues that "the correlation between children and fecal mass . . . is symbolized throughout the tale" (p. 237), and then observes: "children are [for the Prioress] . . . dangerous excreta that have damaged her own body" (p. 238). However, Cohen does not say *how* children have damaged her body. On the other hand, he does remark that "the passage suggests the familiar fantasies of anal rape . . . and, in the mode of disposing of the child's body, an infantile birth theory" (p. 240).

59 Kendrick, p. 50.

60 Norman N. Holland, *The Dynamics of Literary Response* (New York: Oxford University Press, 1968).

61 Stevens, p. 67.

62 After just having called the "mercy multiplie"/"moder Marie" a "stark collocation rhyme," it might be well to quote Stephen Knight's observations: "The word 'mercy' is repeated here so that it almost becomes a jingle, and its absence in the tale is consequently stressed . . . It seems she only thinks of mercy for herself" (*The Poetry of the Canterbury Tale* [Sydney: Angus and Robertson, 1973], p. 143).

63 *Paradise Lost*, X, 1042. When Milton's Eve learns what consequences her and Adam's acts of disobedience will have for mankind—she says: "miserable it is/ . . . of our own Loins to bring/Into this World a woeful Race" (X, 981-84)—she suggests racial suicide in the form of abstinence, a suggestion which Adam rejects as "wilfull barrenness." We will later see how Milton's pronouncements on "wilfull barrenness" can help us with our understanding of Chaucer's own poem.

64 Robinson, p. 735. The *Riverside Chaucer* unfortunately dropped Robinson's observation—unfortunately because in that observation Robinson, unwittingly, pointed in the satiric direction which I investigate in this chapter.

[65] Fisher has made an interesting comment concerning the point of usury. He first observes that before their expulsion from Western Europe "Jews were often bankers and as such enjoyed special royal pretection in England and in other countries. But banking charges and interest could all too easily be interpreted as 'usury'," but he then adds that "usury was forbidden by the Church, although there was no agreement on the percentage at which usury began" (p. 243). Could Chaucer be using the open-endedness of the street as an ironic comment on the openendedness of usury, implying perhaps that "usury" was open to redefinition by the Christian community whenever it decided to redefine it—in parallel to the clergeon being able to sing his own religious song inside the Jewish community? See n. 68 below and the chapter context the note pertains to.

[66] Cohen has pointed to what I think is an interesting connection between the Prioress' feeling about being a nun and her anti-Semitism (although I disagree with the more psychanalytically oriented portion of his observation):

> The Prioress . . . thinks of herself of an innocent chased out of this world. Such an attitude would have its origins, however, not only in the regressive fears of her anality but also in her reality situation. Chaucer has taken pains to depict her conspicuous lack of vocation, leading the reader to surmise that she, like many other women in the Middle Ages, had been placed in a nunnery while still a girl because her father did not wish to give her a large enough dowry for marriage . . . , still another reason for her hostility to the Jews whom she associates with money. (p. 240)

Chaucer's text does not tell us how or why she became a nun, but since in psychoanalytic theory desire for material possessions and bowel content are interrelated, any anality would have to have been caused by her father's unwillingness would to give her enough dowry. See n. 78 below.

[67] Ellis, p. 79.

[68] Commenting on representations of the Jews in medieval religious art, Ellis notes that the "image is that of the torturer, or executioner of Christ

and his followers. Hence, in the N-Town Passion Play the Jews do everything
to Christ that, according to the Gospels, the Roman soldiers did: they scourge
him, mock him, crucify him, dice for his clothes . . . [and] most horribly of
all, when Christ is crucified . . . [they] 'dawncyn abowte [th]e cros' " (pp.
72-73).

[69] Cohen, p. 242.

[70] The phallic role held by the "serpent Sathanas" explains why, as
David has noted, there is no human or divine father figure in the *Prioress'*
Tale—that is, in the actual tale, where Satan acts as a foil for the impregnating
divine father in the hymn to the Virgin. In her comments on Cohen's article
Boyd briefly quotes from Ridley's "Criticism such as this is warped"
paragraph which I cited at the beginning of this chapter, and then remarks:
"Violent sexual imagery is indeed present in [the Prioress' Prologue] and [the
Prioress' Tale], but *these works are the product of the art of literary collage,*
assembled rather than created by Chaucer, the religious imagery part of a
larger context of Scripture, liturgy, and mystical literature existing in the
Middle Ages" (Boyd, p. 47, italics mine).

To me the portions I italicized in Boyd's statement illustrate what is
wrong with the 'inorganic' approach in Chaucer scholarship. First of all, why
treat the Prioress' prologue and tale as separate "works"? I trust I have
shown that the Prioress' tale and her prologue constitute an organic work of
literature, with the interaction between the notions of the impregnating Holy
Ghost and the phallic "serpent Sathanas" merely being one minor example.
Second, but more importantly, I hope I have already demonstrated, and
demonstrated not only with respect to the *Prioress' Tale*, that Chaucer's
violent sexual imagery is not collage but the poet's own literary creation. I
have suggested as one of the controlling images in the *Canterbury Tales* the
Virgil-based cosmic-union picture in the opening lines, lines expressing the
union between spirituality and physicality: using the esemplastic power of

one's imagination in a fusion of Biblical imagery with imagery employed by the most classical of classical poets hardly constitutes collage.

[71] Boyd observes that the fact of the street being open at both ends "makes a vital point to the story: the citizens of this fictional city in 'Asie' are living so harmoniously with their Jewish community that there is free access through the ghetto. This renders the more treacherous the crime which is about to occur, making it a betrayal of trust" (p. 130). I would argue that the vitality of the point cuts two ways. Cohen notes that "the Prioress has the child use his song provocatively, there being no need for him to sing 'wel and boldely . . . as thurghout the Jewerye this litel child cam to and fro' " (p. 238). To illustrate to my students the provocative nature of what the clergeon does, or more precisely, what the Prioress poetically makes him do, I ask them whether they would want a white child to walk through a black ghetto whistling "Dixie."

[72] Alan T. Gaylord, "The Unconquered Tale of the Prioress," *Papers of the Michigan Academy of Science, Arts, and Letters*, 67 (1962), 629.

[73] For a differing interpretation see Lindahl, who observes: "The tales of the three religious speakers [i.e., the Prioress, the Clerk, and the Parson] have moral themes, and thus are especially safe. The Prioress tells a saint's life . . . addressed more to the Virgin Mary than to her fellow pilgrims" (p. 89). I suppose there is safety in a folkloric reading since it does not require a commitment to the text. For discussion of the Prioress' involvement of the pilgrims in and their reaction to the saint's tale, see the latter half of Chapter III.

[74] After noting that the Prioress' "mouth is oxymoronically 'ful smal' . . . and her controversial brooch glistens 'of gold ful sheene'," Kelly observes: "Chaucer uses 'ful' eleven times in his Portrait of the Prioress; I can find no similar concentration of this modifier in his works" (p. 366). Wood comments that in the General Prologue "Chaucer repeats [*ful*] so often

that one is led, however indirectly, to feel that he is in fact protesting too much" (p. 89-90). Could this over-protesting concentration of *fuls* be a hint on the poet's part at the *plena* idea?

[75] Schoeck has made the following observation:

> A fourteenth-century Englishman . . . could scarcely have questioned the laws and the social forces that had excluded the medieval Jew from Christian society . . . But there is in Chaucer's treatment of the Prioress a clear-eyed recognition of the inhumanity of her Tale, its violation of the deepest sense of charity which fourteen centuries of Christianity had been laboring to develop and its failure to carry the burden of charity which is enjoined on all Christians but especially on the religious. The Prioress is not condemned, however; *rather is the poem's objective view one of understanding pity of her: further than this all of Chaucer's compassion could not go.* (p. 265, italics mine).

Schoeck is considered one of the "hardest" critics of the Prioress, but in the portion I italicized he was making a point whose significance he may not have been fully aware of: as I am trying to demonstrate, Chaucer was questioning not so much what the social forces had done to the Jews as what they had done to women like the Prioress, the Christian author's irony being that in the final analysis the Prioress *deserves* the pity, and the reader shouldn't deny it to her, which she denies to the Jews—and denies it to them because their religion allows them, or rather *demands of them*, what her own religion denies to her.

[76] Robert C. Elliott, *The Power of Satire: Magic, Ritual, Art* (Princeton: Princeton University Press, 1960), passim.

[77] David, p. 208. For more specific comments on the Prioress' use of the Jews as religious symbols, see n. 79 below.

[78] Peggy Knapp, *Chaucer and the Social Context* (New York and London: Routledge, 1990), pp. 50-51. Knapp continues: "Chaucer's Prioress belongs to a group of aristocratic women who must forgo the dominant interest of their class in amassing land and providing progeny to inherit it . . . [She] tells a tale about a woman without a man who loses her child but who regains status by a familial connection with sainthood, an only

slightly displaced voicing of the loss of her own potential husband and child.'' If the Prioress comes from a wealthy family, then her father did not wish to give her a large enough dowry for marriage. In that case, her father is a voluntary collaborator in the Church's sexual oppression of females and would deserve to be included in the Prioress' displaced castrations.

[79] Note that I said "religious prejudice" rather than "anti-Semitism." After quoting several anti-Jewish remarks—I said "anti-Jewish," not "anti-Semitic"—from the *Parson's Tale*, Ridley observes: "it is very difficult to see why critics condemn the Prioress for *religious prejudice*, but not the Parson from whom she could have learned it—for men like this priest taught the Prioress. If she, a simple, devout woman, were regularly exposed to pronouncements such as his, she should scarcely be expected to remain completely free of prejudice against the Jews" (*Prioress*, p. 8, italics mine). Although it is difficult for us today *not* to equate prejudice against the Jewish religion with anti-Semitism, we should endeavor to differentiate—and in the portion I italicized in my quotation from Ridley, she seems to be groping for such a differentiation—between racial prejudice and religious prejudice. The Nazis' persecution of the Jews was based not on religious but on racial ideology (the Nazis also persecuted other ethnic groups which they considered undesirable without any regard to religion, e.g, "The Slavs," many of whom, especially in the case of Poles, were Catholic); by contrast, the treatment of Jews by medieval Christians was based on religious conflict. As I noted a moment ago, David has astutely pointed out that "the Jews in the tale are primarily theological symbols." However, the Prioress uses these theological symbols in her psychomachia over celibacy. Or more precisely, she is using the Jews not so much in their function as a customarily preached threat to Christian religion but, instead, as symbols of "multiplication." This makes the Prioress' "anti-Semitism" different from that of the Parson.

CHAPTER III

[1] The term "notorious speculation" is from Dinshaw, p. 156. Portions of this chapter have appeared in the *American Imago* article listed in n. 5 of the Introduction and in my articles, "Sexuality and Self-Recognition in the *Pardoner's Tale*," *Journal of Evolutionary Psychology*, 3 (October 1982), 124-29, and " 'I trowe he were a geldyng or a mare': Chaucer's Pardoner and the Papacy," *Chaucer Yearbook*, 2 (October 1993).

[2] Dinshaw, p. 257, n. 1.

[3] Dinshaw, p. 157.

[4] *Riverside Chaucer*, p. 824.

[5] Monica E. McAlpine, "The Pardoner's Homosexuality and How It Matters," *PMLA*, 95 (1980), 8-22. The following quotation is from from the *PMLA* abstract on p. 5.

[6] Beryl Rowland, "Chaucer's Idea of the Pardoner," *Chaucer Review*, 14 (1979), 143.

[7] Rowland, p. 141.

[8] Jill Mann, p. 146.

[9] McAlpine, p. 13. McAlpine had stated at the outset of her 1980 examination of the Pardoner as a possible homosexual: "It is neither likely nor desirable that such a reading will replace the view of the Pardoner as eunuch; rather, it is hoped that it will shed new light on familiar aspects of Chaucer's rich characterization" (p. 8). I hope that precisely by *not* replacing the view of the Pardoner as eunuch I can shed new light on Chaucer's art of character portrayal.

[10] Dinshaw categorically makes a salubrious statement against interpretations that rely too much on particular medical knowledge, be that knowledge ancient, medieval, or modern:

> Other analyses of the Pardoner's sexuality—that he is a "testicular pseudo-hermaphrodite of the feminine type" (Beryl Rowland, "Animal

Imagery and the Pardoner's Abnormality,'' *Neophilologus* 48 [1964]:
56-60), or a combination pervert, e.g., "a manic depressive with traces
of anal eroticism, and a pervert with a tendency toward alcoholism
(Eric W. Stockton, "The Deadliest Sin in the *Pardoner's Tale*,"
Tennessee Studies in Literature 6 [1961]: 47—seem far more specific
and certain than what is warranted by the portrait and the performance
of the character. (p. 260).

I would simplify Dinshaw's argument by saying that some of the "Other
analyses" simply are not warranted by Chaucer's text (although, as I will
show, Stockton's remark about anal eroticism is not too far off the mark).
What Dinshaw says about Rowland's 1964 article holds true for Rowland's
1979 elaboration of her argument, which, as its title suggests, is partly a
response to Donald Howard's 1976 argument that the Pardoner's sexuality is
unknowable: "an enigma—sexually anomalous, hermaphroditic, contradictory"
(p. 345).

[11]   *Riverside Chaucer*, p. 824.   In 1972 Ross had observed under
geldyng that "the Pardoner should not even have been admitted to a church."
Ross quoted Deuteronomy 23:1, but went on to say: "If these Old Covenant
rules had been enforced, the Church would have been deprived not only of
many of the congregation but also of supremely gifted preachers like
Chaucer's Pardoner" (*Chaucer's Bawdy*, p. 94).   Ross was saying, then, that
the Deuteronomy rule was *not* enforced.   Of course it was not enforced—since
it had been superseded by Acts—but, as I will demonstrate, the Pardoner bases
his behavior on the rules of the Old Covenant.

[12]   Dinshaw cited from Acts, but she did not comment on which
implications the Acts passage may have had for her own re-revaluation of the
Pardoner as eunuch, probably because she was still using the 1957 edition by
Robinson, which did not introduce the seemingly interpretive crux which the
Riverside Chaucer would point to, namely Deuteronomy 23.1.   This apparent
crux will be one of the crucial points in my reading of Chaucer's portrayal of

the Pardoner. McAlpine had observed on what she considered "a conflict in attitudes toward eunuchs in the Old Testament":

> Deuteronomy 23:1, reflecting a literal-minded racial and sexual perception of holiness, excludes eunuchs from the temple, while Isaiah 56:3-5, taking a more spiritual approach, gives assurance that righteous eunuchs are among God's people. The medieval commentators found a solution to this conflict in a statement of Christ's discriminating among congenital eunuchs, involuntary castrates, and "eunuchs who have made themselves such for the Kingdom of Heaven" (Matt. 19:12). Identifying the last group, the voluntary celibates in the service of God, as the eunuchs of Isaiah who will be accepted by God, the commentators go on to invent a second group who will be rejected, as in Deuteronomy: those who, while capable of good works, deliberately remain spiritually sterile . . . Both Christ and the medieval commentators were reacting against the physical determinism of one strain of Jewish tradition. (pp. 10-11)

What McAlpine says about Christ and the medieval commentators reacting against the physical determinism of one strain of Jewish tradition is enlightening, but before we concern ourselves with how medieval exegesis tried to reconcile two differing strains of Jewish tradition, shouldn't we consider what the headmaster of Christian sexology said in Acts? I will elaborate in detail the role which Matthew 19:12 plays in Chaucer's portrayal of the Pardoner.

13 David, p. 193.

14 Lindahl, p. 60.

15 McAlpine, p. 17.

16 Cf. Ross, *Chaucer's Bawdy*, pp. 172-73.

17 McAlpine, p. 16.

18 My argument concerning the causality between the Pardoner's sexual anomaly and his use of false relics to make money is also applicable if Siegfried Wenzel is right in his article on "Chaucer's Pardoner and His Relics," *Studies in the Age of Chaucer*, 11 (1989), 37-41. Trying to "correct a minor but pervasive misapprehension connected with the Pardoner's activity," Wenzel argues that, instead of literally *selling* false relics, the

Pardoner makes money by simply displaying them, "providing some physical contact with them (touch, kiss), and requesting a monetary offering for this privilege (lines 376, 384, 924, 929). Thus the Host is asked not to *purchase* but merely 'to kisse the relikes . . . for a grote' " (p. 38).

I would like to note, however, that the anonymous source which Wenzel quotes does not at all prove his point about mere display. On the contrary, Wenzel's rendering (cited from his own 1988 edition and translation of the *Fasiculus morum*), "*when they open them [i.e., the relics] up*, you will find nothing but the bones of a farm animal," distorts the Latin original: "*si detegerentur aperte*, non invenies nisi ossa alicuius iumenti" (p. 39). By *they*, Wenzel means the pardoners, but the passive voice in the Latin original (correctly translated "when they [i.e., the relics] are opened up") doesn't identify the opener—who, it seems to me, more likely would be the customer who had purchased the fake relics. Besides, the *Fasiculus* speaks about *false pardoners*, whereas we have to assume that Chaucer's Pardoner has been duly authorized.

[19]   Charles A. Owen, Jr., "The Crucial Passage in Five of the *Canterbury Tales*: A Study in Irony and Symbol," *JEGP*, 52 (1953), 304-305.

[20]   Owen, p. 305.

[21]   McAlpine, p. 17.

[22]   McAlpine, p. 17.

[23]   Melvin Storm, "The Pardoner's Invitation: Quaestor's Bag or Becket's Shrine?", *PMLA*, 97 (1982), 813.

[24]   Quoted by Storm, p. 813.

[25]   That *breech* means underpants (cf. *Riverside Chaucer*, p. 202) rather than what we today call breeches is of course important for the sexual aspects of the context presently under discussion.

[26] I said a moment ago that the Host perceives the Pardoner's request as something comparable to to a psychological-castration threat in that it threatens the Host's sense of control over his own life, a control symbolized by his possession of a *purs*, in both senses of that word. Dinshaw makes the following observation concerning a possible castration fear on the part of the Host, in the portion I italicize:

> Harry's response to the Pardoner's invitation to "kiss the relikes everychon" is startling in his vehemence. That final moment between the two pilgrims—the one lacking "naught of manhood" (1:755), the other having "lytill of manhoode" (as the Middle English *Secreta Secretorum* says of eunuchs)—is highly charged with sexual repugnance . . . *Perhaps, sensing something of the Pardoner's lack, the Host fears for his own manhood. . . . But whether or not this moment specifically enacts a Freudian scene,* Harry's response powerfully corroborates the associations I have been pointing to here. In its association of relics and balls, it refers to another medieval discussion wherein relics, balls, and writing are all brought together in a discussion of castration. In the *Roman de la rose*—the text commonly acknowledged to contain, in Faus Semblant, a central source for the characterization of the Pardoner—relics, testicles, and language are brought together in a vivid treatment of the myth of the loss of an ideal as castration. How testicles, relics, and language are particularly implicated in this loss in the *Rose*, and how they gain their gender significance in the *translatio* from the *Rose* into the *Canterbury Tales*, shall now be my concern. (p. 168, italics mine)

Dinshaw and I are of course pursuing different concerns in our respective discussions of the encounters between the Host and the Pardoner: Dinshaw proceeds to deal with the arbitrariness of signs in the discussion, in the *Roman*, between Raison and Amant of the words "reliques" and "coilles," a discussion which provides the source for Chaucer's association of "relikes" and "coillons." I will later suggest that in his associatiing of "relikes" and "coillons" Chaucer parodically plays on Raison's and Amant's discussion (see n. 35 below). In fact, what is going on between the Host and the Pardoner is a little more complex than Dinshaw would have us believe, as the genesis of my own reading(s) of that encounter will show.

When I first suggested an *unconscious* causative correlation between the testicles and the reliques, and a recognition of that correlation *both* by the Host *and* by the Pardoner, in the *American Imago* article listed in n. 1 above (pp. 615-17), I was dealing with the Pardoner as a eunuch. After the appearance of McAlpine's article I applied the unconscious-causative-correlation-plus-recognition-scene interpretation to the Pardoner as a homosexual but not as a eunuch, *mutatis mutandis*, in the 1982 *Journal of Evolutionary Psychology* article listed in n. 1 above. But I didn't remain satisfied for long because in the same year Melvin Storm published his article linking the Pardoner's possible physical sodomy to the spiritual sodomy of wasting the seed of the word of God. Storm's argument has eventually encouraged me to inquire into the *pryvetee* of the Pardoner's underpants, or more precisely, into the *pryvetee* of the Host relating the Pardoner's anus-stained underpants, the *coillons*, existing or not, and the *relikes*. The present chapter tries to reconcile the points I have just listed with Chaucer's tantalizing statement, "I trowe he were a geldyng or a mare," with the mention of the Summoner's "stif burdoun," and, perhaps most importantly, with the Host seeming unduly upset by the Pardoner's request—but also with the Pardoner being rendered speechless by the Host's response.

If the Pardoner, a confirmed cynic, becomes speechless, something extraordinary must have taken place—some kind of "Freudian scene," if I may use Dinshaw's phrase. But the Freudian scene involves a complex overlapping of two simultaneous gender-reversals. If the Host fulfills the Pardoner's request as he perceives it, namely as a homosexual advance, then the Pardoner, who had been the aggressor—the phallic aggressor if you will, although the aggression has nothing to do with the *Pardoner's* phallus—ironically becomes the "text" which, as in the case of Nicholas and Absalom, is being "written on" with the Host wielding the *stilus* (cf. n. 55 in Chapter I), wielding a fountain pen of sorts which provides more stains on the

Pardoner's underpants. But, as I will further elaborate in the body of my chapter, such "writing on" ironically would actually castrate the Host, because the kind of fountain which the Pardoner had consciously appealed to, but which Harry consciously confuses but unconsciously equates with the other kind, is the *purs* alias money bag which gives the Host a sense of control over his life and which the Paroner has just called upon him to unbuckle—so that the "female" Pardoner's own *purs* may bulge (I refer to the Pardoner's desire for plenitude which Dinshaw discusses in her chapter). Thus the castration threat which the Pardoner poses to the Host pertains also to Harry's financial status, as I will discuss. The Host knows that he would be "wasting his money"—in an oblique analogy to the simoniac wasting the seed of the word of God (so that, in terms of the "patriarchal discourse" which Dinshaw discusses throughout her chapter, the gendering of money and the gendering of language, i.e., the word of God spoken by the male, finally converge).

[27] For the connection between the puns in *envoluped* and *semely* I am indebted to Joseph E. Grennen, "The Pardoner, the Host, and the Depth of Chaucerian Insult," *English Language Notes*, 25 (December 1987), 18-24. In his observations on *envoluped*, Grennen notes: "That well-know medieval fondness for finding meaning in false etymology, given currency through the persistent popularity of the encyclopedia known as *Etymologies* of Bishop Isidore of Seville, is likely to be at work here" (p. 19).

[28] By contrast, Dinshaw sees no redemption for the Pardoner, because she sees the Pardoner as a eunuch but not as a homosexual. She observes:

> if the Pardoner is taken to be an effeminate homosexual, as another gloss of "mare" goes, he is, in the normative terms of patriarchal, heterosexual culture, a man who puts himself in the "feminine" position in homosexual intercourse . . . He would thus bodily enact what I have suggested (in Chapter 5 [of my study]) the Clerk and Chaucer imaginatively do: as men who put themselves in the woman's place, they see things from the woman's point of view. For those male figures, such a "feminine" position yields opportunity, a valorization of what is devalued in patriarchal culture, a speaking of and for what is

> silenced; but for the Pardoner, such a position yields not opportunity but torment. In his lacking being he reifies the disturbing suggestion that there is no guarantee of meaning, realizes that there is no fullness and plenitude of signification underneath the wraps of the letter. If, as we've seen in the *Clerk's Tale*, a "feminine" poetic strategy provides a positive, fruitful alternative to oppressive, power-asymmetrical discourse, the Pardoner's strategy, I suggest, would threaten an end to reading and telling tales altogether. (p. 158)

Of course I have not yet addressed the "feminine" poetic strategy which Dinshaw found in the *Clerk's Tale*: I will do so in my next chapter. I do wish to state already at this point, however, that I disagree with Dinshaw's suggestion that the Pardoner's strategy would threaten an end to writing and reading literature altogether simply because of what she perceives as an asymmetrical patriarchal discourse. Contrary to Dinshaw's view, the Pardoner is indeed a man who puts himself in the "feminine" position in homosexual intercourse, but the problem is—and this is something Dinshaw seems to have overlooked—that the Pardoner does so not of his free choice but, instead, because he has been deprived of that choice and, as I will elaborate, tries to avenge himself on God by playing eunuchry and homosexuality off against each other. Once the Pardoner experiences his recognition scene and resulting catharsis, fullness and plenitude *are* possible.

29 David, p. 194.

30 I agree with David's following observation concerning the final scene: "It is a beautiful and understated ending, but it contains the ray of hope that redeems the Pardoner's whole performance and gives it meaning" (p. 203). I do, however, believe that David is oversimplifying a complex situation when he says:

> The kiss of botherhood between the Pardoner and the Host is a comic but meaningful reassertion of the brotherhood of man, which the sworn brotherhood of the three rioters has mocked. Just as the Pardoner has failed to isolate himself utterly from his fellow pilgrims, so no man can willfully withdraw from the Christian communion. If the Pardoner can be pitied by the Knight, the *miles Christi*, then perhaps he may be forgiven by Christ himself. It is at least an open question. (p. 204).

There is the irony that the Knight can function as a *miles Christi* only after the Pardoner has experienced his recognition scene and catharsis, an experience which is triggered by the Host—who is approached for an offering first, because as in innkeeper he is, in the Pardoner's words, "most envoluped in synne."

[31] Glenn Burger is oversimplifying the role which the master of ceremonies plays in this encounter when he observes: "when the Host announces that he 'wol no lenger pleye' with the Pardoner, . . . he silences his adversary, it appears, only to enshrine his own profitable play with the other pilgrims. For the more the Pardoner can be maintained as an absence of potency, the more the Host can assert his own masculinity and moral authority and establish that he is no false copy but the real thing" (1146). Chaucer's Host is much more sensitive to gender issues than Burger gives him credit for, as I will further show in other parts of my study where I discuss passages in which Harry is anything but plugging his "masculinity."

One problem with Burger's study is that, while he tries to provide a corrective to what he calls Dinshaw's feminist approach to the Pardoner, he unquestioningly agrees with Dinshaw's interpretation that the Pardoner is a eunuch but not a homosexual. Another, more serious, problem, closely related to the first one, is that although Burger quotes McAlpine's and Storm's studies of the Pardoner as a possible homosexual, and even though he quotes insights of gay criticism, he refuses to examine Chaucer's characterization of the Pardoner as a possible "mare."

[32] Dinshaw has made an astute observation on the Pardoner's relationship with the Old Testament: "The tavern world of the rioters is the world of the Law. Most of the Pardoner's exempla are drawn from the Old Testament, and he in fact seems to prefer the Old Testament to the New in setting the scene: 'witnesse on Mathew; but in special/Of sweryng seith the holy Jeremy' (634-35). Christ's Redemption is duly acknowledged, but

humankind's original corruption and consequent damnation—imposed by an angry God the Father at the Fall—vividly endure in the Pardoner's rhetoric [in his pronouncements on gluttony and original corruption in 498-504]'' (pp. 117-18). As I will elaborate, the Pardoner even uses Judaism in an attempt to mock Christianity.

33 Dinshaw, p. 164.

34 Cf. Rowland, p. 143, who speaks about the lechery of the goat, but she uses the mention of the goat to support her hermaphroditism-reading.

35 That is to say, while the portrait of the Pardoner is modeled after Faus Semblant in the *Roman de la rose*, Raison's and Amant's discussion of *coilles* and *reliques* is not even needed for our understanding of the exchange between the Host and the Pardoner. Especially since we can hardly assume that the Host has read the *Roman*, Chaucer's pun could even be an attempt to poke fun at the philosophical discussion in the *Roman*: signs, arbitrary or not, lose their meaning when "nothing is left."

36 Dinshaw, p. 164.

37 See Boyd, pp. 166-67, and Ridley, *Riverside Chaucer*, p. 916.

38 *Riverside Chaucer*, p. 917.

39 Fisher glosses *elvyssh* as "abstracted (like someone in fairyland)" (p. 246).

40 Harry had addressed the Clerk in a similar manner when he called on him to tell a tale:

> "Sire Clerk of Oxenford," oure Hooste sayde,
> "Ye ryde as coy and stille as dooth a mayde
> Were newe spoused, sittynge at the bord;
> This day ne herde I of youre tonge a word . . . " (IV 1-4)

In the Clerk's case the Host had hardly been trying to insult the fellow pilgrim. Harry had merely been playing on the contemporary axiom as expressed by the *Totum regit saeculum*: "A maidenly innocence is fitting for clerks" (quoted by Mann, p. 76). The Host's earlier words to the Clerk make his "What man artow?" speech to Chaucer all the more insulting, or at least more hostile.

[41] Cf. *Riverside Chaucer*, p. 918.

[42] The *Riverside Chaucer* notes: "The emphasis on Sir Thopas's chastity . . . is unexpected and hard to explain" (p. 919). Mary Hamel, "And Now for Something Completely Different: The Relationship between the *Prioress's Tale* and the *Rime of Sir Thopas*," *Chaucer Review*, 14 (1979), 251-59, does discuss a relationship of sorts: "My point is simply that Sir Thopas's name associates him with the gemlike hero of the preceding tale" (p. 259). Leaning toward the school of "heartfelt" criticism, Hamel does not address the question of what the strange encounter between the Host and Chaucer-the-poet may add to our understanding of the poet's portrayal of the Prioress.

[43] For critical opinion on Thopas' sexuality, see n. 45 below.

[44] Cf. *Riverside Chaucer*, p. 923.

[45] The irony of Sir Thopas' unmanliness in a tale which abounds with sexual puns and innuendoes (see the Index in *Chaucer's Bawdy* under "Sir Thopas" [p. 255]) has received a good deal of critical attention, but it seems to me that only George Williams has been able to make real sense of the story, in *A New View of Chaucer* (Durham, NC: Duke University Press, 1965). Since this chapter's concern is not with *Sir Thopas*, let me simply quote Ross' comments on Williams' study: "[Williams] includes a revolutionary interpretation of Sir Thopas as a homosexual portrait of the king himself, Richard II (pp. 145-151). Thopas' adversary, Sir Olifaunt, is actually John of Gaunt" (*Chaucer's Bawdy*, p. 13, n. 25). Ross quotes a paragraph "to illustrate the ingenuity of Mr. Williams' argument," a paragraph pointing to sexual symbols, and Ross urges: "There is much more of the same, which I urge the reader to examine for himself" (p. 14, n. 25). Williams may be right, but I hope I have shown that it is possible to make sense of *Sir Thopas*

without reading it as an allegory—by reading it as a tale which Chaucer wrote
(also) for the purpose of palimpsestically informing other parts of the
Canterbury Tales.

[46] Ross, *Chaucer's Bawdy*, p. 207.

[47] The *Riverside Chaucer* also quotes Vincent of Beauvais' "Homo
autem noster exterior de immundo semine conceptus est" (p. 930), but that
Chaucer was more indebted to Innocent III is illustrated by the fact that he had
translated Innocent's *De misericordia condicionis humanae*. Chaucer is
referring to that translation when in the G Prologue to *The Legend of Good
Women* he says that

> He hath in prose translated Boece,
> And *Of the Wreched Engendrynge of Mankynde*,
> As man may in Pope Innocent yfynde.
> (G 413: I have italicized the title of Chaucer's translation)

What do we learn about Chaucer's attitude toward Innocent's contention that
human reproduction is something dirty from the fact that Chaucer changed the
title of Innocent's treatise, a title which literally would translate as "Of the
Wretchedness of the Human Condition," to a title that focuses on human
reproduction? Was Chaucer making fun of Innocent's concern—obsession
might be a more appropriate term—with the reproductive act? Couldn't such
an intent be suggested by Chaucer's statement, immediately following the
"Wreched Engendrynge of Mankynde," about what "man may" find in Pope
Innocent? Isn't Chaucer sarcastically telling the reader to consult Innocent so
the reader can feel wretched about his own engendering?

CHAPTER IV

[1] See, for instance, John McNamara, "Chaucer's Use of the Epistle of
St. James in the *Clerk's Take*," *Chaucer Review*, 7 (1973), 184-93.

McNamara argues that "God has sent external temptations to Griselda in order to test her faith" (p. 189).

2 Cf. Elizabeth Salter, *Chaucer: The Knight's Tale and the Clerk's Tale* (Great Neck, NY: 1962), p. 50. I cannot agree with Salter's stipulation of an exclusively "spritual" reading of the tale (p. 48); see n. 22 below, as well as my discussion later in this chapter.

3 Lindahl, pp. 150-51.

4 In the *Canterbury Tales* Chaucer does subject the aristocracy to fierce satire; see my articles, "'Aurelius' Quest for *Grace*: Sexuality and the Marriage Debate in the *Franklin's Tale*," *CEA Critic*, 45 (1982), 16-21, and, more specifically, "*Gentillesse* and the Marriage Debate in the *Franklin's Tale*: Chaucer's Squires and the Question of Nobility," *Neophilologus*, 68 (1984), 451-70.

5 Although the portion I italicized in my quotation from Lindahl unequivocally claims that Walter decrees that Griselda shall go home naked, Lindahl never makes it clear to unsuspecting readers that such a decree is not carried out.

6 Judith Ferster, *Chaucer on Interpretation* (Cambridge and New York: Cambridge University Press, 1985), p. 104, observes that "when [Griselda] speaks of the possibility of leaving naked, she is much more explicit than Petrarch's Griseldis about the negative implications for Walter's character."

7 In *Chaucer's Bawdy* Ross observes under *maydenhed*: "the patient, patient Griselde, that combination of treacle and tears, . . . gladly relinquishes her maidenhead to Walter, her highborn husband: it is the symbol of her purity and the dowry that she brings to her marriage" (p. 146). I believe Ross underestimated Griselda: as I am about to show, Griselda will turn her "dowry" into a powerful weapon.

8 Dinshaw, p. 136.

[9] Ferster, p. 104.

[10] For discussion of Griselda's reaction to having been abused as a woman, see Dinshaw's comments: "she reveals the sense of having been used. Griselda's demand that she not go smockless ('Ye koude nat doon so dishonest a thyng') . . . is aggressive—very different from her accommodating tone in Petrarch and the *Livre*—her language vivid and biting ('let me nat lyk a worm go by the weye'), her tone even vaguely threatening ('Remember yow, my owene lord so deere,/I was youre wyf . . . ')" (pp. 146-47). I have just argued that Griselda ties her demand that Walter not do "so dishonest a thyng" to Walter's own honor, and I will in a moment argue that Griselda's reference to a "worm" is language "biting" in sense which is much more "threatening" than Dinshaw seems to have been aware of.

[11] Robinson, p. 711. The *Riverside Chaucer* adds, "Cf. Rom. 454, *nakid as a worm*" (p. 883).

[12] Dinshaw, p. 146. For a comparison of Chaucer's tale with its sources see J. Burke Severs, *The Literary Heritage of Chaucer's Clerk's Tale* (New Haven: Yale University Press, 1942).

[13] Ferster observes concerning this scene: "Griselda does not ask to be ordered to keep a dress; she asks to be given one, because she deserves it. Then, in a surprising move, she announces the end of the interview. Her courteous reason ('I don't want to bother you') is self-effacing; nevertheless, rather than waiting to be dismissed, she has taken the initiative and taken control. In shifting from the impersonal 'here/That was youre wyf' to 'And heer take I my leeve' she sheds her role and walks out the door a new 'I' " (p. 106).

[14] Ross has made the following observations: "The stripping in the 'Clerk's Tale' is totally without erotic significance, but that is because the heroine is Griselde, that sexless puppet . . . The pathos in one of her lines here is almost beyond endurance (of heart or stomach) when she pleads 'let me

nat lyk a worm go by the weye' '' (*Chaucer's Bawdy*, p. 213). Chaucer's irony here is that while the stripping is without erotic significance and is so precisely because Griselda had been a sexless puppet throughout her marriage—a point which I will elaborate—during the divorce spectacle she becomes a *vagina dentata* of sorts.

[15] Howard observes that Walter "asserts male omnipotence by testing his wife's submissiveness" (p. 258), but he does not elaborate on the male-female struggle.

[16] Cf. *Riverside Chaucer*, p. 883.

[17] Cf. *Riverside Chaucer*, p. 883.

[18] Lindahl, p. 151.

[19] Robinson, p. 711.

[20] For a differing interpretation of the function of the interaction between the Envoy and the tale see Irving N. Rothman, "Humility and Obedience in the *Clerk's Tale*, with the Envoy Considered as an Ironic Affirmation," *Papers on Language and Literature*, 9 (1973), 115-27.

[21] Cf. *Riverside Chaucer*, p. 882.

[22] Comparing Chaucer's additions unfavorably with the Latin and the French sources, Salter deplores that "the English text throws caution to the winds, and gives us a passage of fervent indignation" (p. 56). Salter cites the Clerk's addition to Petrarch (lines 457-62) and voices her own fervent indignation over Chaucer having thrown caution to the winds: "Chaucer here commits himself to a line of attack which makes fine dramatic reading, but which cannot help the development of the *Tale* as a moral example." Isn't it possible that Chaucer tried to create something that was *more* than "a moral example"—or at least more complex than the moral example Salter was looking for? Perhaps Salter's intentional fallacy is best illustrated by her following statement:

the *Tale* cannot be preserved as a lesson if . . . we are instructed, even encouraged to feel human contempt for the means by which that lesson is conveyed. Griselda may pass without struggle from her one telling, critical comment upon Walter (ll. 852-7) to joyful acclamatation of *his loving provision for her and the children.* (p. 61, italics mine)

I will use the portion I italicized in Salter for my argument later in this chapter.

[23] Cf. *Riverside Chaucer*, p. 882.

[24] In *Chaucer's Bawdy* Ross observes concerning Griselda: "She seems to be a totally asexual creature. Even when she produces children, it is a mechanical and biological process without joy—pure duty" (pp. 98-99). *Quod erat demonstrandum*: under the circumstances, how could we expect Griselda to feel joy?

[25] McNamara observes: "[Walter] goes so far as to assume a divine prerogative in challenging her: 'Shewe youre pacience in youre working' (495). As Bede points out in his commentary on James 1:20, such a challenge constitutes a sin of pride . . . Thus Walter's early self-centeredness appears to have cultivated a disposition that leads to more serious sins later on. Although Walter does not seem to recognize it as such, his willful testing of his wife's patience usurps authority belonging only to God" (pp. 190-91).

[26] Thomas A. Van observes in the article listed in n. 34 below: "the story shows [the *peple*] to be misinformed, vacillating, and ultimately unteachable" (p. 215).

[27] Cf. *Riverside Chaucer*, p. 883.

[28] Ferster, p. 98.

[29] Bernard S. Levy, "*Gentilesse* in Chaucer's *Clerk's* and *Merchant's Tales*," *Chaucer Review*, 11 (1977), 307-308.

[30] Levy, p. 309.

[31] Levy, p. 308.

[32] John M. Ganim, "Carnival Voices and the Envoy to the *Clerk's Tale*," *Chaucer Review*, 22 (1987), 121.

[33] Ferster, p. 111. Ferster notes that Griselda's "denial of her own will is willed" (p. 101).

[34] Thomas A. Van, "Walter at the Stake: A Reading of Chaucer's *Clerk's Tale*," *Chaucer Review*, 22 (1988), 218.

[35] Van, p. 216.

[36] Ferster, p. 178, n. 18. The following indented quotation is from pp. 115-16.

[37] Ferster, p. 112.

[38] Ferster, p. 113.

[39] When Ferster speaks of a "recognition scene" (the quotation marks are Ferster's) at the end of the story, she means it in a sense somewhat different from mine. "As Griselda has told him several times, she has given her will over to him. All the formidable power of her will has gone into conforming her will to his will. Walter has been staring into a mirror for twelve years" (p. 106). Ferster's "recognition scene" is Walter's recognition of Griselda's (in Ferster's words) "meta-will"; mine is Walter's recognition of her unwittingly having revealed to him the motive for his "testing" games. I am of course not saying that Ferster's and my own recognition-scene readings cannot coexist.

[40] In assessing this 'happy ending' we need to remember that, as McNamara notes, "[Walter] does not fully repent of his cruelties toward her, and even after recognizing that 'he so ofte had doon her offence' (1046) he still tries to justify his actions [in lines 1072-78] . . . All this is quite specious, of course, but Walter is *trying to save face* at the end" (p. 192, italics mine). The fact that despite the recognition scene he has experienced Walter is still trying to save face strongly suggests that this paragon of masculine willfulness feels his ego is threatened—or more precisely, his *male* ego, since in his face-

saving speech Walter explains his cruel actions as a test of Griselda's
wommanheede:

> And folk that ootherweys han seyd of me,
> I warne hem wel I have doon this deede
> For no malice, ne for no crueltee,
> But for *t'assaye in thee thy wommanheede*,
> And nat to sleen my children—*God forbeede!*—
> But for to kepe hem pryvely and stille,
> Til I thy purpos knewe and al thy wille. (IV 1072-78, italics added)

Regardless of whether we consider the *wommanheede*/*God forbeede* a stark-
collocation rhyme which the poet uses to suggest that the "God forbeede"
should apply to the "t'assaye in thee thy wommanheede"—in testing Griselda,
Walter had arrogated God's power—we here are dealing with another "open
audience" in which the "povre fostred creature" puts the male-supremacist
monarch in his place.

[41] Dinshaw, pp. 135-36.

[42] Ross, *Chaucer's Bawdy*, pp. 240-41.

[43] Ross, p. 213; cf. n. 14 above.

[44] Mann's translation of "Clericos simplicitas decet puellaris" from
the *Totum regit saeculum* (p. 76).

[45] In part, then, the *Clerk's Tale* is "abreactive fiction"—but not
necessarily in the sense in which Kendrick uses that term:

> The purpose of pathetic, abreactive fictions such as the "Clerk's Tale"
> . . . —or, for that matter, the "Prioress's Tale" . . . —is to work
> through anxieties by repeatedly replaying fearful situations . . . , thus
> gradually leading *the reader* to accommodate himself to a difficult
> reality such as a sudden reversal of fortunes . . . , in short, to lead *the
> reader* to accept his own inability to control his life. (p. 50, italics
> mine)

I quoted some of Kendrick's above observations in my earlier discussion of the
Prioress' Tale, where I spoke of abreactions *by* the Prioress *for* the Prioress,
abreactions whose "purpose" had nothing to do with the reader. In the *Clerk's
Tale*, too, I see the abreactive process in the teller of the story, although in

contrast to the *Prioress' Tale* the abreaction is also for the purpose of the reader—since the story contains an exemplum of Job-like acceptance of one's own inability to control one's life. However, I am at present more concerned with the "purpose" which the tale has for the Clerk himself, and I can agree with Kendrick's following interpretation: "The story of Griselda is an abreactive fiction of total accommodation to the laws of the figurative father, who may stand for the progenitor, husband, political ruler, or God" (p. 48). I can agree with Kendrick's reading if the abreaction includes the Clerk, who is under the *yerde*—in this context of ideas in the meaning of "rod, rule"—not only of an overbearing Host but also of an ever-testing God.

[46] The *Riverside Chaucer* observes: "The Host's stanza is generally held to have been written early and canceled when Chaucer wrote new lines for The Merchant's Prologue containing an echo of 1212" (p. 884). Chaucer probably did write the Host's stanza early, but did he necessarily cancel it? While a cancelation might have made the already easy transition to the Merchant's prologue even easier, the Host's stanza, as I am about to elaborate, sheds a good deal of light on the *Clerk's Tale* as well as on Chaucer's characterization of both the Clerk and the Host.

[47] Ferster comments on the Host's stanza: "Harry Bailly copies the Clerk by echoing his vocabulary of 'purpos' and 'wille' and yet ignores the Clerk's warning that Griselda is not a model for wives" (p. 120). I trust I have been able to show that Harry does *not* in the final analysis ignore the Clerk's warning.

[48] Dinshaw, p. 153.

[49] Concerning the addition see the *Riverside Chaucer*, p. 882.

[50] Deborah S. Ellis, "Domestic Treachery in the *Clerk's Tale*," notes: "Even [Walter's] use of the pronoun—'*thy* doghter'—signals to us that it is Griselda who is expected to pay the price of her husband's 'rest and pees' " (in *Ambiguous Realities: Women in the Middle Ages and Renaissance*, eds.

Carole Levine and Jeanie Watson [Detroit: Wayne State University Press, 1987], p. 103).

[51] If my present argument seems overly 'Freudian,' I refer to Norman Lavers, "Freud, the Clerkes Tale, and Literary Criticism," *College English*, 26 (1964), 186:

> by making the children cease to be, [Walter] has symbolically denied his paternity, *and so denied his mortality* . . . In having his sister raise his children as though they were hers he is fulfilling his unconscious wish that she were actually having children by him. . . . in refusing to acknowledge that the children ever existed ("Ne of hir doghter noght a word spak she" [606]) the same psychic advantages come to Griselda as came to Walter. In addition, with denial of parenthood, their covert father-daughter relationship assumes a more realistic appearance. It is in maintaining such a relationship that they can most subtly act out their incest. (italics mine)

I don't see how Walter is denying his mortality: the Cupid and Psyche myth, which Lavers appropriately cites in the preceding pages, doesn't bear out Lavers' claim of Walter's denial of mortality (Jupiter never had to deny his mortality by *not* impregnating the mortals he philandered with). There are other instances where Lavers seems to be reading Freud rather than Chaucer (note the curious chronological arrangement in the title of his article). However, appearing approximately two years after Salter's saccharinely "spiritual" reading, Lavers' article came as a relief (in turn, a sobering corrective was provided some two years later by Richard A. Lanham, "Chaucer's *Clerk's Tale*: The Poem Not the Myth," *Literature and Psychology*, 16 [1966], 157-65).

Chaucer's literary interest in the subject of incest has been proved, even though in 1987 the *Riverside Chaucer* Explanatory Notes discarded Evan Carton's argument in his article, "Complicity and Responsibility in Pandarus' Bed and Chaucer's Art" (*PMLA*, 94 [1979], 47-61) as "incorrect" and declared the "now widespread view" of there being an incestuous relationship between Pandarus and Criseyde to be "absurd" (*Riverside Chaucer*, p. 1043):

the *Troilus and Criseyde* contributor, apparently, had not yet seen my response-to-Carton-and-follow-up article, "Chaucer's *Troilus and Criseyde*: Narrator-Reader Complicity" (*American Imago*, 40 [1983], 103-113), in which I strengthened the incest-argument by pointing to the narrator's allusions to the Oedipus myth, allusions which had not been in Boccaccio. At any rate, some of the incest-related points which Lavers has made deserve more empathetic attention than they received from Lanham; note, for example, that Van observes: "that Walter's pretended bride is his own daughter at least grazes the taboo against incest between parent and offspring" (p. 20). I will discuss oedipal aspects in Walter's behavior later in this chapter.

[52] Concerning the expansion see the *Riverside Chaucer*, p. 883.

[53] As Valerie Edden observes in her article, "Sacred and Secular in the *Clerk's Tale*," *Chaucer Review*, 26 (1992), 371, "Griselda, unlike other heroines of pious tales, is not presented as putting her trust in God; she does not have any sense of a providential pattern, no assurance that all will be well, in this life or the next . . . her preoccupations are characteristically human and this-wordly."

[54] Salter, p. 45.

[55] Salter, p. 61.

[56] Ferster observes: "The second loss of consciousness may be [Griselda's] deep resistance to this euphemistic interpretation of Walter [as *benyngne*]: The faint enforces silence" (p. 107).

[57] Salter calls the "tenacity of Griselda's embrace" of her children "unnatural" (p. 54). I find Selter's assessment of the scene disturbingly "unnatural." As Ferster notes, "If [Griselda's] maternal instincts were ever in doubt, her unconscious grip on her children erases that doubt" (p. 107).

[58] Ganim has observed:

J. Mitchell Morse, "The Philosophy of the Clerk of Oxenford," *MLQ*, 19 (1958), 3-20, associated the Clerk with Ockhamism, Wycliffism, and other contemporary forms of skepticism or critical reform. "At heart he was on the side of the Wife of Bath, and in mocking her he was also examining, once more and yet once more, his own restless intelligence" (p. 4). The Clerk "breathed an atmosphere charged with individualism and incipient revolt" (pp. 14-15). As convenient as Morse's argument would be for my position [that the tale is carnivalized literature], *it still seems to me that if the Clerk is of the Wife's "secte" it is without knowing it.* (p. 124, n. 6, italics mine)

I trust I have been able to show that as the teller of a feminist *Schwank* the Clerk *knows* that he is of the Wife's "secte"—and *knows* that he is participating in an "incipient revolt." In fact, it might be well to quote Kathryn L. Lynch, "Despoiling Griselda: Chaucer's Walter and the Problem of Knowledge in *The Clerk's Tale*," *Studies in the Age of Chaucer*, 10 (1988), 42: "it is the Clerk himself, in his role as narrator of the tale, who first draws critical attention to the fact that Walter's sadistic tendency to abuse his wife represents *a universal psychological truth*: 'But wedded men ne knowe no mesure,/Whan that they fynde a pacient creature' " (italics mine). In his pronouncement of the universal psychological truth concerning men's treatment of women the Clerk joins the Wife's "secte," but we need to bear in mind that the emphasis is on *married* men: as I have been arguing, Walter becomes a monster because of the "servage"-nature of his marriage. After Griselda confronts him with the recognition of the cause of his behavior, he is cured—cured late but not *too* late. As Levy notes, the Marquis' "lack of *gentilesse* in his scandalous treatment of his wife proves to be merely a temporary aberration rather than a serious defect in character" (p. 309).

CHAPTER V

[1] Ross, pp. 4-5. Small portions of this chapter first appeared in the *Revue belge, American Imago,* and *Annuale Mediaevale* articles listed in n. 5 of the Introduction, and in my essays, "Chaucer's *Merchant's Tale* E 1263, 1854 and 2360-65," *Explicator*, 35 (1977), 25-26, and "The *Parson's Tale* and St. Augustine's Theories on Sexuality," *Explicator*, 42 (1983), 6-8.

[2]   Richard Neuse, "Marriage and the Question of Allegory in the *Merchant's Tale*," *Chaucer Review*, 24 (1989), 115-31.

[3]   Neuse, p. 117.

[4]   I therefore disagree with a comment David has made in discussing a passage later in the tale: "[January] has *pretended* all along that he is marrying primarily in order to save his soul" (p. 177, italics mine). As I will elaborate, the point is that January *is serious* in trying to save his soul through marriage.

[5]   Joseph Mogan, "Chaucer and the *Bona Matrimonii*," *Chaucer Review*, 4 (1970), 130, has observed that "the only *bonum* which January seems to recognize is the *sacramentum* . . . , obviously to legalize and make secure his lust," but Mogan does not connect January's legalization attempt to the old man's use of the idea of marriage as a wordly paradise. But then such a connection would seem to be important mainly for a discussion of Chaucer's use of Augustinian theology.

[6]   Huppé p. 166.

[7]   Arthur W. Hoffman, "Chaucer's Prologue to Pilgrimage: Two Voices," *ELH*, 21 (1954), 2-3.

[8]   I deliberately said that January's inability to impregnate May *is presented as*, rather than *is*, part of his punishment, since Chaucer was sufficiently familiar with contemporary religio-medical lore not to try to suggest that January gets May pregnant: see Margaret Hallissy, "Widow-to-Be: May in Chaucer's 'The Merchant's Tale'," *Studies in Short Fiction*, 26 (1989), 295-304. According to religio-medical lore, conception could only occur if the male seed mixed with the female seed, which was released by the female's orgasm—an event which May presumably never experiences with January. As Hallissy puts it: "Lack of female pleasure, then, was regarded in Chaucer's day as one possible cause of sterility. When May finds Januarie's 'pleyyng' unpraiseworthy, it is more than a simple marital

misfortune without practical consequences: given the Galenic theory, no pleasure, no heir. The ineptness of January's lovemaking, described in such graphic detail, would have sent a signal to the medieval reader that the marriage is likely to be barren'' (p. 303). Intriguing though Hallissy's article is, I think Chaucer did not expect most of his contemporary readers to be familiar with the Galenic theory and, therefore, included as a more easily discernible signal the ''nat . . . worth a bene.''

Moreover, if Chaucer himself believed in the Galenic theory, then we may have a crux with his characterization of the Wife of Bath, who says she has always enjoyed the ''ese/Of engendrure'' (III 127-28), the pleasure of the reproductive act, but who, in Hallissy's words, ''appears to be childless'' (p. 299): did the Wife of Bath practice some kind of birth control, or is she lying to her fellow pilgrims? What further calls into question Chaucer's utilization of the Galenic theory is the fact that the Merchant's story about a man who (ab-)uses his wife, who in turn (ab-)uses him, is intended as a response to the Clerk's story about an atrocious abuser of women: do we expect Griselda, whom Ross has called ''that sexless puppet'' but who gives birth to two children, to have profited from what Hallissy calls the ''fertility factor [of] female pleasure'' (p. 303)?

[9] Malcolm Andrew, ''January's Knife: Sexual Morality and Provocative Wisdom in the Merchant's Tale,'' *English Language Notes*, 16 (1979), 274-75.

[10] Mogan, pp. 129-30.

[11] Donald R. Benson, ''The Marriage 'Encomium' in the *Merchant's Tale*: A Chaucerian Crux,'' *Chaucer Review*, 14 (1979), 48-60.

[12] Andrew, p. 274.

[13] Ross, pp. 126-27.

[14] As Paul A. Olson, "Chaucer's Merchant and January's 'Hevene in Erthe Heere'," *ELH*, 28 (1961), 211, has aptly expressed it, January's marriage is a "phallic Eden."

[15] Elliott, p. 5.

[16] Ross, p. 199. Olson first observes, "When aphrodisiacs and hard work do not give [January] all he had hoped for to find in [his] purchased Eden, he builds an external paradise to complement the subjective paradise he found in May" (p. 207), and then comments: "[January] knows the satisfaction of sexual prosperity, clumsily in the bedroom and then professionally in the garden" (p. 211). Why would January's sexual performance be more professional in the garden, and why does Chaucer write, "And thynges whiche that were nat doon abedde,/He in the gardyn parfourned hem and spedde" (2051-52)? As Jay Schleusner, "The Conduct of the *Merchant's Tale*," *Chaucer Review*, 14 (1979), 241, notes, "[the readers] cannot help wondering what sorts of things can be done successfully in the garden and not in bed?" The answer which I would like to offer is that in the garden January is performing under the auspices of Priapus. In fact, Olson speaks of "the Priapean pear tree" and of "January's phallic garden" (p. 208). The irony is that while in the garden it is easier for January to climax because Priapus' tutelage helps him maintain his *corage* alias erection long enough to achieve orgasm, he still does not produce fruit: Priapus' tutelage helps the flora, but it does not make January's attempt at reproduction "worth a bene." There is the additional irony that the Priapean pear tree in January's garden becomes the scene of his cuckolding. The question now is: will Damian be successful in the Priapean pear tree?

[17] Ross, p. 123.

[18] Cf. De Weever, pp. 106-107.

[19] Elliott, pp. 5-6.

[20] While the pear-tree episode takes place on June 8 (IV 2132-33), Chaucer makes the springtime-ritual aspect explicit through January's pronouncement, "The winter is goon, with alle his reynes weete" (2140).

[21] Cf. Owen, p. 300.

[22] Owen, p. 300.

[23] Ross, p. 200.

[24] Emerson Brown, Jr., "*Hortus Inconclusus*: The Significance of Priapus and Pyramus and Thisbe in the *Merchant's Tale*," *Chaucer Review*, 4 (1970), 31-40.

[25] *Aeneid*, IV, 665-70. Chaucer knew that the Virgilian simile had been modeled after after Homer's simile in the *Iliad* which described the Trojans' crying response to Hector's death, a death which foreshadowed the eventual fall of Troy. Chaucer created his own simile by combining Homeric and Virgilian similes in the description which the Man of Law gives of the reaction of the people of medieval Rome to Constance's departure to marry a man of Islamic faith. Let me quote the Man of Law's simile to show just how familiar Chaucer was with the epic simile, and how adroitly he made use of it:

> I trowe at Troye, whan Pirrus brak the wal
> Or Ilion brende, at Thebes the citee,
> N'at Rome, for the harm thurgh Hanybal
> That Romayns hath venquisshed tymes thre,
> Nas herd swich tendre wepyng for pitee
> As in the chambre was for hire departynge . . . (II 288-93)

This is not the place to elaborate on Chaucer's use of the epic simile in *The Man of Law's Tale*, but I do wish to point out that in his mention of "Hanybal" in that tale Chaucer is allusively utilizing the context of Dido's curse in the *Aeneid*.

[26] Adducing medieval medical lore, Hallissy argues that, even if Damian climaxes inside May, the coital position in the tree is not conducive to conception and May's jumping down from the tree would have caused the seed

to slip out—despite the "fertility factor [of] female pleasure" (p. 303). I doubt that Chaucer had Hallissy's line of argument in mind at any rate, but even if he did the immediate interruption would seem to rule out the fertility factor of female pleasure.

[27] David comments on the Merchant's description of January's roar: "The choice of words throughout the tale is very deliberate. January's later jealousy is pictured as a mother's anxious solicitude for her child. When he sees what is happening in the tree, he roars 'As dooth the mooder when the child shal dye' (2365), a line that prompted Tatlock to comment: 'Nothing is sacred' " (p. 171). As I have attempted to show, the choice of words in line 2365 is indeed very deliberate—but narratively meaningful rather than just sacrilegiously bizarre.

[28] I therefore disagree with Olson's detection of irony in May's "so soore longeth me/To eten of the smale peres grene" (IV 2332-33). Olson observes: "At one level, May is flattering January with the happy suggestion that she is pregnant; at another, she is suggesting exactly where her hunger for Damyan is directed" (pp. 207-208, n. 5). The irony is much greater if May does *not* have the double entendre in mind.

[29] I therefore disagree with Martin Stevens' contention, in " 'And Venus Laugheth': An Interpretation of the *Merchant's Tale*," *Chaucer Review*, 7 (1972), 128, that Proserpina "ultimately prevails. Proserpina is the spirit of spring and May her embodiment." At the arrival of autumn, May ceases to be the embodiment of Proserpina as the spirit of spring.

[30] Neuse, then, was closer to the target than he may have been aware of when he observed: "Claudian's brief mythological epic *De Raptu Proserpinae* (fifth century A. D.) is a major subtext in the *Merchant's Tale* . . . Indeed, Claudian's poem is of enormous relevance to the entire 'marriage debate' in the *Canterbury Tales* . . . Marriage is viewed from the woman's perspective as a kind of rape" (p. 124). I trust I have demonstrated

the relevance the Proserpina myth has for Chaucer's poem, but I would now like to add that in the *Merchant's Tale* marriage is viewed as a kind of rape not only from the woman's perspective. Chaucer, the Merchant, and perhaps even January himself are presenting January's marriage to May as a kind of rape in the old man's fantasies during the wedding festivities:

> in his herte he gan hire to manace
> That he that nyght in armes wolde hire streyne
> *Harder than evere Paris did Eleyne.* (1752-53, italics added)

Surely, Chaucer and his contemporaries were at least as familiar with and interested in the Rape of Helen myth as they were with the myth of Proserpina. While the idea of January "raping" May not so much by marrying her as by purchasing her with his 'Plutonic' wealth is definitely there, what is more important for a story about "hoolynesse"-cloaked lechery is the allusion to Paris' illicit marriage to Helen—illicit because Helen was already married—a marriage which led to the war monumentalized by what has come down to us as the earliest piece of Western literature. Moreover, the poet who wrote *Troilus and Criseyde* was aware of Horace's pronouncement that even before the Trojan War the *queynte* had been the most shameful cause of war: "Cunnus teterrima belli/Causa" (*Satires*, I, iii, 107-108). Chaucer's allusion to Paris and Helen conveys the idea that January's marriage is based on the male's obsession with the *cunnus*.

[31] Kendrick has observed: "[Proserpina] regularly reverses the patriarchal order of things in her own marriage to old Pluto, bringing spring with each of her rebellions against his constraint. Proserpina gives May and all earthly women the ability to *do what they want and get away with it*, to satisfy their illicit desires and put themselves 'on top' (E 2266-75). The Merchant's fabliau inverts the paternalistic hierarchy of both earth and heaven" (p. 116). I believe that I have been able to at least suggest the possibility of a future reversal of what Proserpina has managed to reverse, and

that I have been able to do so without making the Chaucer of the *Merchant's Tale* appear like a male-supremacist. While May is "on top" now, she will literally be at the bottom—at the bottom of a river—after Proserpina herself has returned to the underworld.

³² David, pp. 96-97.

³³ Huppé, p. 148.

³⁴ Robin Grove, "*The Merchant's Tale*: Seeing, Knowing and Believing," *Critical Review*, 18 (1976), 30, has observed on Justinus stepping out of the story being told:

> This is most indecorous, behaving like an audience to *The Canterbury Tales* instead of a character inside it, and Baugh (*Chaucer's Major Poetry*) briskly puts the upstart down: "Chaucer forgets that Justinus could not have heard the Wife of Bath's discourse". I don't know that it's so easy. The Merchant never hesitates to break his narrative bounds if that will serve a purpose, and this effect of reality mutating eerily from one degree to another is quite peculiar enough to be disconcerting, and, at the very moment of reminding us that this is all a fiction, deliver us to its fascinations as a story-being-told, even as it diverts our sense of imaginative responsibility *away* from January and his plight.

I would add that the purpose of the Merchant breaking his narrative bounds is that of diverting, if just for a moment, his imagination away from January to his own plight—without, however, letting his audience know what he is doing: speaking words which actually constitute an interior monologue.

³⁵ Donald Benson, p. 48.

³⁶ Jordan, *Chaucer and the Shape of Creation*, p. 139, quoted by Benson, p. 51. In *Chaucer's Poetics*, Jordan would observe: "the evidence of such . . . achievement as the Nun's Priest's Tale and the Merchant's Tale, to name only two, belies any strong Chaucerian affinity for tightly woven narrative. As all his major works demonstrate, . . . Chaucer's aesthetic impulses did not incline toward univalent cohesiveness and concision. Quite to the contrary, his metier was amplification" (p. 117). I am trying to make a case for amplification *and* cohesiveness in the *Merchant's Tale*.

37 Neuse, p. 217.

38 Olson, "Chaucer's Merchant," p. 205.

39 Peter G. Beidler and Therese Decker, "*Lippijn*: A Middle Dutch Source for the *Merchant's Tale*?", *Chaucer Review*, 23 (1989), 236-50, discuss a brief Middle Dutch play as a possible additional source for Chaucer. Beidler and Decker astutely point out that "In the 'blind husband' versions [of Chaucer's sources, the wife's] answer is that she had committed the act of adultery because she had been told that only by doing so could she cure her husband's blindness. Only in *Lippijn* and in the *Merchant's Tale* is the husband told that his vision is poor" (p. 245). They also note that "In the other analogues there is no such [sexual] explicitness" (p. 244). However, since I have been belaboring Augustinian sexual theology, I would like to question their translation of the cuckold's Middle Dutch lament,

> Want ic habse selve ghesien.
> Ligghen metten bloeten knien
> Ende gingen hem *beide to werke stellen*,

as

> because I saw her myself
> lying with naked knees
> and *both labored hard*. (p. 239, italics added)

At the very most, the Middle Dutch means "both went to work" or "put [i.e., *stellen*] themselves to work (a cognate has survived in the Modern German *zu Werke stellen*, which merely means to perform, i.e., to have something "wrought"): there is no emphasis on effort. Wouldn't it therefore be tantalizing to speculate that Chaucer may have taken the "work" wording from the Dutch farce and, relating it to St. Augustine's sexual theology, incorporated it into a poem which parodically deals with the contemporary notion of marriage as a paradise on earth?

40 Ross has made the following comment under the listing *strugle*: "The word becomes (for the nonce) a synonym for intercourse" (p. 214). I

disagree with Ross because, if January uses the word in the meaning of intercourse, his protestation, "Strugle? . . . Ye, algate in it wente . . . He swyved thee," doesn't make sense: the idea is that, in contrast to the "blind husband" versions where the wife explained the adultery as a means of restoring the husband's eysight, Chaucer has the wife deny the adultery by convincing the husband that his vision is still impaired. It is for the same reason that I don't think May herself uses the word *struggle* in the meaning of intercourse. On the other hand, Kendrick would later observe: "Fabliau wives, like poets, are accomplished at double-talk; they are extremely good at inventing figures and extended euphemisms (such as . . . May's 'struggle with a man upon a tree') in order to deceive their husbands about the true nature of their actions" (p. 90). If Kendrick is right, then there is the ironic twist that May refers to intercourse but does so by using double-talk. In such a scenario, May figures that if January takes the word *struggle* to be a euphemism for intercourse and accepts the reason she gives for her action, then there is no problem, and if he doesn't catch the euphemism, she just will have some more "explaining" to do—which turns out to be the case. At any rate, January walks away from the pear-tree scene believing that Damian did not "swyve" his wife.

[41] Lindahl, p. 152. Lindahl argues that the Merchant's attempt to dissociate himself from January is a pathetic failure (pp. 151-53), and his story a "process of fictional self-abuse" (p. 152).

[42] In a context where I discuss the Merchant's view of January as the view of a professional, it might not be impertinent to quote in length an observation which Bernard Levy has made in his article on "*Gentilesse* in Chaucer's *Clerk's* and *Merchant's Tales*":

> Regardless of how one treats the relationship to the teller . . . , there is a good deal of evidence in the tale itself that the *Merchant's Tale* was intended for a teller who was a merchant. Such evidence can be found in the fact that the "hero" of the *Tale*, January, is a Lombard knight,

> since in Chaucer's time, "commercial and sexual deviousness" was attributed to Lombards, and Janus, from whom January derives his name, "was sometimes regarded in the Middle Ages as the god of merchants and, in Roman times and in the fourteenth century, was treated as the inventor of money and the patron of trade and shipping," as Paul A. Olson, in "Chaucer's Lombard Knight," *TSLL*, 3 (1961), 259-63, has pointed out. Furthermore, as Olson argues in his important essay, "Chaucer's Merchant and January's 'Hevene in Erthe Heere'," *ELH*, 203-14, January, who manifests the avarice attributed to old age in the Middle Ages, treats May more as a possession than as a person, and the deities assigned to the garden, Pluto, the god of avarice, and Proserpina, the goddess of wealth, conform to the commercial ideal established in the *Tale*. (Levy, p. 317, n. 6)

I trust that I have been able to show that, in addition to illustrating the commercial ideal in his tale, the Merchant, or at least Chaucer, employs Pluto and Proserpina for the tale's *sentence*.

[43] Donald Benson, for example, has observed: "Arguing that, unlike the gifts of Fortune, a wife, being God's gift, will endure, the Merchant *gratuitously adds*: 'Wel lenger than thee list, paraventure' (1318). Our controlled ironist appears suddenly to *have broken the rule of the game*, the fiction of agreement and sympathy with January's decision, for the statement, unlike the previous ironies, cannot be read two ways" (pp. 54-55, italics mine). As I am about to attempt to demonstrate, when the Merchant breaks the rules of the game he is being anything but gratuitous.

[44] Stevens, p. 120.

[45] Quoted by Stevens, p. 120.

[46] Stevens, p. 123.

[47] Howard, p. 260. For a thoroughly argued interpretation of the Merchant as bitter and his tale as cynical, see Howard, pp. 260-64.

[48] Kendrick has observed that the *Merchant's Tale* "may be the Merchant's way of putting himself on top by telling a joke on 'himself' (that is, on his inferior or former self, as represented by the newly married, soon to be cuckolded January)" (p. 60). Kendrick doesn't say what she considers the

Merchant's inferior or former self. As I have tried to argue, through his abreactive fiction the Merchant may be able to overcome his former sexual inferiority, which is indeed represented by January, but I have also shown that not everything about January is representative of the Merchant himself: the teller strongly dissociates himself from his character's willfully erroneous view of marriage.

[49] Cf. Ross, p. 67.

[50] Ross, p. 149.

[51] Robinson, p. 768. The *Riverside Chaucer* lists "269 unidentified" (p. 958).

[52] Ross observes under the heading *abhomynable synne*: "The Parson cannot bring himself to name this terrible sin—'thylke abhomynable synne, of which that no man unnethe . . . oghte speke ne write.' Nonetheless, it is openly referred to in the Bible (see Romans 1:26-27), he says, and we are led to guess that he refers to homosexual acts. The good Parson continues, with perhaps more knowledge (or curiosity) than is seemly: 'this cursednesse doon men and wommen in diverse entente and in diverse manere' (I 909-910)" (p. 33).

[53] Ross, p. 205.

[54] I have changed my mind concerning the conclusion I offered in the 1983 *Explicator* essay listed in n. 1 above.

[55] Cf. *Riverside Chaucer*, p. 963.

[56] Howard has observed: "perhaps we should not chide the Parson for what he doesn't do, but we never see him do or say anything kindly—he doesn't intervene when harsh words and insults are exchanged [and] leaves it for the Knight to make peace at the end of the Pardoner's tale" (pp. 378-79). Lindahl notes that the "Parson—labeled a Lollard by the Host—isolates himself from the other pilgrims, *condemning the telling of tales* (10. 3134) and refusing to speak with those who utter oaths" (p. 34, italics mine). While

Chaucer is merely showing the Parson's strictness when he reports him as condemning the telling of tales, we do wonder how Chaucer as a literary artist felt about such a condemnation—and how he really felt about the Parson whom he had created in telling the *Canterbury Tales*. As Lindahl discusses (pp. 34-36), the Parson doesn't seem to have too many friends among the pilgrims who censure him "for excessive piety and [tell him] to keep his thoughts to himself" (p. 36).

[57]   Actually, the *Knight's Tale* might deserve the benefit of being examined in the light of Chaucer's theme of the springtime ritual. Lorraine Stock's article listed in n. 97 of Chapter I is a promising beginning.

BIBLIOGRAPHY

Adams, George E. "Sex and Clergy in Chaucer's 'General Prologue'." *Literature and Psychology* 18 (1968): 215-21.

Andrew, Malcolm. "January's Knife: Sexual Morality and Provocative Wisdom in the Merchant's Tale." *English Language Notes* 16 (1979): 273-77.

Augustine, Saint. *The City of God against the Pagans.* With an English Translation by George E. McCracken. Cambridge: Harvard University Press, 1957.

Bachman, W. Bryant Jr. "Mercury, Virgil, and Arcite: *Knight's Tale,* 1384-1397." *English Language Notes* 13 (1976): 168-73.

Baum, Paull F. *Chaucer: A Critical Appreciation.* Durham, NC: Duke University Press, 1958.

Beidler, Peter G. and Therese Decker. "*Lippijn*: A Middle Dutch Source for the *Merchant's Tale*?" *Chaucer Review* 23 (1989): 236-50.

Benson, Donald R. "The Marriage 'Encomium' in the *Merchant's Tale*: A Chaucerian Crux." *Chaucer Review* 14 (1979): 48-60.

Benson, Larry D. "The 'Queynte' Punnings of Chaucer's Critics." *Studies in the Age of Chaucer, Proceedings, No. 1: Reconstructing Chaucer.*

Eds. Paul Strohm and Thomas J. Heffernan. Knoxville: University of Tennessee Press, 1985: 23-47.

————. Gen. Ed. *The Riverside Chaucer*, Boston: Houghton Mifflin, 1987. Based on *The Works of Geoffrey Chaucer*, Ed. F. N. Robinson, 2nd Ed. Boston: Houghton Mifflin, 1957.

Bowden, Muriel. *A Commentary on the General Prologue to the "Canterbury Tales."* New York: Macmillan, 1949.

Boyd, Beverly. Ed. *A Variorum Edition of the Works of Geoffrey Chaucer.* Vol. II. *The Canterbury Tales.* Part 20. *The Prioress's Tale.* Norman and London: University of Oklahoma Press, 1987.

Brown, Emerson, Jr. *"Hortus Inconclusus*: The Significance of Priapus and Pyramus and Thisbe in the *Merchant's Tale."* *Chaucer Review* 4 (1970): 31-40.

Burger, Glenn. "Kissing the Pardoner." *PMLA* 107 (1992): 1143-66.

Carton, Evan. "Complicity and Responsibility in Pandarus' Bed and Chaucer's Art." *PMLA* 94 (1979): 47-61.

Clark, Roy Peter. "Christmas Games in Chaucer's *The Canterbury Tales."* *Studies in Short Fiction* 13 (1976): 277-87.

————. "Squeamishness and Exorcism in Chaucer's *Miller's Tale."* *Thought* 14 (1974): 37-43.

Cohen, Maurice. "Chaucer's Prioress and Her Tale: A Study of Anal Character and Anti-Semitisim." *Psychonanalytic Quarterly* 31 (1962): 232-49.

Condren, Edward I. "The Prioress: A Legend of Spirit, a Life of Flesh." *Chaucer Review* 23 (1989): 192-218.

Curtius, Ernst R. *European Literature and the Latin Middle Ages.* Trans. W. R. Trask. Princeton: Princeton University Press, 1953.

Dane, Joseph A. "The Prioress and Her *Romanzen."* *Chaucer Review* 24 (1990): 219-22.

Davis, Norman, Douglas Gray, Patricia Ingham, Anne Wallace-Hadrill. Eds. *A Chaucer Glossary*. Oxford: Clarendon Press, 1979.

David, Alfred. *The Strumpet Muse: Art and Morals in Chaucer's Poetry*. Bloomington: Indiana University Press, 1976.

DeNeef, A. Leigh. "Robertson and the Critics." *Chaucer Review* 2 (1968): 205-34.

De Weever, Jacqueline. *Chaucer Name Dictionary: A Guide to Astrological, Biblical, Literary, and Mythological Names in the Works of Geoffrey Chaucer*. New York and London: Garland Publishing, Inc., 1988.

Dinshaw, Carolyn. *Chaucer's Sexual Poetics*. Madison: University of Wisconsin Press, 1989.

Edden, Valerie. "Sacred and Secular in the *Clerk's Tale*." *Chaucer Review* 26 (1992): 369-76.

Elliott, Robert C. *The Power of Satire: Magic, Ritual, Art*. Princeton: Princeton University Press, 1960.

Ellis, Deborah S. "Domestic Treachery in the *Clerk's Tale*." *Ambiguous Realities: Women in the Middle Ages and Renaissance*. Eds. Carole Levine and Jeanie Watson. Detroit: Wayne State University Press, 1987: 99-113.

Ellis, Roger. *Patterns of Religious Narrative in the Canterbury Tales*. London and Sydney: Croom Helm, 1986.

Ferster, Judith. *Chaucer on Interpretation*. Cambridge and New York: Cambridge University Press, 1985.

Fichte, Joerg O. *Chaucer's "Art Poetical": A Study in Chaucerian Poetics*. Tübingen: Gunter Narr Verlag, 1980.

Fisher, John H. Ed. *The Complete Poetry and Prose of Geoffrey Chaucer* New York: Holt, Rinehart and Winston, Inc., 1977.

Frye, Northrop. *Anatomy of Criticism*. Princeton: Princeton University Press, 1973.

Ganim, John M. "Carnival Voices and the Envoy to the *Clerk's Tale*." *Chaucer Review* 22 (1987): 112-27.

Gardner, John. *The Poetry of Chaucer*. Carbondale and Edwardsville: Southern Illinois University Press, 1977.

Gaylord, Alan T. "The Unconquered Tale of the Prioress." *Papers of the Michigan Academy of Science, Arts, and Letters* 67 (1962): 613-36.

Grennen, Joseph E. "The Pardoner, the Host, and the Depth of Chaucerian Insult." *English Language Notes* 25 (December 1987): 18-24.

Grove, Robin. "*The Merchant's Tale*: Seeing, Knowing and Believing." *Critical Review* 18 (1976): 21-38.

Hallissy, Margaret. "Widow-to-Be: May in Chaucer's 'The Merchant's Tale'." *Studies in Short Fiction* 26 (1989): 295-304.

Halverson, John. Ed. *Geoffrey Chaucer: The Canterbury Tales*. Indianapolis: Bobbs-Merrill, 1971.

Hamel, Mary. "And Now for Something Completely Different: The Relationship between the *Prioress's Tale* and the *Rime of Sir Thopas*." *Chaucer Review* 14 (1980): 251-59.

Harder, Kelsie B. "Chaucer's Use of the Mystery Plays in the *Miller's Tale*." *Modern Language Quarterly* 17 (1956): 193-98.

Hieatt, A. Kent and Constance Hieatt. Eds. *The Canterbury Tales by Geoffrey Chaucer*. Selected with Translations and Notes by the Editors. New York and Toronto: Bantam Books, 1964.

Hieatt, Constance B. Ed. *The Miller's Tale by Geoffrey Chaucer*. New York: Odyssey Press, 1970.

Hoffman, Arthur W. "Chaucer's Prologue to Pilgrimage: Two Voices." *ELH* 21 (1954): 1-16.

Holland, Norman. *The Dynamics of Literary Response*. New York: Oxford University Press, 1968.

Howard, Donald R. *The Idea of the Canterbury Tales.* Berkeley, Los Angeles, London: University of California Press, 1976.

Huppé, Bernard. F. *A Reading of the Canterbury Tales.* Albany: State University of New York Press, 1964.

Jordan, Robert M. *Chaucer and the Shape of Creation: The Aesthetic Possibilities of Inorganic Structure.* Cambridge, MA: Harvard University Press, 1965.

————. *Chaucer's Poetics and the Modern Reader.* Berkeley and Los Angeles: University of California Press, 1987.

Jordan, Tracey. "Faerie Tale and Fabliau: Chaucer's *The Miller's Tale.*" *Studies in Short Fiction* 27 (1990): 87-93.

Kelly, Edward H. "By Mouth of Innocentz: The Prioress Vindicated." *Papers on Language and Literature* 5 (1969): 362-74.

Kendrick, Laura. *Chaucerian Play: Comedy and Control in the Canterbury Tales.* Berkeley, Los Angeles, London: University of California Press, 1988.

Kerkhof, J. *Studies in the Language of Chaucer.* Leiden: Leiden University Press, 1982.

Knapp, Peggy. *Chaucer and the Social Context.* New York and London: Routledge, 1990.

Lanham, Richard A. "Chaucer's *Clerk's Tale*: The Poem Not the Myth." *Literature and Psychology* 16 (1966): 157-65.

Lavers, Norman. "Freud, the Clerkes Tale, and Literary Criticism." *College English* 26 (1964): 180-187.

Le Comte, Edward. *Milton and Sex.* London: Macmillan, 1978.

Levy, Bernard S. "*Gentilesse* in Chaucer's *Clerk's* and *Merchant's Tales.*" *Chaucer Review* 11 (1977): 306-318.

Lewis, C. S. *A Preface to "Paradise Lost."* London: Oxford University Press, 1949.

Leyerle, John. "Thematic Interlace in 'The Canterbury Tales'." *Essays and Studies*. London: John Murray, 1976.

Lindahl, Carl. *Earnest Games: Folkloric Patterns in the Canterbury Tales*. Bloomington and Indianapolis: Indiana University Press, 1987.

Loney, Douglas. "Chaucer's Prioress and Agur's 'Adulterous Woman'." *Chaucer Review* 27 (1992): 107-108.

Lynch, Kathryn L. "Despoiling Griselda: Chaucer's Walter and the Problem of Knowledge in *The Clerk's Tale*." *Studies in the Age of Chaucer* 10 (1988): 41-70.

Mann, Jill. *Chaucer and Medieval Estates Satire: The Literature of Social Classes and the General Prologue to the Canterbury Tales*. Cambridge: Cambridge University Press, 1973.

McAlpine, Monica E. "The Pardoner's Homosexuality and How It Matters." *PMLA* 95 (1980): 8-22.

McNamara, John. "Chaucer's Use of the Epistle of St. James in the *Clerk's Take*." *Chaucer Review* 7 (1973): 184-93.

Miller, Robert P. Ed. *Chaucer: Sources and Backgrounds*. New York: Oxford University Press, 1977.

Milton, John. *Paradise Lost*. Ed. Merritt Y Hughes. Indianapolis: Odyssey Press, 1962.

Mogan, Joseph. "Chaucer and the *Bona Matrimonii*." *Chaucer Review* 4 (1970): 123-41.

Neuse, Richard. "Marriage and the Question of Allegory in the *Merchant's Tale*." *Chaucer Review* 24 (1989): 115-31.

Olson, Paul A. "Chaucer's Merchant and January's 'Hevene in Erthe Heere'." *ELH* 28 (1961): 204-14.

————. "Poetic Justice in the *Miller's Tale*." *Modern Language Quarterly* 24 (1963): 227-36.

Owen, Charles A., Jr. "The Crucial Passage in Five of the *Canterbury Tales*:
A Study in Irony and Symbol." *JEGP* 52 (1953): 249-311.

Partridge, Eric, *Shakespeare's Bawdy*. Rev. Ed. New York: Dutton, 1969.

Perri, Carmela, "On Alluding." *Poetics* 7 (1978): 289-307.

Richardson, Janette. *Blameth Nat Me: A Study of Imagery in Chaucer's Fabliaux*. Den Haag: Mouton, 1970.

Ridley, Florence H. *The Prioress and Her Critics*. University of California
Publications: English Studies No. 30. Berkeley and Los Angeles:
University of California Press, 1965.

Robertson, D. W., Jr. *A Preface to Chaucer: Studies in Medieval
Perspectives*. Princeton: Princeton University Press, 1962.

Ross, Thomas W. *Chaucer's Bawdy*. New York: Dutton, 1972.

————. Ed. *A Variorum Edition of the Works of Geoffrey Chaucer*. Vol. II.
The Canterbury Tales. Part 3. *The Miller's Tale*. Norman, OK:
University of Oklahoma Press, 1983.

Rothman, Irving N. "Humility and Obedience in the *Clerk's Tale*, with the
Envoy Considered as an Ironic Affirmation." *Papers on Language and
Literature*, 9 (1973): 115-27.

Rowland, Beryl. "Chaucer's Idea of the Pardoner." *Chaucer Review* 14
(1979): 140-154.

Rudat, Wolfgang E. H. "Aurelius' Quest for *Grace*: Sexuality and the
Marriage Debate in the *Franklin's Tale*." *CEA Critic* 45 (1982): 16-21.

————. "The *Canterbury Tales*: Anxiety Release and Wish Fulfillment."
American Imago: A Journal for Culture, Science and the Arts 35
(1978): 407-18.

————. "Chaucer's *Merchant's Tale* E 1263, 1854 and 2360-65."
Explicator 35 (1977): 25-26.

————. "Chaucer's Mercury and Arcite: The *Aeneid* and the World of the
Knight's Tale." *Neophilologus* 64 (1980): 307-19.

————. "Chaucer's Spring of Comedy: The *Merchant's Tale* and Other 'Games' with Augustinian Theology." *Annuale Mediaevale* 21 (1981): 111-20.

————. "Chaucer's *Troilus and Criseyde*: Narrator-Reader Complicity." *American Imago* 40 (1983): 103-113.

————. "*Gentillesse* and the Marriage Debate in the *Franklin's Tale*: Chaucer's Squires and the Question of Nobility." *Neophilologus* 68 (1984): 451-70.

————. "Heresy and Springtime Ritual: Biblical and Classical Allusions in the *Canterbury Tales*." *Revue belge de philologie et d'histoire* 54 (1976): 823-36.

————. " 'I trowe he were a geldyng or a mare': Chaucer's Pardoner and the Papacy." *Chaucer Yearbook* 2 (October 1993).

————. "The Misdirected Kisses in the *Miller's Tale*." *Journal of Evolutionary Psychology* 3 (April 1982): 103-108.

————. *The Mutual Commerce: Masters of Classical Allusion in English and American Literature*. Heidelberg: Carl Winter Universitätsverlag, 1985.

————. "Ovid's *Art of Love* and Augustinian Theology in *Paradise Lost*." *Milton Quarterly* 21 (1987): 62-65.

————. "The *Parson's Tale* and St. Augustine's Theories on Sexuality." *Explicator* 42 (1983): 6-8.

————. "Reading Chaucer's Earnest Games: Folk-Mode or Literary Sophisticaton?" *English Language Notes* 29 (December 1991): 16-19.

————. "Sexuality and Self-Recognition in the *Pardoner's Tale*." *Journal of Evolutionary Psychology* 3 (October 1982): 124-29.

————. "Spenser's 'Angry Ioue': Vergilian Allusion in the First Canto of *The Faerie Queene*." *Classical and Modern Literature* 3 (1983): 162-82.

Ruggiers, Paul G. *The Art of the Canterbury Tales*. Madison: University of Wisconsin Press, 1965.

Salter, Elizabeth. *Chaucer: The Knight's Tale and the Clerk's Tale*. Great Neck, NY: 1962.

Salzberg, Albert C. "A Jew Teaches Western Literature." *CEA Forum* 19 Nos. 3-4 (1989): 20-23.

Schleusner, Jay. "The Conduct of the *Merchant's Tale*." *Chaucer Review* 14 (1979): 237-250.

Schoeck, Richard J. "Chaucer's Prioress: Mercy and Tender Heart." Repr. in Richard J. Schoeck and Jerome Taylor. Eds. *Chaucer Criticism: The Canterbury Tales*. Notre Dame: Notre Dame University Press, 1960: 239-55.

Schweitzer, Edward C. "The Misdirected Kiss and the Lover's Malady in Chaucer's *Miller's Tale*." *Chaucer in the Eighties*. Eds. Julian N. Wasserman and Robert J. Blanch. Syracuse, NY: Syracuse University Press, 1986: 223-33.

Severs, J. Burke. *The Literary Heritage of Chaucer's Clerk's Tale*. New Haven: Yale University Press, 1942.

Stevens, Martin. " 'And Venus Laugheth': An Interpretation of the *Merchant's Tale*." *Chaucer Review* 7 (1972): 118-31.

————. "The *Canterbury Tales* for a New Age." *Review* 11 (1989): 36-70.

Stock, Lorraine Kochanske. "The Two Mayings in Chaucer's *Knight's Tale*." *Journal of English and Germanic Philology* 85 (1986): 206-21.

Storm, Melvin. "The Pardoner's Invitation: Quaestor's Bag or Becket's Shrine?" *PMLA* 97 (1982): 810-18.

Turner, Frederick. "A Structural Reading of the *Knight's Tale*." *Chaucer Review* 8 (1974): 279-96.

Utley, Francis Lee. "Robertsonianism Redivivus." *Romance Philology* 19 (1965): 250-60.

Van, Thomas A. "Walter at the Stake: A Reading of Chaucer's *Clerk's Tale*." *Chaucer Review* 22 (1988): 214-24.

Virgil. *P. Vergili Maronis opera*. Ed. F. A. Hirtzel. Oxford: Clarendon Press, 1963.

Vulgate. Roma: Biblioteca de Autores Christianos, 1959.

Wasserman, Earl R. "The Limits of Allusion in *The Rape of the Lock*." *Journal of English and Germanic Philology* 65 (1966), 425-44.

Wenzel, Siegfried. "Chaucer's Pardoner and His Relics." *Studies in the Age of Chaucer* 11 (1989): 37-41.

Williams, George. *A New View of Chaucer*. Durham, NC: Duke University Press, 1965.

Wood, Chauncey. "Chaucer's Use of Signs in His Portrait of the Prioress." *Signs and Symbols*. Eds. John P. Hermann and John J. Burke, Jr. University, AL: University of Alabama Press, 1981: 81-101.

INDEX